THE

SHAYṬĀN

BRIDE

SUMAIYA MATIN

THE

SHAYṬĀN

BRIDE

A Bangladeshi Canadian
Memoir of Desire and Faith

RARE
MACHINES

Publisher: Scott Fraser | Acquiring editor: Julie Mannell
Cover designer: Laura Boyle
Cover image: arcangel.com/Rebecca Massey
Printer: Marquis Book Printing Inc.

Library and Archives Canada Cataloguing in Publication

Title: The shaytān bride : a Bangladeshi Canadian memoir of desire and faith / Sumaiya Matin.
Names: Matin, Sumaiya, author.
Identifiers: Canadiana (print) 20210167971 | Canadiana (ebook) 20210171065 | ISBN 9781459747678 (softcover) | ISBN 9781459747685 (PDF) | ISBN 9781459747692 (EPUB)
Subjects: LCSH: Matin, Sumaiya. | LCSH: Muslim women—Canada—Biography. | LCSH: Muslim women—Canada—Social life and customs. | LCSH: Muslim women—Canada—Social conditions. | LCGFT: Autobiographies.
Classification: LCC HQ1170 .M38 2021 | DDC 305.48/697092—dc23

We acknowledge the support of the Canada Council for the Arts and the Ontario Arts Council for our publishing program. We also acknowledge the financial support of the Government of Ontario, through the Ontario Book Publishing Tax Credit and Ontario Creates, and the Government of Canada.

Care has been taken to trace the ownership of copyright material used in this book. The author and the publisher welcome any information enabling them to rectify any references or credits in subsequent editions.

The publisher is not responsible for websites or their content unless they are owned by the publisher.

Printed and bound in Canada.

Dundurn Press
1382 Queen Street East
Toronto, Ontario, Canada M4L 1C9
dundurn.com, @dundurnpress 🐦 f 📷

For Ammu (Mother)

The whole of my life summed up in three phases:

I was raw

then
I was burnt

now,
I am on fire

— Rumi

Tarid al'Arwah Alsharira /
The Exorcist

(طارد الأرواح الشريرة)

I didn't see the exorcist, but I heard he'd dropped by and brought with him a *ta'wiz*, a silver locket containing a small scroll with verses of *Ayatul Kursi* to ward off evil. The locket with the *surah* was attached to a black thread. The *ta'wiz* was supposed to be wrapped around my arm or worn around my neck.

It must have been early in the morning or late in the night when he left it for me. I must have been sleeping. I wondered if he had entered the bedroom and watched as I lay there on one of the two beds, the one by the large window next to the veranda. That window was usually open at all hours, the thin linen curtains blowing occasionally when the breeze could eke its way through the humid Dhaka streets.

I must have been on my back, legs spread apart, each breast sliding away from the centre of my chest, open and unguarded. Or maybe I had been on my right side, in the fetal position with my knees up to my chest, head over my bent arm, as if I was back in the womb again. It must have been then when he hovered over me, holding his palms open to the sky, reciting prayers, then gently placing his clammy hand on my forehead. Whiff of sandalwood incense. Performing *ruqyah*, reciting the words of the Quran to confront the jinns with bad dispositions and the jinns sent by everyday sorcerers to afflict humans.

I heard the lilting Arabic verses that were so distinct and familiar to me. A tonic of solace, trust, and mystery soaking into my ears, soaking into the saliva filling my gaping mouth as I half slept. These words were a remedy, despite any incoherence from the flawed delivery of the reciter. My heart was either conditioned or naturally inclined to find the breaths between them, a space to rest, like the pulpy pillow I laid my head on.

Or maybe I had heard nothing but the rattle of the rotating blades of the fan overhead.

The haze and my disorientation were much less bothersome to me than the sharp flicker of light between my eyelids. I twitched awake, only to hear fading footsteps.

Had it all been a dream? I wondered.

What I knew was that in the morning, when I got off the stiff bed, drowsy and suffering some sort of memory distortion, I found Sweety Khala standing there in her floral *salwar kameez*, wavy black hair in a bun. She turned her body to the mattress and, suddenly and hastily, pulled it up with all the strength she had, revealing the black string attached to a silver locket. She carefully moved one of her hands toward the amulet and snatched it from where it lay, releasing her other hand from the mattress. She let the mattress tumble like a falling skyscraper while keeping her eyes fixed on me, almost unblinking. She opened her right palm slowly to reveal the *ta'wiz* she was now holding.

"Put this around your arm," she said. "It will protect you from what you've been stricken with."

"No," I said in a sharp tone. I turned away from her. We stood there under the rotating fan blades for a few more minutes.

"From what do I need protection? I'm fine," I said.

"You claim you're in love," she replied, widening her eyes, and with all her weight on one hip, which indicated she had diagnosed me with some certainty, but that there was more she was probably trying to figure out. "It's not wise, to be so eccentric. It's not normal, however you're behaving."

I pushed her hand away with my own — what felt to me like moving boulders but was really a slight tap. I hadn't eaten for days. I was really weak. She held onto the *ta'wiz* tighter, as if her life depended on it.

"All the men we've suggested, you've rejected. You just lay there, and don't consider anything we say. Sometimes you're a monster, yelling loudly and pushing us away."

She explained that these were all the symptoms of *sihr*, someone else's ill intentions sent my way, or perhaps the interest of a jinni who wanted to make a home of my body, or who had fallen in love with me.

As she explained, I thought, *I believe in jinns, too*, made of smokeless fire, living alongside humans in an unseen world. I did believe that certain powers could be sent to influence a person to behave in ways that were not aligned with their true, deepest nature, that would make their battle within themselves to manage their misguided yearnings even harder. However, the agony I felt came not from jinns, but from one source and one source alone: being co-erced to do something I did not want to do.

As my thoughts unravelled, intertwined, and spun like thread, a young girl stumbled in. She was a maid, and her name was Bilkis. She was wearing a pair of brown capris with holes in them and a pink shirt with a rainbow printed on it. She had dark-brown tumbleweed hair. Her front tooth was crooked, and her skin seemed brittle. Bilkis kept her eyes on me as she shuffled in my direction holding a glass of water, which she presented to me with-out comment.

I peered over the rim of the glass. I was parched and could already feel the slimy water in my mouth. Amid the miasma of se-crets, fading sounds albeit moving mouths, and the furtive glances, I wondered if someone had put something in this water.

"At least drink this," Sweety Khala said, pointing to the water. "It's Zam Zam water from Mecca, brought back from *Hajj*."

The Zam Zam water came from a well in Mecca, east of the *Kaaba*, the holy building toward which Muslims around the world pray five times a day. Prophet Ibrahim's wife Hajar had found it in the hot, dry desert, where no one thought water existed, and used it to feed their son Ismail.

It was holy water that I, too, revered, yet when I extended my hand toward the glass, I retracted. Such were the times, where my trust was always wavering, where I couldn't believe what people were telling me — not completely.

What did I think and how did I feel about being told that I was possibly possessed by a jinni? As Sweety Khala had pointed out, it was true that I presented with quite a few symptoms of a person possessed: aches in my heart and my head that were constant and far-reaching; my occasional dreams of falling off buildings, which lingered like an unattended urge; trailing whispers, sometimes in the distance and sometimes close.

It was, at first, all too ridiculous. A diagnosis based on an observation, so sudden, and imposed by everyone. But as they increasingly exposed me to their hopes and the concerns of their own agenda, I realized that perhaps all these years I had not known them as well as I thought I did, and there was a larger world about which I had not been very aware.

The time was strange, but all I knew and wanted was for it all to be over.

When Bilkis handed the glass of water to me, I thought for a moment, *What would happen if I knocked the glass out of her hand?* Perhaps it would have looked like I was exactly what they thought I was: *crazy.* During this time, I had become particularly aware of and attuned to how I was being perceived and the multiple ways my actions and words could be used to suggest a truth about me that I wouldn't be able to erase. What was this truth? It was fleeting and defined by the perception of groups of people. So, given the intangibility and conditionality, I decided then, despite my every urge, to grab the glass and take a sip.

I thought to myself, *Allah knows my heart.* Whatever is right, whatever is real, will ultimately surface.

"Fine, put the *ta'wiz* on me," I said in a kind of rebellion, or maybe acceptance. For, somewhere within me, I knew it didn't matter, anyway. No talisman or amulet could shape what would happen; only Allah's will.

At the time I was perceived as going astray from Allah, but it was then that my faith had deepened the most.

Disclaimer:
This is not a rescue story.

The Shayṭān Bride

When I was a young girl living in Dhaka, Bangladesh, I heard about eccentric women who were possessed by jinns. These jinns had very fine and thin bodies, and were often hard to trace. There were good ones and bad ones. The bad ones were akin to the devil, the Shayṭān.

How I understood Shayṭān in Islam was that he was once Iblis. Iblis was created by Allah, or God. He was regarded as an angel by some and a jinni by others. When Allah asked Iblis to bow down to Adam, Iblis didn't obey. Some believe this was because of arrogance and envy, as he felt he was superior to Adam, who was made of mere clay. Others believe his refusal was because he believed in bowing down to one God only, no one else, and especially not another one of God's creations. Iblis was then banned from Paradise. Instead of repenting, Iblis decided to take vengeance by making it his mission to lure humans into their lower instincts, into doing evil. Some Sufis think Iblis represents unrequited love, as his love for monotheism was misunderstood by Allah and he was cast away. Other Sufis believe his behaviour only demonstrated what happens when one does not look at the inner qualities of another, and judges them only from the outside, deducing their own self as greater. Some also see Iblis's dark light as the beacon to follow, to transcend superficial worship.

In all of these interpretations, it seemed Iblis eventually became Shayṭān. Shayṭān's heart is inflamed with an anger so reckless that it creates discord and inevitable corruption. He is the master then of all the ill-dispositioned jinns, whom he commands to afflict humans in different ways.

The eccentric women that were talked about displayed all the signs of Shayṭān's meddling and were therefore considered possessed. Like Shayṭān, they were thought to be nefarious. What were the markers of their rebellion? In their mannerisms, they were highly lethargic, solitary, or disinterested. They were often forgetful or appeared ill. They turned down their men for sex or didn't love them anymore. Their hearts were filled with disgust and hate. They heard or saw things others didn't. They dreamt often of being summoned or of other peculiar things. Their bodies often ached, or had involuntary movement. They rejected all their suitors, saying they were too ugly or had some other defect.

There was also the kind of eccentric woman thought to be infected with *ishq*, a reckless passion, an undying desire to obtain one's beloved. They fell in love with men or other women with no regard for whether their desires would be socially acceptable. They ignored the consequences their desires would have on their bodies, their families, and their religion. This audacity or carelessness was so preposterous that the only explanation was meddling from an outside force that had somehow found its way in. Those they loved were considered shapeshifters, sometimes in the form of humans, animals, or even an untraceable shadow. These jinns preyed on women whose hearts were pure, naive, and easily able to feel what others felt. They sometimes seduced women who were meant to be the brides of other men, good men.

One specific story I heard was that of a jinni who stole a woman on her wedding night. He picked her up from where she lay, sleeping next to her new husband, and put her in a treasure chest that he had brought with him. The bride was never found.

I always heard stories of women both in the city and nearby villages who weren't married despite being of marriageable age, or who had run away because of a jinni. The stories of their possession by jinns, or their love affairs with them, were passed through whispers.

Who are these women? I wondered. *The ones who are always named alongside the Shaytān?*

There were many incarnations of this same story, and sometimes the women were considered victims — thought foolish, naive, not prudent enough, and therefore vulnerable — and other times simply deserving of whatever ill fate. About those latter ones, I heard plenty of people say, "Well, you know, she was just asking for it."

At the end of the stories, the moral or warning was always the same: never end up like these women, stay vigilant, and do simply what you're supposed to. Always.

When Ammu warned me that I should be good and maintain my honour, I wasn't sure if her purpose was to console or warn me. I also didn't know that in other lands outside of Bangladesh there were women with similar stories, with details that were different. I decided to name all these women as one woman. An essence. I called her the Shayṭān Bride.

I imagined the Shayṭān Bride burning like the flames of the Darvaza crater in Turkmenistan, the one that people call *the gates to hell*. Her fire wasn't the substance of what was in Iblis's heart — vengeance — after he became Shayṭān. It came from a longing that could never be put out, for both love and life, one and the same. I imagined her walking the earth as if she didn't have to anticipate any turn or fall, as if there were no limits or bounds as to where she could go. She didn't accept everything she was told. She asked questions. Did her assuredness lack remembrance of God? Was it driven by an image she had of herself, a type of self-aggrandizement or entitlement? No. It was possible that through her choices, she found herself often in the depths of sin, but her falling is what grew her faith. She trusted herself, even if she made mistakes.

Yes, I imagined the Shayṭān Bride as forewarning, but not as terrorized by the bad jinns, the sorcerers, her human or non-human lovers, or even the Shayṭān, like they said. She moved freely and in ways most others didn't because they weren't sure how, or they were afraid, or such freedom of movement existed entirely outside the spectrum of their imaginations.

Ṭiẏā pākhi / Parakeet
(টিয়া পাখি)

It started over twenty years ago, with a vague conversation in the living room of a spacious house on Lalmatia Street in Dhaka. I had a parakeet at the time, South Asian rose-ringed with vivid green plumage and a striking red beak.

Parakeet seemed perceptive, bobbing its head here and there as if to agree — or disagree — with the shared thoughts of comers and goers, its beady yellowish-white eyes bouncing across the room. Most of the time, however, it sat quietly, watching me as I swam through the air on the indoor swing Abbu had built me.

I remember swinging amid the murmurs of Ammu, Abbu, and my maternal uncle, who I called Boro Mama; they went back and forth like a fencing duel on the potential gains and losses of moving to a new country: Canada.

At the time, Abbu didn't really want to go. He had a stable life in Dhaka, solid employment, a home, and the warm quilt of family, including his eleven siblings, wrapped around him.

"The people there may be too different," Abbu said. "We're content where we are."

Abbu, like his father, my Dada, was a man of faith, thinking often about the afterlife and how to prepare for it. Although Abbu was an electrical engineer by trade, he spent most of his youth under betel trees in the fields of Rajshahi University studying philosophy, psychology, theology, and literature, jotting down key insights into a small brown leather notebook. One of his favourite reads was Hemingway's *The Old Man and the Sea*, through which he learned to articulate integrity as well as *sabr*, which means *spiritual steadfastness*, a particular patience in Islamic philosophy.

He valued the adoption of a simple mindset. Disorder confounded him, so he explored and made sense of it by gaining knowledge from a range of scholars, experts, and artists. A true polymath.

Dada went to Calcutta Alia Madrasah, later known as Aliah University. Fluent in Arabic, he carried the verses of the Quran in his heart, shared them with his students as a professor at the same university. He eventually came to be regarded as an adviser in matters of both faith and the material world.

He died a year after the 1971 Liberation War. Abbu didn't have a photograph of Dada, so I've never seen what he looked like. Nevertheless, Abbu seemed to carry an image of his father that he could conjure upon any and every conundrum. Before he spoke, he lifted his eyebrows as if he was asking some invisible manifestation, "Baba, tell me: what would you do?"

"*Duniya*," Abbu would begin, squinting as if Dada were only just barely out of sight, "it's just a passing dream. Why do we need so much when we have everything here?" Pointing to his heart, pointing to his head, pointing to the sky. And I trusted that Dada would probably have said and done the same things.

Parakeet must have loved Abbu. When he arrived home after a long day of work, Parakeet would predictably turn its head and make an indecipherable sound, as if to alert me. I'd jump off my swing and run to the door.

"How was your day?" Abbu would ask.

To which I'd smile and pull his arm to play. Abbu was a busy man, but like Parakeet, he'd keep his eye on me from afar, never with judgment, only compassion and pride.

To Boro Mama he'd say, "My daughter has everything here that she needs."

Yet, my mother, Ammu, disagreed. She'd been convinced by Boro Mama that there was a world grander than ours. For her, its sparkling newness contained unlimited possibilities — even its ambiguity was there for her to graft her own dreams onto.

"We can stay with my sister. She says Canada is livable and even magical — mammoth buildings, lush greens, nicer people, cleaner streets, and mostly made up of something called snow. She says there's no better place."

Ammu had four sisters. One lived in Canada, one in the United Kingdom, and the other two in Dhaka, who would eventually move abroad, as well. She also had a couple of uncles in Australia, Europe, and the United States. Whenever they visited, they brought suitcases of gifts — the softest sweaters, the most unique fragrances, handbags of various opulent styles and textures. It was an entire ritual, relatives and the domestic help all gathered around while the suitcases were opened and the gifts were revealed one by one, sorted, and then handed out. Everyone wide-eyed and wondering what new fabric or appliance would be unveiled. If they were lucky, the gifts would be American or European brands, like the celebrities modelled on television.

Equally intriguing was the elusive accent of a person who spoke English as if it was their mother tongue, suggesting a refined sense of status and knowledge about the true size and contents of the world. For Ammu, migration was a rite of passage, if nothing else.

To Ammu's frustration, Abbu replied, "You can get the same things here, if not more. There will be new opportunities, but they're not worth more than a sense of home."

Parakeet listened to them both go back and forth in the living room, watched the hot *cha* simmering in their hands. An uninvited guest to the conversation, a spectator, but never in violation of confidentiality. A proper parakeet, not mischievous in any way.

Sometimes though, Parakeet and I would share a glance when we knew that a lie had been spoken, or perhaps a quip, as both animals and children are astute that way.

On Ammu's side was Boro Mama, who'd planted the idea in the first place. He was a man of expansion. When he entered a room, his chest would lift and open, his chin always up, his well-built arms with hands snug in his pockets, not shyly but with a self-assuredness earned through a confidence that was frequently praised and admired. Not a very tall man, maybe he was five foot eight or so, but the way he moved, swiftly and with purpose, made everyone follow.

Boro Mama often made the family decisions, large and small, sometimes to the point where others may have not had a say, but he was trusted. "He will do the right thing," they'd repeat among each other. "He always does the right thing."

He revered self-sacrifice; he was his father's right-hand as a young child during the family's migration from newly independent India to East Pakistan, and then later, as an adult, during the Liberation War, when East Pakistan became the separate country of Bangladesh. Plunging into lakes and taking shelter in abandoned homes while the leaves ruffled under enemy footsteps, the far-reaching screams and shallow whispers, gunshots, bullets, bodies — only with his instruction did my family survive.

To the sisters, Boro Mama was an absolute authority, one promotion short of God. When he would enter the living room to find his siblings indulging in black-and-white films he would yell, "This is a waste of time! Feeble, what they teach in those films. Fantasy." His ideas and opinions were absolute and went unquestioned.

Just the hint of his voice would cause everyone to scurry out of the room and hide, as if they'd done nothing, seen nothing, felt nothing — not just in the moment, but ever. Their put-on blank expressions offered Boro Mama the opportunity to project that which he found beautiful, interesting, comforting — whatever confirmed what he already knew and, in so doing, affirmed that he always knew what was best.

Perhaps to him he was only doing what any eldest brother should do, what was expected of him. When the family settled, he made it a point to arrange the weddings of all of his sisters, with their enthusiastic support, one by one, and to good respectable men, before he married his own wife.

This included Ammu, who loved to eat too much and was just a bit too short, reasons for suitors to withdraw their proposals. "A little *rasugullah*, my brother called me," she said. Still, these "flaws" were very much compensated by her creamy glowing skin and the rosiness in her cheeks, her subservience to her elder brother, her master's degree, and everything else that indicated a good, respectable woman.

"He was an engineer. What more could I have asked for than a man of respectable profession?" Ammu said about Abbu. "And he was a man of faith. Your Boro Mama thought he was a good human being."

So, when Ammu saw Abbu from the rooftop of her mother's white house in Rajshahi, pulling up in the tangerine rickshaw, the corners of her mouth lifted slightly. Abbu caught her glance and smiled back, and then quickly lowered his gaze, to protect himself and her, *astag furallah*, and as if to say *your majesty*, for Ammu had that effect on others; especially on him.

Perhaps it was true that Boro Mama was a decent match-maker. For on the walls of our Dhaka home there were plenty of photographs of the romantic sort. In one of them, Abbu and Ammu were sinking deep into flower fields, Abbu placing a red rose gently behind Ammu's curly black hair while she smiled coyly. In another, Abbu is placing a gold chain around Ammu's neck as she beams into the camera, glowing like the planet Venus. Ammu in a royal-blue silk sari and chunky black heels, standing next to Abbu, much taller, with his shoulder-length hair and light-cerulean collared shirt, me in a frilly white lace dress, hair short like a boy, on his shoulders. We are touring India. In these photographs, Abbu's lips are always curved tenderly, his eyes always in reverie, as if he were actually in heaven.

Ammu and Abbu were so different in personality, Ammu much more gregarious and concerned with matters of everyday life, and Abbu a little more pensive, an intellectual and lone wolf. Somehow, however, they made a union, a match, and it had a great lot to do, Ammu said, with the "clear judgment of your Boro Mama."

When Ammu was pregnant with me, they'd all expected a boy. Perhaps Ammu thought her brother would be disappointed by my birth, but he wasn't at all. With me, I remember Boro Mama being a similar way: an adviser of sorts, gentle mostly but also stern at times. "And only," he said, "for her educational good."

Despite his demanding work as an engineer, he found himself on most days with Ammu holding me, admiring the glint of my iris, within which he saw his own. I was born the shade of a creamy frangipani (plumeria) and near weightless like one, too, and so he'd often pick me up, throw me into the sky.

"Think bigger than you are now," Boro Mama said to Abbu. "If you move to Canada, your daughter will get a better education. And not just that. She'll meet better-quality suitors, more educated, worldly, and therefore wise in every sense. There will be much she can pass on to her future children."

Abbu at the time had also received an offer for a well-paying job in Jeddah, Saudia Arabia. If he accepted the offer, he'd receive not only the title of chief engineer, but also a grand house for us to live in. Despite the temptation of luxury and ease, Canada was still seen as the ideal. It was the West, after all.

Every school year, the top-three ranking students would get a medal. During one of these years, I was wearing a silky light-blue dress. At the awards ceremony I saw, from behind the stage, rows upon rows of parents and teachers. I bounced up and down in anticipation, praying underneath my breath for my name to be called. And it was. I made my way to stage, my view fixed on the three twinkling medals. I wanted the gold but that year I got the bronze. The excitement of my heart rose to the volume of the claps, and they sounded like thunder that gained momentum then faded to hush. The headmaster stooped down to my little body and put the medal around my neck. The weight of it pulled my neck down, and I could feel my chest sink with it. As elated as I was, I still thought I could have done better. I imagined Boro Mama's face, then Ammu's and Abbu's. I wanted their smiles almost as much as I did the metal.

Later that day, I sat at my desk, reading over instructions on how to do long division because I was determined to improve. My Boro Mama hovered behind me, watching me work while my feet dangled from the chair. I pressed the lead of my pencil deep into the paper, almost piercing through it, scratching my head from time to time and biting my lip.

"You carry the one over like this," Boro Mama said, using his hands to demonstrate the action. Learning was important to him, and he planned to send his eldest son, just an infant then, abroad when he was older, to become more global and well-educated in every sense.

Half circle, loop. I followed suit.

"Good, good," he said. "Good, good."

I didn't search Boro Mama's face like Ammu often did, nor did I mind his presence. I was fond of his company more than I was nervous. I narrowed my eyes like a fishing line to better catch the numbers floating on the page. Boro Mama sat next to me as if he were helping me scout out my prey. He was a protector, a friend. A part of me would always want to make him proud.

"Good, good," he said. "Nothing will stop this spirit."

When I looked into his eyes, I often saw a benevolence that rose from ashes of loss and defeat. The humble understanding that one could always have to rebuild. This much I deduced as a child from the stories Ammu had shared about Boro Mama during the Liberation War. In one of these stories, Boro Mama; my maternal grandfather, whom I called Nana; and the rest of our family were taking shelter in Nana's friend's house. Like Nana, this friend was Urdu speaking and culturally ambiguous. He kept the family hidden in the most discrete corners of his home and brought them food while the government forces shuffled outside his door. It was during one of these times that Boro Mama, seeing the chaos and uncertainty of the future, decided that he would go back to newly independent India, where they had emigrated from, to find a place for the family to live. So, he embarked on a solo trip, disguising himself. On his way he decided he would stop by one of their old family homes, just to relish it, before leaving it for good. He headed to Kushtia.

In the family home in Kushtia, not too far from Shilaidaha Kuthibari, where Rabindranath Tagore, the Nobel Peace Prize laureate, once lived, Boro Mama touched the walls with his hands, now soiled with the dirt of negligence, and sniffed for the lingering smoke of cigarettes he had inhaled many weeks before. He lay down on one of the uneven beds and folded his arms over his eyes. He would listen for the faint tête-à-têtes between his father and mother, or sisters, now tucked under the floorboards and layers of wall paint.

Miles away, Nana sensed that his son was in trouble; he had the inkling Boro Mama would indeed return to Kushtia, so he himself left to track him down. By the time Nana got to the house and entered it, he could already hear the footsteps of government forces gathering around the place. He ran through each room hastily — open doors creaking and swinging, his heart pounding — until he found Boro Mama snoring on a bed.

Nana shook him awake. "What are you doing here? We have to go!" Nana said in a loud whisper.

Then they heard the gunshots, and the smell of burning tires wafted to their noses. Boro Mama and Nana looked at each other as if it could be the last time, and bolted through the door in front of them, hurling any object in their way — old tables, photographs in frames, handmade boxes with handwritten letters — until they found their way through the back door. They ran without looking back, pretending not to hear the shouting behind them, or see the rising smoke. Until they did.

And there it was: their home burning to ashes, soon to be scattered under people's feet. It had been set on fire by the government forces, or maybe enemies that had informed the forces, the flames obliterating the lifetime they'd shared. The tears in Boro Mama's eyes unable to put them out. The gunshots fired again, and they ran.

So, when Boro Mama offered his advice we all trusted he was streetwise. He knew the secrets of resiliency; he had built his life all over again, and had hoped to do the same for all his kin.

I only vaguely remember the intensity of the diverse opinions on moving to Canada. Boro Mama, Abbu, Ammu. My memories of that time are like dreams that stay with you when you wake up in the morning, the fine details lost. What remained was a kind of lineament of both the stress and excitement of that time — which in Dhaka also seeped into our clothing, our skin, glistened through our shirts, *lungis*, *salwar kameezes*, and saris, impressed their promise on all of our movements and fluctuating voices.

One day Boro Mama strode through the door with a cardboard box of *ladoos* in one hand and paperwork in the other, and a smile that spread across his face. A few days later, we had more visitors — Ammu and Abbu's siblings and cousins, my first and second cousins, neighbours, friends, and even strangers. They sat in groups in our living room: their high-pitched laughs that later turned sombre. A celebration and a mourning, and I struggled to understand what was really going on.

It wasn't too long after the 1991 Bangladesh cyclone — one of the deadliest in history, which, like a wild carnivore, swallowed the Chittagong District whole as if it were a sacrificial lamb — that we would emigrate to Canada. The aftermath of the cyclone was the result of mismanagement and poor planning by authoritarian military governments and their civilian successors.

Near the time of our departure there seemed an impending feeling that homes would continue to be broken, and by forces greater than us. As a child, I didn't know that the country was just recovering from years of oppression, torture, and loss. Political instability, military rule and repression, the rise of fundamentalism based on politicized religion, famine, and starvation. Outside the doors of our home, as I sat my little bottom on sticky but slippery rickshaw seats, I saw more Nike shoes on people's feet, faces of Hollywood celebrities sneaking onto billboards and some television screens, more of my neighbours on the streets with suitcases saying goodbye to their loved ones. People were leaving. The world was evolving.

Parakeet must have known that some great change was coming, for that clever bird somehow slipped out of his cage and flew to every corner of the house, only occasionally stopping to rest on the windowsill. We chased it for days, but it would not return to its cage.

As a six-year-old, I didn't know I had already started grieving. While the family dreamed of the gains that would come with moving, there was also much to loose. Wayfaring down the streets, being greeted by everyone we saw, invited over for *cha* spontaneously and at various times of day, sitting on the balcony into the hours of the evening, the cars beneath us jamming — near-death collisions but no big deal — their volume and intensity comparable to my family's passionate debates as we sipped tea and ate. There were the stall owners in Newmarket or Gausia, calling out to us, telling us about the latest sale, only to catch our momentary glares. Also, the Bangladeshi news anchors who'd greet us every morning and evening from the television set, usually women and often in lively-coloured, body-hugging saris, perfect hair, pristine faces, moon-eyed, and speaking impeccable proper or *shubdo* Bangla. I'd try to figure out what they were saying while Ammu rolled up balls of curry-soaked rice in the palm of her hands and pushed them into my mouth.

I'd also lose the wooden swing that Ammu had to chase me off when scolding me about my flagrant dilly-dallying, like during the mornings of *Eid al-Adha*, the Muslim Feast of Sacrifice.

One of these *Eids*, I was a hot mess: my dark-brown hair in tangles, dirt beneath my fingernails, and my blood ecstatic with sugar I'd snuck from the kitchen.

The car horns were memorable that day. They were loud even for Dhaka; they rang out in obnoxious harmony.

"Good morning, good morning!" "*Eid Mubarak*!" I heard these greetings through the walls; they came from the streets outside. I could already taste the marmalade-hued *amriti* sweetmeat. I could already smell the nutty *chiraunji* and fruity *kewra* in the traditional Mughlai flatbread. Just the idea was enough to make me salivate. I wanted them in my grubby little hands. I could already see the middle-aged and old men in their *chikan*-embroidered *dopalli topis* biting aromatic *paan soparis*, areca nut wrapped in vibrant green betel leaves. There would also be shops where cow, goat, and sheep *Qurbani* meat could be purchased. Sometimes, during the rainy season and floods, the blood of these slaughtered animals would flow to the peoples' feet. I could imagine the vermilion water, its ripples dancing to the rising melody birthed by the catgut strings of mango-wood *dotaras* and from the bamboo flutes.

"*Alhumdulillah! Alhumdulillah*, for this incredible feast!" the people would shout.

Yet there I was, trapped inside, Ammu running after me with a broomstick in her hands, her voice hovering above my naked body as I ran to and fro. The tap had been on, water gushing out like a geyser from the ground. I still hadn't jumped in the shower but, as part of *Eid* etiquette, I had to be clean. So, she chased me like a poacher in a children's movie, and I ran past my swing, giving it a slight push. It soared as high as her voice when she's perturbed.

"*Shaytān mey!*" she shouted, which meant something like *devilish girl*, to point out my misbehaviour.

Behind her fuming frame, I noticed street beggars at the door lining up for food. During this holiday, we gave out goat meat, one-third for the home, one-third for relatives, and one-third for the poor. Our stovetops were running while the beggars had their palms out, their wrists extending toward the cracked window. Ammu's eyes followed mine and then she took a deep breath, let out a sigh. She melted into her disappointment, a grimace and then a tear, and, before more tears could trail down her face, I sulked diligently back to the mess I'd made.

This is the Ammu I would often see peering into her mirror, choosing peach for her lips and a pink powder for her cheeks. Kohl was too much, so she let her eyes be. Her brown eyes like mahogany obsidian. I imagined the fine lines around her mouth when she smiled were a trace to a lineage of queens, perhaps aristocratic blood. She possessed an aura of divinity. I loved seeing her in her golden sari. It was the crunchy kind, and reminded me of a chocolate wrapper. I hoped that one day I'd be as beautiful as her.

"I'm sorry, Ammu," I told her, and she peered into my eyes as if to say, "What kind of daughter have I made?"

I'd been escaping Ammu all morning but now that I was close, she didn't even try to clutch me, for maybe she knew that I'd always be loyal, and that I wouldn't be able to tolerate any sadness of hers. I could sense it in her downturned palm that she placed on my back, a gentle tap that felt momentarily like a hot needle on the edge of a flame.

Under this roof, Ammu and I tested each other always, the limits of our rebellion and love. However, it was now the beginning of a time of goodbyes, to the house and all its memories and lessons made.

Leaving Bangladesh also meant losing Sweety Khala, Ammu's younger sister. With her, I'd spend many of my hours, picking mangos from trees, visiting garment stores, or just sitting on the balcony dipping cake *rusk* in tea as she told everyone her stories. She was like a second mother to me, taking me everywhere she went, including on her honeymoon when her new husband would have to be extra patient with receiving her attention.

I'd also lose Nani, my maternal grandmother, who would roam around her white house in Rajshahi with the keys to all the rooms tied to the end of her sari, jingling. She'd often barge in on me on the balcony, pocketing dried mango with my sticky fingers. She would open her mouth to yell — exposing her tongue, orange from chewing copious *paan* — but would instead chuckle. Soon after, I would, too. We'd sit there under the sun after, Nani on a straw mat doing *dhikr*, pushing vibrant green *tasbih* beads with her wrinkled fingers, while I twirled in circles like a dervish to the holy words muttered under her breath.

I also had to say goodbye to my friends, one in particular who feels out of focus now but was, at the time, very distinct and incredibly important. He dipped his bread in water like it was milk. I remember that this nonconformity intrigued me. He, too, had a special bond with Parakeet — he'd hover over the cage observing the bird for long minutes in silence, as if he was counting its feathers. I'd stand there beside him, inspecting him inspecting the bird with the same kind of fascination. I was too young to desire him, but the feeling was something like desire, yearning for a shared closeness. I remember thinking, *If we leave, will I find him again?*

∞

I don't remember the details leading up to our departure to Canada, but I do remember the sensations were similar to what I felt when Ammu rushed to her socials, hopping houses, trailing away on elusive rickshaws painted bright yellow, orange, and maybe blue, the tail end of her uniquely patterned saris floating in the air.

Once I chased after her, not wanting to be left behind, my arms reaching out for her *anchal*, getting two inches closer, then falling. I looked down to see my oversized black sandals holding my tiny feet, and then up again to the back of the rickshaw disappearing around a street corner.

"Ammu! Ammu! Ammu!" My words must have hung like wet laundry on a clothing line, lifted in the air by winds during the arrival of a storm, forgotten but needing to be tended.

As I continued running, I looked to my left and then right. There were men half-sleeping like corpses, bodies covered by plastic bags, rotting food, and the smell of apathy. I saw also women with babies on their hips, searching like hungry zombies for an ounce of compassion from the travelling Dhakaiyas. I was overwhelmed by the darkness of the oncoming evening, engulfing me with all the other people on the street.

Thud! I fell. I sat on my little bottom and my half-open eyes caught a fuzzy glimpse of my legs. My knees were bloodied. My mother was gone. She came back eventually. She always did. But in those moments, the time after her leaving, I experienced her departure with a sort of desperate finality usually reserved for death.

We finally caught Parakeet and put him back in his cage, but it wasn't too long before he was out in the world again. Parakeet wasn't allowed to come to Canada with us.

One otherwise uneventful evening, Abbu and I picked up Parakeet's cage and brought it to the front door. Abbu turned the doorknob and went into our mini-porch. The late-afternoon sun had cast shadows on the ground. Golden hour was approaching. Abbu sat the cage down on a steady chair. He slowly opened the cage door, then navigated his sturdy hand in. Parakeet flinched and waddled away on its perch. Abbu clutched Parakeet swiftly but gently, then pulled his hand out of the cage. He stood upright, rotating his own body in a careful circle, allowing the bird to take in its surroundings in full. Abbu raised his arms to the sun, with Parakeet between his still-cupped hands.

He looked over his shoulder at me for a moment or two, as if to ask, "Are you ready?" I don't know if I did anything. I'm not sure what I responded. He slowly inched his hands away from each other before releasing them to his sides. I watched Parakeet falter at first, near-spiral in a slight free fall, my heart thumping, until it opened its wings, its striking shamrock-green feathers like a dab of paint in the rosé sunset, scooping the air and pulling itself up then away, soaring, soaring, gone. I whispered *"Jao pakhi,"* and nothing more. What had been done was done. Goodbyes don't need to be spoken to be goodbyes.

Conversations with Trees

I remember the time the bear passed the house in Thunder Bay — not growling or threatening, but stopping to stare, as if he'd come only to pass judgment. It was an elegant house, a white-brick diamond, bordered by garnet roses, amethyst lilacs, and emerald bushes. Peering over it was the regal Mount McKay, so when Ammu, Abbu, my one-year-old sister, and I arrived from Dhaka, it seemed nothing short of majestic. It was during the tail end of winter that this happened. A winter that takes you in like a hug, albeit one you squeamishly accept but don't necessarily want. It was the first time I saw snowflakes. These little angels — they fluttered from the sky onto my eyelids, dancing the whole way. I was a little human explorer, wobbling about in an astronaut snowsuit across large fields of snow and slippery ice.

In Dhaka, the gravel ground bites your feet, the sun's rays whip your back as you navigate a maze of cars, cows, and beggars.

In Thunder Bay, only stillness. Rows of houses deep in slumber and acres upon acres of wild.

Annabelle, who was as white as Christmas, didn't welcome me. Could I blame her? I didn't speak the language of the blue- and green-eyed children. Not the way they did. My Ahsan Khalu, who is Pori Khala's husband, drove my cousin Zahara to Annabelle's house every other Saturday, in a fancy car, for a playdate. I was never invited.

I didn't quite understand why, as I thought Zahara liked me. She, her younger sister, and I would often hide out in the furnished basement, playing radio using a tape recorder we had found in one of the dusty old trunks. I was the host, and they were my callers. Each would dial in, asking a random question, and I'd follow up with either an answer or my own questions. I would speak a combination of Bangla and English words. Questions ranged from how to best remove unwanted hair from the face to how to best survive a world war. The topics were endless, as were our giggles, so we kept our voices down before our mothers got too curious about our antics.

However, when Annabelle was over, it was as if I would disappear. Annabelle and my cousin would scurry over to the living room, to the zebra-printed couches and fluffy white carpet, and lay their toys all over. A good mystery, a hard-to-crack code; I remember listening intently to the vibrations of their words, unconstrained by their malleable mouths. Their playdough lips changed form — round, trapezoid, oval — swiftly and without hesitation. Now, when I tried to speak, my tongue would just hit the roof and sides of my mouth, the sound stuck behind my tonsils. I gulped the words down. As I moved closer, Annabelle and my cousin looked up to utter what sounded like a question or comment. I remember nodding, smiling, frowning, and shaking my head in response. They exchanged glances, glared at me for a moment or two, and chuckled. They continued to play while I escorted myself to the sidelines.

I watched them; awkwardly aware I'd been uninvited. It made me feel perverted. It made me feel like a voyeur.

In school, I sometimes felt a similar way. When the boys and girls played soccer in the gymnasium, I waited for them to say a word of invitation, perhaps reach out a hand, but they didn't.

In Dhaka, I had gone to an English-medium school and was familiar with the twenty-six letters of the English alphabet. Abbu had read me stories of great authors and books such as *Lambs' Tales from Shakespeare*. However, it was in Thunder Bay that I truly began experimenting with the sound of each letter, peering at myself in the mirror while shaping my lips, then by myself and in secret, putting the letters together to form words. Beautiful words. Strange words. Odd-sounding words. Funny words. I rotated my wrists like a symphony conductor, stretching the dots of ink into lines across paper. The cursive writing reminded me of the Arabic letters I often sketched, as well as the way a sari flows. It became a love affair, between English and me. The mere act of writing and uttering, and in secret, it was something very special.

I didn't know then that Bengalis had fought many battles to preserve their language, that language in Bengal, both pre- and post-India's separation from the British, was a means to retain individuality, dismantle other oppressions, to encourage the uplifting of humankind with creativity and connection. A whole Renaissance once. Bangla as the poetry of the people's hearts, their dignity, and their freedom from oppressors.

As I courted English, my ability to recognize Bangla letters gradually faded. My understanding of Hindi and Urdu also became secondary to English. It was how I would connect to this new land.

However, when Ahsan Khalu and Pori Khala's Bengali neighbours visited and I heard them speak Bangla, the lyrics of Ammu's lullabies returned. I'd waft into the lingering memory of her embrace, me cradled within her arms, her curly black hairs stroking my supple face, rocked ever so gently as I fell asleep. Never feeling alone and always loved.

In Thunder Bay, Abbu would frown while nudging the lasagna in front of him like it was a carcass. Sometimes he'd walk over to the window to stare into the blizzards, periodically turning his head to catch a glimpse of my tiny eyes floating along the edges of the dinner table. Abbu was especially fond of reminiscing after long days of job hunting that seemed to impose his mood on the house, the gravitas, even the speed at which shadows moved across the room. When he returned to the dinner table, he'd share his distaste for the interviewing process. "I have experience, and I'm fluent in English," he told Ahsan Khalu. "They just keep asking for Canadian experience. What does that really mean?"

As the years passed, the disappointment in his eyes melted into a steadfast river of responsibility.

I often found myself in Ahsan Khalu and Pori Khala's glass greenhouse. My mouth slightly gaped, I'd marvel at the mid-morning sun, its peach rays diffusing into transient clouds above the sharp edges of the triangular glass structure. When inside, I tiptoed just high enough to dip my fingers into flowerpots and touch the damp soil, inhaling deeper for the buoyant jasmine smells. It was mystical, this place, and within it, all the miracles birthed. Abbu and

Ammu joined Ahsan Khalu and Pori Khala in this pyramid second home, planting, watering, chatting, with their bright-ginger garden gloves and linen tweed hats. In the greenhouse, I mused at the buds when they bloomed into flowers, and sulked when they didn't, not understanding what conditions prevented the flourishing of a plant's soul.

One day, as I picked up one of the watering cans and twirled, sprinkling the water around me, leaving a bit of a puddle, I saw her, the Shayṭān Bride, briefly. Just as likely an illusion as an authentic vision, makes no difference, she appeared almost daydream-like, prophecy perhaps, divine warning, my own neurosis. For a fragment of a moment I saw her, or I felt like I saw her, sauntering past the red geraniums, her naked back, waist-length hair. Then she was gone. It was a vague moment trapped in a memory that sailed aimlessly onward. Had she come all the way from Dhaka to here? In what way did that world and this one overlap? Then I forgot about her.

Jungle

We stayed in Thunder Bay for a little more than six months. After Thunder Bay there was Toronto. It was still the early nineties when we moved near the intersection of Jane and St. Clair for a short while, into a house on a hill. The school I was enrolled in there was where I first spoke English in a public setting. It happened one typical afternoon during class, when we were making storybooks.

I remember waiting in line at the front of the class, where my teacher was handing out a package of markers, crayons, special notebooks, and stickers. I was wearing a navy-blue knee-length dress and standing behind two blond boys, who periodically turned their heads to me and chuckled then whispered something to each other.

Perplexed, I speculated what they had been talking about, and then one of them pointed and shouted, "It was probably her! She looks like she farted."

"Shhh," the other one said.

"Oh, she doesn't know English," the first one replied.

The laughter of the boys grew, and I stood there just listening. They had no idea that I understood everything they had said.

Later on, after I finished putting together my storybook, I ran up to my teacher, a Greek woman with curly dirty-blond hair that she kept in a low bun, perpetually flushed cheeks, and a green scarf that she always wore around her neck regardless of the season. I handed her my storybook, pointed to the passages I had written and complicated illustrations I had added, and, without much thought, unleashed a few sentences. All the children around me dropped their pencils, as they had never really heard me speak before. The colour evaporated from the teacher's face, and she stopped the class to share with everyone what I had said. I remember this moment poignantly, for it was as if I had been waiting, just waiting, to finally reveal what I had been creating, and it wasn't until I'd finally spoken that I properly understood that for the better part of a year I'd been waiting for my turn to participate.

Shortly after, we moved to Jungle, the area of Lawrence Heights in North York. Just four months prior to our move, my brother was born.

Jungle was a cluster of low-rise public housing apartments and bungalows. We moved into an apartment in the interior, where people said the wild ones lived. The belly of the beast, they warned, was behind the steps of the elementary school that I attended. The steps led to a path that, when followed, took you into Bagot and Dorney Court, which the other children called "Faggot and Horny Court."

"My mom says that once you go in there you never come back the same," one of my classmates told me.

"It's where they sell drugs. Where the bad men live," the other classmate said.

Jungle looked and felt so different from bare Thunder Bay. The streets were filled with women in hijabs and *abayas, ankaras* and *agbadas,* and the men in *kippahs* on the outskirts of the neighbourhoods. There was always a community potluck, where I'd find sweet, salty, pungent dishes, and Motown beats on the P.A. system before the morning announcements started. Jungle was a biome of people from all over the world, living together in entwined ways. Its nickname obviously racist. To the outsider, it was sometimes misunderstood. Within it was my adolescence, which I also experienced the same way.

Jungle was where Rukhsana, Fatima, and I would run to the rusty tire swing during Quran class recess on Saturday mornings. Each time Fatima pumped the tire swing forward, we'd all laugh a little louder. The higher I flew, the closer I felt to the tip of Mount Qaf, which Allah held in place along with the sky and earth. Sometimes my hijab would fall from my head and I'd fling it away to see if it could reach another realm.

In my elementary school, my teachers would sometimes ask me to stand in front of the class and share the knowledge I had gained from all the books I read. They were aware that, otherwise, I'd perhaps become a nuisance, waving my arms incessantly in the air, pleading for permission to answer every question. I became the class assistant, an unofficial substitute teacher sometimes, delivering lessons on wide-ranging topics: how volcanoes erupt, how snow forms, how people digest. During recess, however, I sometimes created trouble, punishing boys who teased girls by throwing dodge balls at them and then running away, as a type of playground vigilante. Mrs. Seidu, my grade three teacher, who had emigrated from Sierra Leone and had a husband from Ghana, was rather fond of me. She would come over for samosas and then biriyani at our house, discussing the immigrant experience with both Ammu and Abbu. Sometimes we would visit her, too, and delight in flavourful *waakye*.

Ammu and her friends from all parts of the South Asian, African, and Western Asian continents would also organize get-togethers in each other's homes, decorated with colourful tapestry and unique objects that were not available in Canadian stores. They played Farsi and Indian music. We'd all fill our mouths with *mantu*, biriyani, and kabobs while watching Bollywood films. We'd also gather in a circle and twirl our arms to traditional Afghan music, and then the young daughters would demonstrate their new belly-dancing skills.

I would play Karam and Ludo with Abbu and Ammu while a cricket match was on our television in the background. On the same day, I'd ask them to buy me expensive Wayne Gretzky skates and the brightest Maple Leafs jersey I could find.

In the same neighbourhood, mothers worked long hours in factories and fast-food chains while struggling to make time to help their children with homework, fathers were deported and families separated, and teenagers were told to avoid wearing certain colours, as they could be mistaken for a gang member and shot dead.

I looked forward to our trips to BiWay every Saturday, and the McDonalds beside it that sold soft-serve ice cream. BiWay was my favourite because it was the only store where Ammu would spend a little more freely. In Thunder Bay, Pori Khala would take Ammu to the fancy stores. She'd pick up shirts made of twill, silk, cotton, or poplin, rubbing them between her index finger and thumb.

"Hmmm," she would say under her breath, her lips pursed, the same way Ammu inspected the fine details of gold in the hustle bustle of Dhaka's Newmarket shops. Pori Khala would investigate the sweaters next, made of cashmere and wool, and then her fingers would slide along the vertical ridges of solid corduroy, which too required time and careful attention. Ammu and I trailed behind her for hours until we found ourselves at the cash register. Pori Khala would have a couple of pieces cradled in her chest, Ammu's hands would be empty. Ammu would look at the tags hanging from Pori Khala's selection, and her face would crumple like a pop can. "We'll go to a different store," she would say to me.

I would stretch my arm outward, reaching to feel the sweater Pori Khala held. Its softness as subtle and serene as a thousand sleeps. At BiWay, I could find my own version of such things.

One day in BiWay, as Ammu pushed the shopping cart through the aisles and I jumped on and off it, I noticed a pair of bright-pink snow pants from afar. I pointed instantly, then turned my face to Ammu with a slight pout and raised eyebrows, as if to say *I want this*. Ammu, very mindful of what we spent, first shook her head, and then I pleaded, "Please? It's pretty!" As I said this I imagined the thrills that I'd get sliding down the great green hill next to our apartment while wearing them.

"No!" Ammu said. "We're in a new place and we have to be careful with what we spend."

I jumped off the cart and ran to the pants, brought them back, and dumped them in the cart. "Please, please, please!" I said. "I want to toboggan."

Ammu by now was flustered. She also had my younger sister in her arms and was looking through a pile of mismatched socks. My sister began crying and Ammu's face became flushed pink.

I stomped my feet, then decided to negotiate. "I'll clean my room, or the living room. I won't make any more messes."

Ammu looked up from the pile of socks and squinted. "Fine," she said. "But only because you're my eldest." Then she ruffled my hair.

These became my favourite snow pants.

In Jungle, there was always a buzz of activity in our apartment. Ammu was working for the first time, as a classroom assistant; she had never done so in Dhaka. She was also taking classes at the local college to upgrade her English and learn teaching skills. There were often papers scattered across our tangerine sofa and the Persian rug where we sat. Ammu and I scratched our heads and scribbled with our pens, moved by creative spirit and a roaring tenacity. I had now become Ammu's English tutor. We spent countless hours practising so she could find employment and pay for things like my Superwoman Barbies.

Over the years, despite all her efforts, I'd hear Ammu say from time to time, "I didn't get the job." Wrinkles on her face forming and deepening, the queen of Dhaka would sometimes look as tired as a rag doll. I would find her often on the *jai-namaz*, crying. She worked part-time for years, the permanent positions always, in the end, given to younger, whiter, and less experienced Canadian university graduates.

Seeing how busy Ammu was, I would often drag our green plastic bucket into the bathroom tub and fill it with water and detergent, as well as one squirt of shampoo, just to add a fruity scent. I'd tug the overflowing bucket of water out of the bathtub with every ounce of strength I had and use it to scrub the floors, imagining myself as Cinderella. When Ammu would open the apartment door, she would see the floor sparkle like the white of teeth. The smirk pressing on her cheeks. My acts of service always opened the door to Ammu's heart.

Abbu, at the time, was often out, searching endlessly for employment. He was also enrolled in college to complete a new degree in computer programming, which helped him successfully apply for a position that was more aligned with his skills, although in a totally different field. Abbu had started off with a door-to-door sales job, despite having been a distinguished engineer before emigrating. We had entered Canada during the tail end of a recession. On his feet all day, he was often tired when he got home, unable to play with me like he used to in Dhaka. During this particularly arduous time of our lives, when Abbu was often gone for most of the day, I sometimes sobbed, longing for his gentle presence and words of advice. When he was there, my world always did change for the better.

For example, there was the time when I got eliminated from a spelling bee. There were annual competitions, and this particular year I had made it to the semi-finals. During the critical moment, which at the time felt like it would determine my future, I was asked to spell *Jedi* — the *Star Wars* Jedi — which was not a familiar term to me, as I didn't have cable television and didn't visit movie theatres to watch Hollywood films with my family, like some of the other students did.

It was terrible, that dryness in my mouth when I couldn't spell this random word that everyone else knew so well. Ammu's lips were turned down the entire car ride home. Later she said to me, "You are so irresponsible! How could you fail? You spent all summer riding that bike, instead of practising!"

It was true; I had done that. It was a new bike that Abbu had gifted me with the money he had made. I fell while riding it a good ten times or more, but I had been so determined that summer to learn.

"I know that you like trying new things, challenging your mind," Abbu had said.

When Ammu stood there, her arms across her chest, Abbu manoeuvred in between us. He turned to Ammu and said, "She may not have won the spelling bee, but she learned how to ride a bike. That's certainly something."

Then he turned to me. "Congratulations, my dear."

In our little family, there was also my two younger siblings, with whom I played school, teaching them different topics. For them, I once organized our very own Olympics. Couch cushions overturned to practise our gymnastics on and smooth socks to slide through the hallways as if we were figure skaters. Of course, my siblings also received front row seats to all the movies I'd act out in different costumes.

It was all a world of play and wonder; of new beginnings.

The apartment we lived in had four windows. Ammu and I both took to staring out of them. I loved to watch animals and people walk by, and Ammu, well, she liked to watch me. It was her daily ritual to keep an eye on me as I sauntered to and from school, as though her watch could protect me from all the world's dangers.

From all of the windows, I could see a surrounding patch of green grass embellished in dozens of bright-yellow dandelions. I'd dance through them often, stopping to pluck and smell, then blow the puffy seedlings away. It was my little secret garden, like the kind Ahsan Khalu and Pori Khala had in Thunder Bay, the one in their grand glass greenhouse. I must have made a thousand wishes, now drifting to every corner of the earth.

I wish for a saxophone.

I wish to climb a volcano to see the lava.

I wish to see Billy at the library again.

I wish for Ammu to pass her ESL test today.

One day, from one of these windows, the one facing the back of the elementary school, Ammu saw me get picked up by a stranger, and her protective watch could not prevent it.

It happened during winter. I was coming home from school for lunch in my new snow pants. I saw Ammu's face peering, as usual, from the windowsill. I went past the hill I often tobogganed down, which now stood as an observer, witness to me counting my steps as my boots crunched the snow. I also passed the daycare playground, the red and yellow slides and rusty blue monkey bars still wet from the earlier snowfall.

With my depth perception misled, I dipped my right boot so deep into the snow that I just couldn't lift my leg up anymore. Trapped, I yanked, pulling myself backward and thudding onto my little bottom, my gloveless hands stinging. I continued to pull and pull but my leg wouldn't move from out of the snow. Beyond my blurry vision, the taste of salty tears and snot on my lips, was Ammu at the window like a mannequin. Twenty minutes passed of me trapped and writhing in the snow with my hands and feet stinging from the cold, and then a fuzzy shadow appeared from behind and grew. I turned around. The shadow belonged to a man who I thought of as Viking because he was broad boned and red bearded, with heavy gladiator arms, the way Vikings had looked in books I had read. He brought his colossal stature down so that he was on his knees. His chest was eye level to me.

"Do you need help?" he whispered, gutturally.

I nodded.

"Where do you live? Where are your parents?"

I pointed to the window where Ammu stood watching.

"Do you want me to take you home?" he asked.

I wondered if I should say yes. Although, from afar, Ammu's expression seemed unchanged, I thought how alarmed she would be if I went with him. My stomach panged with the guilt of how I may cause her to question her ability as a mother if I was brought home by a stranger, although I could not articulate this at the time. I also worried I would disappoint her by ignoring her motherly pleas to stay away from strangers. At the same time, it seemed a matter of survival because the frost, its bite feeling like death.

If the Viking did take me, Ammu might at first shout and scream. She would think that I had made myself vulnerable to this man's innate tendency for something she called *rape*. Rape was something she referenced in plenty of indirect ways, as well as its consequence: shame and disgrace. When she'd see it on television screens — this mysterious thing that looked like men who were animals and women that screamed — she'd put her hands over her mouth or widen her eyes, a cavernous caution. When the characters brought their lips together and kissed, she also had this same reaction. And during conversations with her friends about young women and men, the message was persistently the same: *Guard your body or there will be consequences.*

I didn't know then that these warnings and whispers were not particular to my family. It didn't seem like a bad message as a child, but what stuck was the strange sensation of power and responsibility over my own body; the understanding that my awareness of it should be so great, but at the same time, knowing women's and girls' bodies could, in an instant, almost become disposable at the hands of men, people, and the general world.

I wished Ammu would not worry so much, but then I wondered if she should worry more. Was there such a thing as too scared when it came to rape?

I decided to let him help me.

The Viking picked me up with his thick arms, pulled me over his shoulder, and marched toward the building. The hard bone of his shoulder pressed into my stomach. My head bobbed as quickly as my heart pounded, and as quickly as he took his steps. I sniffed his musk. Was Ammu thinking the man had kidnapped me? Was she frantically searching for me now? What had she been afraid of that she hadn't come down herself? Or did she not realize I was stuck? What if the government takes me away, like what my class-mates said happens to some children?

My stomach knotted. The urge to scream was there but I gulped.

When he reached the building gate, he climbed up the stairs to the third floor where we lived. The closer the Viking got to our apartment door, the more my toes stung. I decided then that as much as I told myself that Ammu didn't come down because she didn't love me enough, or I wasn't worthy enough, she was probably just too scared and confused by what it all could have meant. It was also possible she couldn't leave the apartment because of her newborn son, my younger brother, or my growing toddler sister, who needed her to stay.

When Ammu answered, the Viking immediately and pointed-ly asked her, "Is this your daughter?"

Ammu nodded, her eyes frantically searching his face and then mine. It was a look I recognized, concerned for my well-being, but also hers, and then the opinion of the rest of the world, and how the situation must have looked.

"She was sitting alone in the cold out there in the snow. You'll have to take better care of her. And these snow pants, they look very big. You should buy her ones that fit."

I began to squirm myself out of his grip as a method of resist-ance to his recommendations. He had brought me home — why did he feel the need to make speeches? Teach lessons?

Viking pulled me down from his shoulders. I hated him sud-denly. Ammu was a busy woman. In between her long study ses-sions, she made us meals that we wanted. With a duster in one hand and my bookbag in the other, she simultaneously cleaned the entire apartment while checking that I had read my books. She worked part-time, sewed clothing for her neighbours, took driving lessons, made biriyani for Ramadan *iftars* to serve people at our local mosque, organized socials, and babysat for friends.

"Thank you," Ammu told the Viking softly, and then brought me inside. She closed the door.

I thought Ammu would ask more questions of both him and I, but she didn't. Instead, she pulled a wool blanket over my legs. She was shaking. In that moment, I wanted so very much to pull the wool blanket from my toes and wrap it around Ammu instead. The impulse was tantamount to my longing to rip my own heart out of my chest and place it at her feet, as that's where the gates to heaven would be. And somehow, in this moment, I realized all I actually wanted was for her to never stop loving me, and her forgiveness.

One day I was playing dodgeball with a handful of the other girls and boys at school. We were playing near a special tree on a hill, where the other girls said Bloody Mary was buried.

"I dare you to call her name three times," they said. "Do it in front of a mirror."

I wondered then if Bloody Mary was a *jinniyah*, a female jinn, like the ones I heard about in Dhaka. Curious, I followed the girls to the bathroom, where they stood outside the door. I hastily ran to the mirror. The stalls were grey, the tiles were stone, and the porcelain sink was only a few inches from my pelvis. I stood there, my hands shaking but my chin upward and eyes straight.

"I will be brave. I will be brave," I said to myself. I slid my fingers over the sullied mirror as the giggles of the girls outside grew louder. I called out "Bloody Mary! Bloody Mary! Bloody Mary!" but nothing happened. So, then I said, "Shayṭān Bride! Shayṭān Bride! Shayṭān Bride!" expecting to see a woman with long black hair, maybe some blood on her lips dripping down to her breasts, but, once again, nothing. There was no magic, no metamorphoses, just my plain reflection in the unremarkable school bathroom. The hinge of one of the stall doors squeaked. I noticed the piece of toilet paper under my feet. The recess bell rang. I ran out of the bathroom. All the other girls were gone.

Not too long after this incident, I was traversing home, following the grey pavement trail, as I always did, passing the row of marmalade-orange–brownish houses, over the silver railing bridge, down the street, Ammu in the window, as usual, peering at me. The whole journey down there was a pounding on my abdomen walls, my body calling attention to itself.

At home, I saw the blood that came from between my legs. I nonchalantly told Ammu, who wrinkled her face, then spent the rest of the day and evening pacing back and forth. I wanted to tell her about Bloody Mary, that it could have been her doing, or maybe the Shayṭān Bride, who could have paid a visit without my knowing. But also, that I had heard about girls bleeding from my friends.

Instead, I asked her, "What's wrong?"

"Why did it happen so fast? You'll have to be more careful," she replied. There were wafting clouds above our heads, signalling that things had changed.

Then she cried.

Where did it come from, this concern, this anguish, that would now never go away? I resented her for this sadness and also myself for causing it. At the same time, I could also feel what she did: the tenderness of an open wound. Ammu was like an ocean, and I a river; we were connected, with no end or beginning. Bodies of blood, bodies of water, Ammu and I flowing into each other. I wondered if God got angry when the capacity for life was not appreciated.

Abbu bled in the brain a few years after. It was a brain hemorrhage from falling on ice and hitting his head. The bad news came to me while I was in the middle of fourth-grade French class, learning the appropriate use of prepositions to signify figurative locations.

"*Dans la situation actuelle*; *dans ces conditions*," said Mr. Dubois, as he chalked the blackboard. The librarian, Mrs. Evans, whose outfits were often embellished with scintillating beads, knocked on the door asking for me. She took me to the office, where Ammu stood with an obscure look, my eight-year-old sister, with her pink-and-white floral dress and curly black hair, holding her hand.

"Your Abbu is in the hospital," Ammu said, the franticness on her face spreading out and suspending in the air around her.

I don't remember how we got to Toronto General Hospital, but when we did we floundered through aluminum doors toward the elevator. I saw a herd of nurses barging through hallways and turning corners, some pushing patients in wheelchairs and others holding clipboards, making their rounds. Perhaps one or two of them smiled, rotated their heads to say hello to others, but most looked onward and forward. Like robots, they seemed preprogrammed and deterministic.

The room that we entered had two hospital beds, each sheltered by periwinkle-hued plastic curtains. We were escorted by a nurse with distinguished auburn curls, past the first bed to the second. When the nurse moved the bed's curtains, I saw Abbu lying still and pale like a marble statue, his head angled toward us, the tip of his nose diagonal to his right toe. He had needles in the veins of his hands, masked by white tape and attached to a half-full drip. His body at the time did not do justice to the force of his character inside.

When Abbu realized we were there, the corners of his mouth became slightly upturned, and there was a glint in his eyes like the sun's reflection in water. We moved closer to him.

He opened his lips slowly. "I almost died," he said. "But I'm alive, *Alhumdulillah*."

I could tell from the faintness in his eyes that he had been somewhere else, seen something that none of us had.

"Our lives, they are not long. We have to remember what's important. Think about life, think about death."

I picked up Abbu's hand — once thick, large, durable, now limp and lying loose. Afterward, as a person who had almost faced death, Abbu would remember his one crucial priority: his duty as a father to protect his children through *Deen*.

Abbu became increasingly preoccupied with my online activity and phone chats, my trips to school and back, the way I spoke, and the way I dressed. How many times I prayed, or what I was reading.

"Did you read the news?" he would ask. "Have you learned about this ... or that ... What are you doing to play your part? There are terrible things happening in the world right now. I want you to think about them critically."

In retrospect, at the time I didn't know much of what was happening in the broader context of the world, let alone the country. What Abbu wanted me to think about specifically was my Muslim identity and what it meant in this new place we were in, how the world was shaping who I would eventually become.

Instead, all I felt was restriction. *You can't go here. You can't do that. You have to protect yourself.* Stricter curfews, more confinement, and monitoring. A type of informal surveillance of my behaviour.

Why are you monitoring me? I thought. *As if I'm going to do something wrong. Have I done something wrong?*

I didn't know then that the whole of Canada is shaped like a panopticon, with law enforcement and the government at its centre. Muslims would be increasingly monitored without having information on who was observing and what they were concluding — leaving them with a heightened awareness about the perception of their behaviour. The surveillance of Muslim men and their families like a curse that removes the focus from the faith itself, and all you're left with are delusions.

"Don't text or publicly say anything related to religion because you never know who is watching or listening."

"You should take off your scarf when you're in this region …"

"No hijabs for photo identification."

"Are you sure you want to keep a beard when you go for that job interview?"

"I think you should remove your experience at that Islamic organization from your resume."

"Probably best you don't travel at this time. You're more likely to get pulled over at the airport with that last name …"

"If I were you, I wouldn't share my family or marital problems with these white people. They might call the cops."

"Don't pray frantically in public."

Years into my adulthood, I would go to *Masjid* Toronto on Dundas Street, often at lunch and after work. It was a special place for me, where I parked my preoccupations with everyday worldly life, the same way I put away my shoes at the entrance before going in. This was where, as I sat on the carpet cross-legged or put my head down in *sujud*, I remembered I was more than the mortal body I found myself in. It was where I met a Bengali Imam who showed me photographs of his first daughter, who had just completed her studies, gotten married, had a child. "This country," he told me, "made dreams come true."

On one particular day at this important place, I saw something different: ordinary Torontonians holding signs that read "Say NO to Islam!" They were crowding around the mosque entrance, fuming, loud. Everyday people for whom I once most likely opened a door or gave up a subway seat, maybe even a job, unconsciously. As I briskly moved past them to open the mosque door and enter, my palms became drenched in sweat and there were tears at the back of my eyes, waiting to be released. But I wouldn't. This was once a place of safety; now it was where I'd be watched.

In Jungle and beyond, people watched Muslims, Muslims watched each other, and Abbu watched me.

During my adolescence in Jungle, the more confined and restricted I felt, the more intriguing the world on the other side of our apartment windows appeared. For most of my childhood, I retreated to the various planes of my mind, where I stored and pondered ideas I had read about in books and sketched characters and developed storylines for scripts. I played the stories out on the back of my eyelids like a film reel before I slept. Sometimes, if I fell asleep before a story ended, I'd physically act out the remaining scenes in the morning, with imaginary people, dancing with walls and talking to pillows. Ammu caught me smooching the wall once and scolded me for this very disturbing behaviour.

Now, in adolescence, this internal playground was just not enough. I remember the strong inclination to interact with the world and its people in a more tactile, physical way. The mysteries I started to become fascinated with were that of the heart, for I often felt mine tug, sometimes without explanation. My heart's language was layered; its expressions quite particular but still in synonymity with each other. Like similar notes of music that were quite unique by themselves. Notes that needed a form of expression. Such is adolescence for most, I suppose.

Each time I did something unacceptable, my fate of confinement became more sealed. My middle school graduation night was one such time. I was the class valedictorian and had also won about ten awards. I was wearing a beautiful lavender silk dress and was excited to dance with my friends. When the after-party dance segment started, I was elated. The sounds of the bass and the twinkle of the fairy lights put me in a trance. I knew I couldn't stay for the entire dance, and that I'd have to get home before ten o'clock. I'd enjoy the moments I had, for there was much to be proud of, and I had been good. I was surely deserving. I spun periodically, wondering if this would be when I could also dance with a prince.

After perhaps only about half an hour of being immersed in the magical fog of various hues that filled the place, I caught Abbu storming in with eyes that had a tint of red in them. Although the room was dark, I was certain everyone around me would see the interaction we were about to have. Abbu grabbed my wrist and escorted me out the door, without looking back. My peers stood still, just observing. He moved with such thunder, I struggled to keep up, my feet almost slipping out of the ivory-hued sandals I wore. The edges of my dress trailed on the floor as I left.

Outside the school gymnasium, some teachers and students hovered around Abbu and I in a circle. The new makeup from Zellers I had eagerly applied earlier, purple eyeshadow and blue tinted mascara, were wiped away by my distress. I fell to Abbu's feet with my wrist still in his hands and cried "Why?" I was usually quite composed, but not this time.

The entire year leading up to this moment, Abbu had patrolled the school grounds before school started and after it ended, to ensure I wouldn't run off with troublesome friends. Sometimes my classmates would see him standing outside our classroom window just looking on, point and laugh, then shout, "Oh, look, your Paki dad is following you again!" The teachers would ask me later, "Is something going on at home?" My heart would pound, afraid of being taken away from the person I loved most, so I'd lower my eyes and pray for something else to divert their attention.

So, on my graduation night, when my teachers asked again if I was all right, suddenly I realized I was being watched like a spectacle. Oh, what they would deduce about Abbu, with their lack of understanding, and how they could hurt him with their ideas — and by hurting him, hurt me. As for me, I was also embarrassed that I couldn't be *normal*. I eventually wiped my tears and left with Abbu, although I was enraged with him and would be for months to come.

So, that summer, as I was under continued lockdown, I watched from my window. I saw the sun leave, disgruntled, and I retreated to its shadows. It's where I would now stay. The world, which I had imagined would become grander as I grew, shrivelled. The darkness trickled in.

Although my heart didn't quite understand at the time why I had to experience what I did, something many of my friends hadn't or wouldn't, I learned that my confinement was meant to be a mitigation to the worst thing that could happen: me forming any kind of sexual repertoire with anyone. If a young woman had any sort of entanglement with a young boy or man before marriage, it would do great damage to the perception of not just her, but her entire family.

As a young girl, the connection between joy and family dishonour made no logical sense to me. I had only one desire: to explore the world and pursue what called to my heart. And I wondered, too, why it was that boys could follow this desire with less caution or discretion and I, who had always been more well-behaved than any of the boys in my grade, could not.

Regardless, I saw the implications of this unfold the very next day after graduation, when I sneaked out of my summer science program to see my friends because I had missed the graduation dance. Abbu called the father of a friend of Afghan descent, who was supposed to drop me home, who told him I had not shown up at all. The father went on to tell Abbu about my shamelessness, not out of concern for where I had been and if I was okay, but to reinstate his own accomplishment, given his own daughter's relative obedience, clearly a source of pride related to his own self-image. As he told Abbu that he himself had done a better job of raising his daughter according to certain values, and that Abbu had failed, I watched Abbu's eyes lower and his face wrinkle. This friend and her father weren't particularly religious, nor did they seem to spend much time pondering mortality, afterlife, or ethics, like Abbu often did. Yet, they seemed to speak with such authority on these subjects. Furthermore, they didn't even know Abbu the way I did.

Abbu said nothing to him or me after that discovery of my betrayal, even if my friends were girls, good girls, overachievers. Inside, I reflected on how I had once again disappointed him. To love him, to be loyal, I'd have to sacrifice joy, exploration, discovery, or find it in more acceptable forms.

I couldn't understand how I was supposed to see the volcanoes, the moon, the girls and boys who unveiled interesting secrets, and the marvels of humans and the world, when all I could feel was shame for having unintentionally hurt others because I was pursuing the trajectory of my own curiosities and imagination. Is it in moments like these that young girls begin to lose sight of their inner desires and needs, because they become conditioned to focus on others instead? The precautions they need to take to not hurt other people, for they would be punished in some way. I would learn that this certainly exists across cultures, it just looks different.

As a young girl becoming a woman, I also learned the importance of restraint as protection. I studied the concept of *taqwa*, or God consciousness, so I could remember Allah more often and be more mindful of how I moved through the world. But still, my heart sometimes reigned on its own terms.

Javier, for example, who lived on the same floor as us with his single mother, sometimes rode his bike in the park in front of our building, his big black dog running loose behind him, all the neighbours complaining. We often stared at each other from afar, but never spoke. As we both gained years, I saw him less in the park and more often in the stairwells of the building, with the backdrop of graffiti and amid a strong stench of weed. His bloodshot red eyes and purple arm. I remember galloping down the staircase once, passing by him, when he looked up at me.

"Stop," he said, and I did, my right foot hanging in the air until I brought it down, softly.

I thought then that I would tell him how I had felt about him since I first laid eyes on him years ago, which was *intrigued*. Now my lips trembled as I finally dared to speak.

"Do you want a joint?" he asked before I could say anything. He seemed dazed.

The little hairs on my arm stood to attention. I thought I saw an outline of the Shayṭān Bride hidden behind the smoke. Her wild black hair and a seductive poison-malachite green sari. Did she say to stay or to leave? I would do the opposite. I knew I shouldn't spend time alone with boys, especially ones with purple arms. Abbu and Ammu were a few doors down. If they saw me there, they would panic, so I hurried away.

The pull was tremendous. What was he like? What music did he listen to? What books did he read? Why did he have a purple arm? How did he feel about the complaints he got about his big black dog running on the streets unleashed? So many questions.

I didn't know then that a few years after that, Javier's mother would stop me in the building hallway. She was a Latina woman who looked younger than her son. "H-have you se-seen m-my son?" she would stammer. "I haven't been able to find him for days. I am worried about him."

I would look into Javier's mother's puffy eyes. "No, I'm sorry," I would reply.

She'd take her leave, mumbling, "I've lost my son."

Javier never did come back to his mother, the building, or me.

In later years, the stairwell where Javier used to sit would become the spot where I would change out of my loose, modest clothing — baggy checkered shirts, track pants, and windbreakers — into short skirts and tank tops, as this is what most of the girls in the neighbourhood wore. This way of dressing only seemed normal. At the time, the modest fashion industry wasn't popular or as easily accessible; social media hadn't exploded. There was hardly any representation at all when I turned on television screens or picked up books from library shelves. Abbu would catch me one day and sternly say, "This doesn't happen in Bangladesh or any other Muslim majority country."

He'd point to an imaginary painting of a memory, a recollection of Dhaka as he had left it. Memories of migration that get a shrine of their own, that are worshipped, and that diaspora is expected to live up to, all while globalization washes up the shores of almost every country in the world.

At the time he was trying to explain *haya*, a particular bashfulness that protects you from the harm that comes from drawing too much attention to yourself, and which applies to men, too. A whole spiritual philosophy that in application is often misunderstood. It would only be years later that I would better understand this.

I would wear the hijab to ground my focus in the holy month of fasting and prayer, to instill in me discipline for spiritual endeavours. At the time, I was only wearing it when praying and during religious observances; however, I contemplated wearing it permanently and out of choice. I thought I would take baby steps, trial it. Perhaps it would help me reclaim my faith, given the prevalent ideologies about Muslims at the time, which were so shallow they might as well have been lies. I wanted to find a way to better connect to Allah.

One day at work, with this cloth on my head, my co-worker Scott had asked, "So, why are you wearing this? What's the purpose?"

Scott was in his forties with a voice of deep slumber.

"It's a personal quest, to help me mentally and spiritually this month, and perhaps beyond," I told him.

"I am curious to know what led you to this," he continued to probe. "Certainly, I would hope it isn't because you were forced to.'

I was telling him more about the holy month when Anna, another co-worker, moseyed into the meeting room. A tall Polish woman in her early fifties, she wore cat-eye frames and coral beads around her neck.

"What are you two talking about?" she asked, pouring herself a cup of coffee — the aroma of roasted beans settling in the air, all three of us straightening our spine to its sharp hit.

Scott and I looked up at her, and Scott said, "Just about the hijab and Ramadan."

"Oh, yes." Anna sat down at our circular table, one leg over the other, red mug in one hand and the other pushing back her glasses, which were gliding down her nose. "I find it interesting when Muslim women who don't wear the hijab speak for the entire community of Muslim women." Anna sipped her coffee and looked me straight in the eyes, as if either searching for my approval or questioning whether I should be speaking on the topic at all. I couldn't quite tell just yet. She'd studied this stuff, she reminded us, her observations were educated.

"I don't know if not wearing it makes you any less Muslim. It's not as black and white as it looks on the outside. There are many reasons why women may or may not wear it. There's culture.

There is also the factor of choice. At the end of the day, no person can tell you what is in your heart," I said to her.

"Regardless, I do this work in the community, and I just find it disturbing because you are more racialized when you wear hijab versus when you don't. Those who won't wear it are more passing."

I would agree with her about racialization and visibility, but then wonder about the brick she had now laid in building some theory of internal faith and outer appearance, and the relationship between that and the colonial frame. Really, the construction of it all. Regression versus modernity, religious visibility versus progression. I would wonder how this cloth on my head, which brought me closer to faith, now signified where on some elusive battleground I stood. Did I want to be associated with being modernized and progressive, or the ideal, pristine Muslimah who didn't make mistakes, or the oppressed victim needing help? And why were these options my only choices? Did my decisions have space for nuance? Wasn't I complicated? Hadn't I multiple dimensions that grew and retracted at any given moment, depending on where I was and how I found myself and who I wanted to be and how I would evolve personally, professionally, ideologically, spiritually, sexually?

Anna continued talking, telling me about a woman she knew, who she once worked with, who booked speaking gigs on the topic of veiling when she herself didn't veil. This woman spoke about the damage caused by Bill 62 in Quebec, preventing a person with a face covering from receiving or delivering a public service. As this bill targeted people in the public sector, doctors couldn't practice, nor could nurses, public school teachers, or other public sector professionals.

"She got the limelight, she did, but what does she truly know about their experience?" As Anna continued to speak, I stopped listening, as I had nothing to learn from her about my faith. The conversation was more political in nature. Instead, I'd think about governments taking away choice, like the choice taken from women across the world who were killed for not veiling, like the choice taken from women across the world who were ostracized for veiling. The paradoxical relationship between women and clothes, religion and clothes, race and clothes, women and religion, women and race — they circled like the shore circles the ocean.

As I left the office that day, through the elevators toward the exit, a male colleague swiftly ran ahead to open the door for me. Later, in the subway, a young woman gave up her seat for me. I basked in the sudden politeness, exasperated by the kindness of complete strangers. Were they reacting to my hijab? Did wearing a hijab make me a different person? Unconcerned with how my clothing sat on the curves of my form, the tightness or fit, I would indulge in a freedom nestled privately underneath the layers.

I remembered being a young girl and flipping through young girl magazines in the Barbara Frum Library and noticing the titles of the articles:

"How to Attract a Man"

"What Your Eyeshadow Means to Him"

"Ten Tricks for an Unforgettable Blowjob"

Wow, I had thought at the time, sitting in the magazine section of the library with my mouth gaping, *there is so much to do.*

Under these layers, I felt free from that. Yet, climbing down the steps of the bus at my stop, a disgruntled man pushed past me and I hit the railing. I knew distinctly that his behaviour was a reaction to my clothing, my religion, my race, my gender, my gender expression, and my culture — and, beyond that, both my refusal to hide these parts of myself and the desire within me to both perform and even amplify these aspects of myself. Is this how all my Muslim sisters felt, the ones who wore the hijab or niqab or *abayas* every day in the streets of Toronto? I wouldn't know. I could only speak for myself.

Sometime during the months that followed, I was at Queen's Park Circle, at the reception of Ontario's new premier. Among the civil servants, myself included, passersby, and neighbours, there were a few holding signs that said "Send back the Muslims." I would wonder then about the paradoxical nakedness that could also be felt beneath this cloth, the vulnerability. I would wonder how hate speech could be allowed so easily on these grounds.

Eventually, I would come to my own understanding of what veiling meant for me, which was deeply intwined with my feelings about how others perceive me, how they relate to me, and what clothing would signify to me. What role clothing would play in my own understanding of faith, and how it could possibly bring me closer to Allah. Although I had a choice about it, for which I was grateful, I would acknowledge then that both its presence and its absence on my body told a story. For it seemed to me, no story would ever be completely mine. No, could never be completely mine.

Whether it was a sari, hijab, or short skirt, as a woman I would always find myself in the middle of a battle, aware my body was always at risk of becoming some political tool, and still a pivotal way of conveying my internal self to others. That the answer to who you are can shift — sometimes I would be totally confident in who I was, and a new thing would happen to destabilize that notion of selfhood. Walt Whitman once said, "I am large, I contain multitudes." I would realize this truth about myself, too.

I'd realize that was all the reason for me to develop my own — to a degree autonomous — relationship with my body and with clothing, separate from all other people and influences. As challenging as this is.

One day I stood at the window and reflected on Jungle's complex biome: the way the buildings stood, the way the ground lay, the way the people moved. A small of piece of Canada, and it was our *home*. I had a letter in my hand addressed to Abbu. Through the window, I saw him heading toward me. He was pushing a shopping cart, returning from Fortinos in Lawrence Square Mall with a small amount of groceries.

I, in that moment, with whatever tenacity I was thought to have, was not prepared for what I'd do that day: to give him this letter I thought was important. In it I expressed that I wanted to know why he had changed since his brain hemorrhage; how he seemed to me, at times: overly involved but increasingly disconnected; how on the *jai-namaz* I felt most grounded but also scrutinized, as if my actions were being noted by the passersby in addition to the angels who took notes of people's deeds; whether he really continued to see me as a good person; why it mattered that he did; how I just wanted to fit in, to have friends; that my friends were a connection to the great big world that I so much wanted to explore; and that I hoped to restore our relationship and I wanted to know what I had done wrong.

The rain hammered the windowpane. I massaged the letter with my fingers. I heard a knock on the door, and then it creaked open. Abbu strolled in, drenched.

He turned toward me and, in a half-hushed tone, said, "My dear, can you help me put these away?"

I looked back at him, holding the letter behind my back. "Abbu, I am afraid of …" I muttered.

Abbu dropped his groceries on the floor and took off his jacket as if he hadn't heard me until, finally, we looked at each other, like two friends who hadn't seen each other for years and had finally met again. I was frozen, studying Abbu's flushed face and damp hair. Eventually, I took a deep breath.

"No," I said, and left. I just couldn't take the risk.

Abbu stood there utterly confused.

In my room, I ripped up the letter.

∞

In the fall, I started grade nine at a new school outside of my catch-ment area, for its enriched program in mathematics, science, and computers. The students were whiter, richer, and, as I was told by my teachers and advisers, a lot more studious, which was what I needed to develop and grow further.

Although the thrill of passing the placement test was great, I couldn't predict how out of place I would feel at the new school, where the students wouldn't look like me or, most likely, relate to me. I also didn't know that nostalgia would set in. I'd long to see the familiar faces of my old friends in Jungle. I hadn't been prepared for the change.

I wondered then if this was how Abbu and Ammu had felt, living in a place when their minds and hearts were still somewhere else. Or perhaps their loyalty was split between all the places they had lived. Was it possible to live in more than once place at the same time? What is it then, that makes a place home? Is it the memories, familiarity, resonance, or the holding of a passport? Later in life, I would wonder the same about relationships, how people stayed in them while perhaps wanting to be somewhere else, or leave them while still living in them in their minds. People could also split with-in themselves, live out different, contradictory aspects of who they were, sometimes without awareness. In all these cases, what role did our minds play in how we escaped or tried to recreate the sense of a particular belonging or safety or what we desired? How did our minds help us survive separation?

During my first year of high school, I would often leave my classes early to wander around Jungle, searching for my old friends along those familiar streets. Soon after, my family and I would leave the neighbourhood and move to another one in North York.

A bungalow-style home in a predominantly Italian neighbourhood, red-bricked with a large lawn where Ammu would eventually plant her roses. On the other side of our driveway would be
where Abbu would busy himself with gardening, sprouting vegetables to keep us stocked for the summer seasons. We'd have plant
pots inside the home, too, of various colours with unique herbs and
flowers Abbu and Ammu would scavenge from garden centres all
over the city. Photographs in frames of times gone by hung on the
walls, as well as Islamic quotes and tapestries. A new *almari*, the
type of shelf Bangladeshi folks keep their ceramics and crystals in,
along with figurines for decorative show. Our family continued to
build our new home, but I would continue to return to Jungle.

Amaranthine

One day, during my first year in high school, I met Bhav. I was in grade nine and fifteen years old, visiting a friend who lived on Jungle's outskirts, near the intersection of Lawrence Avenue West and Caledonia Road. The time was almost five o'clock, right when my curfew was, and I was late to get home. So, when I opened my friend's apartment door, slightly frantic and a bit distracted, I was in no mood to entertain the man who asked me all sorts of questions.

He was sitting casually on the tattered admiral-blue carpet in my friend's hallway, wearing white Nike sneakers, beige slacks, and a white T-shirt with a checked brown collared shirt over it. He had a quiet self-assuredness resting between his blush lips. I caught his brown eyes as he ran his fingers through his hair, ruffling it slightly. His wide back was leaning against the off-white wall, unbothered and still. He blinked little, so I decided to outstare him for a few minutes. I wondered who he was and what he wanted.

We were on the third floor of this worn-down building, with a half-operating elevator. The paint on the wall was cracked and the carpet seemed two decades old. The man didn't seem to care. In fact, he remained nonchalantly sitting on the carpet at my feet the entire time we spoke.

"Hi," he said, a little monotone, but gentle.

I said nothing but continued to stare. A minute later my friend, who was behind me, stepped through her apartment door and stood next to me. She saw us locking eyes and commented, "Oh. I see you've met Bhav."

I remained standing and he sitting, neither of us flinching. My friend continued talking, telling me that Bhav was her neighbour, that they were good friends, and that he was sitting there in a vagrant manner only because he was waiting for another friend who would be meeting him soon.

"Oh. Nice to meet you," I finally said.

"I like your legs." He finally let out a smile, peering up from where he was. I rolled my eyes in response, adjusting the vibrant red summer dress I wore. Although his comment irked me as a greeting, I appreciated the way he looked at me from where he sat, in slight awe, as if I was a sovereign.

"Is that the first thing you tell women when you meet them?" I asked, claiming womanhood although I was only fifteen at the time. "So typical."

I turned away from him and looked at my friend. "I have to go."

"No, stay," I heard him say. I turned back to him. He was still sitting but was flashing a smile now. "You'll have to give me the opportunity to ask you more questions."

I raised one eyebrow. "And why would I do that?"

His smile grew into his face. He began, asking me how often I visited the area to see my friends and whether I liked it, to what music I listened to, and what I liked to eat. Although the questions were the basic get-to-know-yous, it was as if the dingy old hallway became the site of an excavation. The unearthing of mysteries, the revelation of hidden, significant artifacts, and the persistent toil of diggers. The feeling was such. He asked these questions and more, all while sitting, and I stood there answering them, not sure exactly why, my hands dancing in the air as I spoke.

He didn't give me much of an opportunity to ask questions of my own, and at the time I believe I didn't really care to. I had to get home. Still, I learned a few things, one being that he was a few years older than me, and he seemed to be the pack leader of the group of young men who my friend was friends with. "The village boys," she called them.

Usually people would ask "Where are you from?" even the non-white ones, but I certainly didn't. My attention, narrow like the hallway that we were in, settled on the hair strand that fell on his forehead, his baritone voice, how he waited for me to finish my sentences before asking another question. The way the corners of his lips lifted gently when he retreated to a memory or thought.

As a young Muslim girl, would it have been important to ask him about his religion? I didn't ask, as I didn't think I would see him again, or that this complete stranger would play any significant role in my life at all. Furthermore, in those days, I would be more curious about his beliefs only as demonstrated by his actions and not any declared identification. I'd learn later, from my friend through a passing comment while we were on the phone, that he was Sikh but not really practising — though it still didn't matter to me, anyway.

I didn't even ponder at the time what he might have thought of me, but I would learn later from him that he thought I was exceptionally beautiful, but, more significantly, that I was humble and down to earth.

Instead, when I left, I said, "Okay. Maybe I'll see you again, or maybe not." I hurried away, cognizant that I would possibly miss the bus.

The year was 2001. The internet was a burgeoning phenomenon, and we were just learning its codes, the abbreviations, and slang. Y2K was supposed to have happened, but it didn't. Bhav became my first MSN friend. Our casual exchange of introductions and pleasantries soon found their way into chat boxes and emails. Both of us were romantics in the traditional sense so we wrote each other letters. Some of the letters were written on lined pages or computer paper but once in a while one of us would get fancy and use manila pages.

> Hi,
>
> How was your day? I hope better than mine. College classes are so boring. They teach you things that you'd eventually find out anyway once you're in the world. But of course, you probably wouldn't relate. You're the biggest nerd I know.
>
> Bhav

> Hey,
>
> Oh, shut up. Although, I have to admit, I was a bit bored in class, too, today. My classmates talk about things I have no interest in. What is happening with your friend Anya? You said she

wasn't doing okay, and that you were helping her out with something.

Sumaiya

Hi nerd,

Yes, just some family things. I took her out for ice cream, and we talked about it. She is better now. What would you rather talk about?

Bhav

Hi Bhav,

That's good. I am glad to hear it. I like that you're always looking out for your friends. How do your friends tolerate your boring dad jokes, though?

Sumaiya

Morning,

Haha with the dad jokes. You know you like them. Better than not being funny at all. I like helping others out, because I had a tough time growing up and couldn't share much with my parents. What about you? What makes you sooo quiet?

Bhav

Hi Bhav,

I just had my drama class. Did you know, I do an excellent King Lear? I don't know why I am so quiet. I guess I just don't like talking much unless there's a point. But yeah, when we talk, I end up saying a bunch of nonsensical nothingness.

Sumaiya

Hi,

Nonsensical is good. You should smile and laugh more. It looks good on you.

Bhav

Our messages were simple but consistent. They sometimes contained proper sentences, other times slang and abbreviations. Each time we wrote, we peeled layers to further understand the other. Over time, our letters got kinder and deeper. Bhav would come to my window, after midnight and before sunrise, I'd throw him down a basket, tied to the tail end of my Georgette *orna*. In it, he'd leave another letter, which I'd pull up and excitedly read when he left. Sometimes he'd bring snacks, including spicy cinnamon hot tamales that he said reminded him of me. For months that eventually turned into years, we continued like this, writing our hearts away.

An outsider would probably have found Bhav mundane. Just a basic guy, a twenty-one-year-old tradesman who liked his fast food daily and played a lot of hockey. Maple Leafs jerseys, open-collared shirts, and Timberland boots. A strange passion for eating fluffy white jumbo marshmallows. He only went to college and not university because he wasn't a fan of the abstract or theoretical, just what he could touch, smell, and see, and whatever was practical. The youngest of three brothers, but the most responsible. He wore dark-black sunglasses, even indoors. What was he hiding? What was he insecure about? Despite the glasses, he seemed to have an impeccable attention to detail.

One day Bhav brought me to his favourite place, a park in the city by a river I'd later learn is the Humber River. This river extended to the area where I'd later live, where I myself would go to pray for him. At the time, we renamed it ourselves and referred to it as the Getaway.

At the Getaway, we made our way from the parking lot to the bridge, where Bhav pulled out a penny from his pocket and gave it to me. He held one, too, in his other hand. We stood on the bridge and watched the current slide past granites, pebbles, and fallen branches. There was some surrounding greenery, some amaryllis buds.

"I've come here almost every week of my life," Bhav confessed. "It's my favourite place. I come whenever I need to think. Like when I was younger, and my mother and father fought."

The timber boards creaked. My ankles rubbed against the inside of my boots. A lingering aroma of damp dirt and cedar.

Bhav went on to tell me that his father often hit his mother, and that this was very hard to see growing up, that they fought quite a lot, and were now separated and not speaking, despite living under the same roof.

Bhav looked down at the copper penny in his open palm with the small, hard callus. He shut his palm tight. He hunched over the bridge rail. I imagined him then, the little boy, standing in the corner of a room watching his father raise his hands in the air over his mother and the terror in his mother's eyes. I imagined Bhav still, just whimpering in the shadows.

"That must be so hard. How could they live under the same roof but not speak?" I asked.

"It is, but you know, they can't actually separate. It's not something we do in our culture. And you know, they're both older. Where would they go? We don't have any family here."

I nodded, then said, "I could never imagine living with someone, seeing and hearing them, but not acknowledging their existence or them acknowledging my own. It would be a type of eventual disappearance, a burial while still being alive, wouldn't it?"

I didn't know then what I would learn later, that in the coming years, despite all the technological devices that would be developed to bring people closer, many would wonder if they truly were seen. That love was just as complicated as it was simple, and it was expressed in a multitude of ways, and sometimes not at all, despite it existing. That a simple change in circumstance, however trivial or tragic, that could leave two lovers riven.

At the time, I only thought, *I will never let this happen. No, not with someone with whom I had made a commitment.* Just of optimism and anticipated endurance.

"Also," Bhav continued, "our parents need their sons."

I moved in front of Bhav to where I could better read his face.

He told me then about the cardboard boxes of rotten avocados and tomatoes, kept for days, just in case meals were no longer available. The tattered dusty sweaters folded square and stacked in every corner, just in case it got cold. The dusty glass shelves that held twenty, thirty, fifty ceramic figurines like precious moments that lingered on for so long they were no longer precious. His mother hoarded these things. To throw away her objects was akin to her disintegrating until she ceased to exist. To Bhav, however, the objects obscured her existence and signalled, to his horror, that it was as if she were slowly becoming the objects while simultaneously ceasing to be his mother.

"It's her mind. She forgets things, doesn't process things, she doesn't throw anything away. I can't control it. I can't fix it. She won't accept my help."

I speculated, *Maybe this is how she copes with —*

"I'll share another secret." Bhav interrupted my thoughts. "Something more interesting. Did you know I'm a *deshi*?"

"A what?' I asked.

Bhav told me about all his karate lessons. My eyes travelled to the silver *kara* dangling on his arm, the marker of a warrior, and a gift from his father.

"It's about the mind more than anything. Cultivating a higher level of human character to prevent an attack before it actually occurs," he explained — I wondered whether to me or himself.

I asked to see his moves. He contracted his chest and narrowed his eyes. A deep bellow, his exhale and vocal cords married at the right time. He brought his right elbow to my face ever so seriously, then pulled it away in a roar that shook the leaves of surrounding trees. I watched it all happen, then laughed along with him.

Bhav reached out for my hand, brought me closer to the rail of the bridge. "Let's make wishes together," he suggested.

He closed his eyes, his dark-brown lashes twice the length of mine. He blew onto one penny and I blew onto another. We threw them into the half-frozen water. I didn't ask him what he had wished for. I just looked at the side of his face, noted his attention drifting with the cascades. He wasn't thinking of himself. His mind was at his home with his mother and her terrible mausoleum of superfluous collections. I didn't know then this was Bhav's greatest gift, to be thinking of others often and how he could be of service of them. I moved in closer to his body, which was trembling, just slightly.

During the six months after Bhav and I met, I found myself increasingly pleasantly surprised by his thoughtfulness. He showed up often to my school with an assortment of gifts, anything and everything he thought I might need or perhaps want: notebooks, electronics, shoes, books, food, flowers, chocolates. The list was endless, and even extended to my family and friends. The gifts always came with a note.

Thought you could use this.

Remember, you told me you were looking for ...

This might help you with …
This made me think of you …

I thanked him but also often declined, as I had been taught to refrain from taking gifts from men. Bhav, however, was impossible to escape, and it was true, he had become a good friend.

On the days where I was able to meet him for a stroll in the park, or for lunch by the school, we'd often find ourselves immersed in a laughter so loud that for us it deafened the rest of the world. One day we found ourselves on a stroll at Earl Bales Park, not too far from Sheppard and Bathurst and intersecting with the West Don River. The park was once farmland, so as we moseyed through the vast green space, I imagined the animals that once roamed there. I looked for the ancient trees.

"Look at those two. I wonder what they're talking about. They seem so deep in conversation," Bhav said, pointing to a man and woman sitting on a cart that was slowly moving through the field we were traversing.

The cart was like a park ranger cart, cobalt blue, four-wheeled, two-seater with a pull-out back. I followed his eyes to the woman who was driving the cart with a zig zag line of sight, and the man next to her with pursed lips as if he was hyperventilating. This middle-aged couple were most likely park employees, although they weren't wearing uniforms. Periodically, the woman brought her hands to the air with a toothy grin. The man then leaned in and grabbed the wheel. The woman pushed him away. They laughed, then, suddenly, they both shifted their torsos away from each other. The woman's jaw thrusted forward. The man extended his arm to touch her hand on the wheel. Within the five minutes that we observed them, it seemed that so much had occurred.

"Yes, I wonder, what could they be talking about?" I played along.

"Well, since we don't know, let's explore the possibilities," he proposed, then simpered in contentment.

"Okay," I replied. "I'll be the woman, and you the man."

We spent the next thirty minutes continuing to observe the couple on the cart, inspecting every curve of their lips, swerve of their sight, and muscle twitch. We replaced their words with our own, role-playing various scenarios and using various accents, including our favourite to make fun of the British.

"So, while we're on this chin wag, I do have to tell you something," I said, flipping my hair like the woman in front of us. "I did something terrible."

"What did you do?" Bhav asked, pretending to reach for the steering wheel. "Don't give me any codswallop now."

"My prom date — she died," I whispered. "It was gruesome. At the base of the pond, she was found."

"Blimey, you don't say! Well, that date went all to pot. What a shame! How did it happen?" Bhav exclaimed, pointing his nose to the air.

"They suspected she had some type of poisoning," I said, waving my hands around.

"Was it true? Had she been drunk and sick?"

"No, just bloke," I answered. "She was so boring, I just had to do it. Put it right in the wanker's bottled water, then crushed the bottle after she drank it and put the bottle in my bra."

"Well, I am gobsmacked!" Bhav exclaimed. "You're a monster. So, what are you doing to do? Aren't the police on your tracks?"

"Bugger all. I'll do bugger all. They'll never suspect it's me."

After this improv in our most ridiculous British accent, we dropped our bodies on the green grass field, holding our stomachs as we had laughed too hard. "Bloody hell!" "Brilliant!" "What rubbish!"

Bhav and I spent most of our time trying on different accents and expressions. People-watching, wordplay, silly little things. We also had to see each other during carefully carved out segments of time, and often in secret. It would be trouble if anyone saw us. Those of the opposite sex were not supposed to spend time together, especially alone. This would make it much easier for the Shaytān to intrude and influence them. Yes, our world was limited, but there was an abundance of ways we remained amused and content with each other's company as friends. At Earl Bales Park, as we looked at the wide sky over our heads and raised our arms to it, it was as if the world beyond reach could actually be ours, not just in our minds, dreams, imagination, or wishes.

I had just started the tenth grade when the 9/11 attacks happened. After finding out in class as it was announced over the P.A. system, I emailed Bhav about it. At the time, he was skipping his college class to spend time with one of his friends. He read my email and suggested we meet to talk about it.

I told him that when I navigated the hallways of my high school, I felt the layer between the inside and the outside of my body crack, leaving everyone to see everything — my organs, my psyche — and it was all spilling out, as if there were something physically in me to expose. The links in a chain connecting who I was to the Al-Qaeda that might and could live in me, like a secret birthmark or undiscovered genetic mutation. But, looking back, there wasn't anything. I was just a teenager.

"If that happens, they'll see just how pure you are," Bhav assured me.

I told him about the rising tensions between the Jews and Muslims at school, the former being more predominant, and the friend from my middle school, originally a student at Forest Hill, who now also went to this high school and had warned and implied, while eating her *mantu* in the girls' bathroom, that it was truly safer to be white.

At the time, I had shrugged her off, but she seemed to have vocalized something that lay dormant in all of us. A particular framework of superiority and inferiority imposed on the world and over time; how things worked, apparently, according to white European men.

Later that day, Abbu found me in my room listening to music. He sat across from me with a frenzied look. "What do you think about what happened?"

I answered, "Nothing," afraid any response of mine would affect him in some way, in this very challenging time.

In the years to follow I'd increasingly see acts of violence, prejudice, discrimination, and hate toward Muslim people or people who were mistaken for Muslim. Irrational fears related to Islam as well as perception of people based on race, ethnicity, or physical presentation. I would begin to feel Islamophobia as something other than conceptual — a phantasmagoric force that I could simultaneously feel physically as an aspect of my body to overcome.

In these years, there would be a lot happening in the world around me, both in Canada and abroad. I'd learned about the sacred spaces that were contaminated — garbage thrown, vandalism, a pig's head left at a doorstep. I'd understand this when hearing the claim that Muslims were having children as demographic warfare, that Muslim women's hijabs were being pulled off as they travelled down the street or boarded buses. The slurs, the names, and the disrespect and ridicule of religious figures and religious practices that were the centre of family unions, personal resilience, sense of spirituality, and life purpose. Detainment with assumption of guilt, security measures that displaced people and separated them from their families, biased immigration practices, and public debates about religious attire that women were wearing — as if to suggest that controlling women's clothing and bodies would lessen the number of terrorists in the country. Having to let go of the essence of who you were in order to be welcomed into a country that had built its identity on inclusivity. The rhetoric, as well, putting *Islam*, religion of peace, before parts of words, names, and sentences that implied violence and human politics.

As I thought about this, an entire galaxy folded inward into a speck of absolute everything compressed into nothing, and a memory came of a time where it wasn't like this.

Bhav and I spent days, weeks, months like this, as friends, until it came into my consciousness that perhaps what I was feeling was what they call romantic love, my first true experience of it. Was that what it was? I asked myself this question when Bhav visited me at school after a dance performance of mine. I was wearing my burgundy *sharara*, looking like a gerbera daisy, still sweaty from dancing. After watching the performance, he met me behind the school with a red rose in his hand.

"Congratulations," he said, handing me the rose.

The rain started to drizzle on us both. He took my silk *orna*, curved it to a loop, threw it over my head. It slid down my waist and soon rested on my hips. With it, he tugged me forward to his chest, as if lassoing me like a cowboy, the way they did in the Bollywood films. When close to Bhav, I studied his skin, the hue of Jaisalmer sand, the muscles on his arms like the hill ranges of India, and the space between his shoulder blades the width of the Ganga river. My chin chaffed on the merino wool of his beige sweater. I whiffed myrrh, patchouli, and citronella. I savoured the shiny black beads trailing his jagged jaw. The goosebumps on his neck. His feather eyelashes and lava lips. The rain thrashed the rooftops of the surrounding cars. Waves ran up and down my body like musical notes on a piano. Bhav's body near mine felt strangely familiar, as if I had known every inch without even having explored it.

If I stayed away, I would deny myself this. The yearning to un-
ravel this great mystery of my heart started to take my sleep and
sometimes my appetite. When alone, in the middle of conversations,
or running to catch a bus, just a caress of the gentle wind against
my cheek stirred in me an anxious fretting. When would I see him
again? How could I shorten the minutes between now and then?
In social gatherings, among family and friends, when my attention
would drift to memories of one of our silly jokes, or the recollection
of Bhav's cologne, I would burst out in random laughter or a tender
grin. To the outsider, I must have appeared as somewhat of a lunatic.

These yearnings, they were indeed different. I tried to count
my crushes, but they never quite felt like tangible possibilities
as they fell outside the scope of marriageability. Bhav wasn't
Muslim but there was still some racial and cultural familiarity. For example, I sometimes compared Bhav to the Italian boy
in my high school whose band played in the background while
I read spoken word poetry. He invited me over and presented me with spaghetti and meatballs doused in marinara in his
mother's kitchen. Then, later, as I joined him in the living room,
he took off his shirt to seduce me, except, upon seeing his pale-
white chest and wiry blondish armpit hairs, I screamed and ran
out the door. He followed, chasing me half-naked. "What did I
do?" he yelled. He didn't feel so much like a Bollywood hero, the
way Bhav did, with a certain depth, foreseen commitment, and
seriousness, out of both duty and self-inclination.

When one of Bhav's friends learned that he and I were spending time together, and said, "Oh, her, she's hot; but be careful, that
means she's loose," Bhav took the knuckles of his fists and pounded
them on his friend's face, warning, "Don't you ever say shit about
her character, or this friendship is over." The bravery and pursuit
of justice, despite any friendships or other affiliations, made me
respect Bhav more.

It wasn't just because I felt Bhav's actions were particularly tender toward me that I began to desire his constant presence. It was that I admired him. He could risk what was important to him or what he depended on to live by what was right, fair, and compassionate. To me this signalled a type of integrity. The valour was not necessarily about physical strength but the strength in making oneself vulnerable to speak up, correct a wrong, or even face one's own shortcoming in a situation. Apologize. It was as if he could die for a cause, and in that, I could live for one. Such was the intensity of the devotion I began to feel, a pull like no other, to be recognized and protected for the woman I was innately — the woman I would become.

"You're the eldest daughter. I know you don't have an older brother, and I know you can't always share everything with your father or mother, because you are afraid of disappointing them," Bhav said. "It's important to me that both you and the world don't lose sight of who you are, which is innocent."

"Yes," I replied. We were on the phone. Through the handset, his voice was cracking.

I cried that night, hearing the echo of Bhav's words, while wrapped in my fleece blanket. It was as if part of his life purpose had become to honour me.

For a young woman who suddenly had to pay attention to her widening hips and developing breasts, what she had implied to this boy or that boy, or against which girl she was more or less, and all the other makings of adolescence, to have a protector who looked out for my best interests, was only a gift. So, I wondered then, *Is it possible that Bhav is an angel sent down from Allah to earth?*

I often felt the presence of beings, neutral or benevolent, at the base of my feet and behind my head, as I slept or right before I woke up. In Islam, it is known that angels are often around, that there are particular ones that also take note of our daily behaviours and utterances, even thoughts. I wondered if Bhav was also an angel but just in human form. He wasn't Muslim, but did seem to usher me onto a path that was more aligned with the vision he had of me, and the vision felt very much aligned with who I was at my core. I thought perhaps that he had a gift of foreknowledge, a third eye.

So, six months later, we were both back at the Getaway standing on the bridge. It was the end of January and the edges of Bhav's car windows were laced in snow. I took off the leather glove from one of my hands and brought my fingers to his pink nose. I wiped off the snowflakes.

"Come here." He cupped my face with his hands, and leaned in. His chin grazed my nose. He blew gently on my eyelashes. The snowflakes danced off my lids, and then, as he lowered his chin, somehow, we found ourselves more closely embraced. Was it the warmth of each other's bodies during the cold chill that drew us in? Or were the parts of ourselves that had existed long before our bodies ever did finally meeting each other, after having been separated, in the same way both Socrates and Islam had described soulmates?

As I was lost in my whirling thoughts, I felt Bhav's soft lips on my forehead. I tiptoed to lift myself up from the ground to kiss his forehead, too, but could only find his lips. And so, that is when it happened — our growing friendship became something else. The warmth in my mouth and running through my flesh was like a soft electric current. We kissed there on the bridge for almost twenty minutes, forgetting the cold. Bhav tasted like roasted coffee.

Our friendship now contained a particular fondness. Our sole purpose was putting a smile on each other's faces.

In the weeks leading up to Bhav's birthday, I could not sleep, pacing back and forth frantically, wondering how I could even get him a gift worthy enough, a gift he deserved. Abbu had asked that I focus on my studies instead of work. I was penniless. And then it struck me, while I was gulping mango juice and flipping through a Nancy Drew novel, that I could create a castle made of his favourite thing: marshmallows. So, I bought a few packs of marshmallows and toothpicks with whatever money I had and began to create. The castle was perhaps half a metre long and ten layers high. I added towers and, right in front of the portcullis, a throne, on which I placed a marshmallow king with a crown. My second challenge was getting the castle to Bhav, as I'd have to meet him a bit farther away from my home that day. I was determined. On March 28, I ambled down a long and winding street to Bhav, carrying the gigantic concoction, wearing fancy heels, and having dabbed on shiny plum lip gloss. The journey was toilsome, and the heels were torturous, as I tried to keep the castle from toppling over. I did manage. When Bhav saw me in his rear-view mirror, carrying the castle, which I'd covered with aluminum foil, he ran out of the car to help me, and placed the castle on the trunk. He looked on with anticipation as we unveiled my creation.

"A castle for you, my king." I bowed.

Bhav ogled the castle.

"Well?" I asked.

He finally reached his arm out to grab mine then pulled me in close to his chest, put my head on it.

"I love you," he said, for the first time.

When Bhav put the masterpiece down on a park bench and we both admired it, I told him, "Don't worry, I got you covered," and pulled out two big bags of jumbo marshmallows from my purse. I handed him the bags. "For us to eat, so your castle can stay intact, my king."

Bhav smiled. "I see you've thought of everything."

We spent the rest of the afternoon with his head on my lap, me dropping marshmallows into his mouth, as if they were falling clouds, and him trying to catch them like dreams. I ran the fingers of my other hand through his hair, always silkier than my own. *Cafuné.* I then gently rubbed his ear lobes, a caress I knew would bring him some calm.

So, there we were, under the sky.

Bhav had a habit of bringing disposable cameras with him wherever he went. Sometimes he would pull them out of his pocket in an ad hoc manner. For example, when my mouth was filled with spaghetti, or when we were playfighting, or as I diverted my glance when I was shy, Bhav would snap candid photographs and I'd be frustrated, other times delighted. The ones we took together, however impromptu, were the ones that I most looked forward to. When Bhav developed the photographs and shared them with me, I asked to keep them for a week or so, as I couldn't risk Abbu and Ammu finding them. He agreed. Instead of storing them, say, under my mattress or in a locked suitcase, I placed them in scrapbooks that I would create. Underneath each photo, I would write a short description, sometimes about the real accounts and other times for our amusement out of my imagination. The scenes would have to be connected, to tell a bigger story about us and our world. I would sometimes include poems, and other times sayings that only we knew. Under one photo, for example, I wrote: "This is a photo of the world's greatest monkey giving me the world's most famous monkeys. All the monkeys involved are ridiculously silly, but um, still quite astute." The text was under the photograph of me holding the three "Hear No Evil, See No Evil, Speak No Evil" monkey figurines in my arms, with my eyebrows slightly raised, as if to say, "Why this?" But Bhav, he always had a reason.

I titled these albums "Unbreakable," determining this to be our one, unified name, like the way the Hollywood couples had their individual names amalgamated. Brangelina, Bennifer, Spederline.

I surprised Bhav later with these books. "Our stories," I said. "They are here. One day, though, I will capture our story in a real book."

Bhav smiled. "I have no doubt that you will."

"Tell me, though," I asked him — we were on a bench by his apartment building, across from the small convenience store where we often went to pick up ice cream — "don't you get tired of taking these photos?"

Bhav turned his face to me, as the young children with water guns ran past us and the Soca music played from the speakers nearby. "No, never. Whatever happens, I want us to have memories. It's how we will come back to each other, always. It is what our children will see. Why do you think I save all our letters and our emails?"

To an outsider looking in, it might have been strange that Bhav and I were speaking of exclusivity and marriage at such a young age, for I was only sixteen at the time. How could two people with such limited world experience know anything about life and its challenges, and what it took to sustain a long-term relationship? A marriage. These details did not matter to us, as long as the *niyat*, or intention to be together, was there. Our desire and commitment to each other would be like the waters of Niagara Falls, where Bhav and I often visited. The water that came from the last ice age, that was enough to cover all of North America. Durable, ancient, organic, creating its own path.

I hadn't consciously thought about this then, but would contemplate later, that being with one love, and one love only, seemed to be especially encouraged for women; as if having a past would reduce her in some way, whereas the same didn't necessarily apply to men. I wondered how much this drove people to stay together, drove women to love hard and men to protect their honour. Save women before they *fell*. I wondered also if in

Bhav's and my case it was more a stubbornness to prove that love truly exists. Perhaps we knew deep down that as humans, we were all broken after having been separated from the origin of where we came from. That life itself was the beginning of the journey to death. And that by looking for *the one* and never separating, we were searching for a certain wholeness along the way to it. Relationships, connections, therefore, were a way to restore that broken bond between ourselves and a power greater than us. Marrying our partner was considered to be fulfillment of half of our *Deen*, after all.

As Bhav and I sat on a park bench across from the ice cream store, I could see sketches of our future in his eyes. Under the warm Canadian sun, I wondered how I had been so blessed.

I closed my eyes and imagined my wedding to my beloved as I always had: not in a long, trailing white dress, nor a ravishing red sari or *lengha*, with layers of gold jewellery. I imagined not crowds of photographers, people, family, or even friends. I saw only the profile of my lover's face in my periphery, as we were both looking ahead at the grand open space before us. We would be on a cliff. I would be holding my lover's hand in mine, and we'd take slow steps together to reach the edge. It was then that we would turn to face each other. We'd take a deep breath, both at the same time, and push our bodies over, not letting go of our hands, nor shifting our eyes. What happened after, in my vision, I didn't see. It was just the simple act of falling, allowing ourselves to fall without letting go, without knowing what lay ahead. Oblivious to the dangerousness of the cliff, rocks from surrounding mountains, or whatever lay below — none of this mattered as much as our willingness to take a risk, together. This represented to me the space between wonderment and security. Being drawn to the soul of another person and the possibilities of union without worrying about what I would have to let go of as a separate individual, including sometimes my own ideas and the safety they provided me. It represented a willingness to abandon predictability at times, and be open to the unknown, because that was where growth and expansion happened.

This was what I had imagined, what I strove for with Bhav. Yes, marriage would happen with Allah's will and for Allah's purpose, but what was important was never dimming the spark of desire between us along the way.

I found myself, then and after, continuously speaking Bhav's name to all of my friends. I often repeated God's name before I slept and when I woke, when in fear and when in hope. When in gratitude or amazement. However, now it seemed that it was the syllables of Bhav's name in between my *tasbih* beads. In all my emotions, everything I felt or experienced, he was both an adviser and a witness. A healer, too.

I heard in both his words and saw in his actions nothing but the ninety-nine names of Allah. Al-Hafiz (The Guarding One), Al-Badi (The Unique One), and Al-Wadud (The Loving One). These names of God were more than theology. They were attributes of God in all living things, including Bhav.

Then, one day during the month of Ramadan, the month I usually avoided Bhav for fear of breaking my fast by a careless gaze of longing or an inclination to kiss, I sat in the neighbourhood mosque with my family. We were listening to a *khutbah* on the basics of faith and practice. Sometimes during these *khutbahs*, if the tone of the imam seemed to inspire any kind of fear or had traces of condescendence, I would have to try harder to focus my attention. If the tone was indeed just a little more loving, my chest would expand, my ears would perk up. I would no longer be drowsy; I would listen more attentively. So, on that particular day, there was an imam with the most earnest of voices. As he described the experience of another Muslim who had recently been to *Hajj* in Mecca for holy pilgrimage, I was in awe.

"It is one of the most gruelling journeys you would ever have to make," the imam explained. "But it's that physical, emotional, and spiritual struggle that will bring you closer to your Creator."

How would it feel to be even closer?

"Remember, my sisters, if you are under the age of forty-five, you'll have to get a *mahram*," the imam then advised. "A *mahram* is someone in your family whom you can't marry. It could also be your husband, but, of course, he has to be Muslim."

It was then that I could feel my slightly cupped palms fold and close into a fist, the wooden *tasbih* beads in them hard against my skin. The back of my throat was dry. I thought, *How would I even do this significant pilgrimage without him?*

I had been aware that Bhav wasn't Muslim, but at the time he disclosed he was Sikh I had seen him only as a friend, even an acquaintance. Now that we had declared our commitment to each other, I would have to find a way for us to marry and experience *Hajj* together.

So, that day, after the mosque, I ran home to the computer and turned it on. I looked around to ensure no one else was nearby. My fingers shaking, I clicked on the icon for the internet. In the search box, I typed in, "Who can Muslim women marry?"

I discovered that Muslim men could marry women of the Abrahamic faith and that Muslim women couldn't marry outside of the faith at all. Both weren't technically allowed to marry anyone who wasn't monotheistic.

The screen became fuzzy and I almost vomited. This to me, was illogical. If Muslim men continued to marry outside of the faith, then who would be left for Muslim women to marry? And I didn't believe young Muslim boys or men would even think twice before they made these decisions, the way girls and women would, considering all of the repercussions.

That much I knew then, that although our traditions were once based in logic, if those traditions handed responsibilities and special considerations to boys and men, and those boys and men lacked awareness of their privileges or a certain conscientiousness, then there wouldn't be a point of sustaining those traditions in the first place. Otherwise, what purpose would they serve the community long-term? I suppose I could have thought this about patriarchy in general, even outside of this faith context. I participated in it, too, sometimes, while still asking myself, *How is it fair that men get away with more while giving up less?*

The tide of moral outrage that washed over me then brought with it a deep sadness. It was technically forbidden to love Bhav.

It was true, though, that there were differences between our faiths, Bhav's and mine. Although both were monotheistic, the differences were in how God was visualized, in the guiding scriptures, and in the articles of faith. It was true that Bhav's mother often prayed to an image of a Guru with her open palms touching each other, as he had shared. My own Ammu's hands were often cupped, palms facing the sky. Both closed their eyes though, searching for the face of God within the wells of their heart, letting God's presence fill up all of the space around them.

Alongside the question about *Hajj*, there were other questions, too: How would we explain the differences in our faiths to our future children? What about certain practices that for me would be considered *shirk*? What about pork or alcohol? How would our families get along?

Abbu once told me the story of Sumayyah bint Khayyat, who was a slave in Mecca. She was one of the first ones that accepted Islam without having any kind of class protection. She soon became victim to torture, simply for her faith. She was tied up and left under the sun for hours or submerged in containers of water. She endured all sorts of pain and was repeatedly forced to renounce what she believed. I remembered that in some of the books I had read, her limbs were attached to two camels that pulled her apart. A pointed spear then flew across the air of blinding desert sand, piercing and tearing through her reproductive organs.

I remember seeing the passion in Abbu's eyes, and feeling the fire in my own core, learning about this woman of conviction and fierce bravery. Sumayyah was able to stand up for what she believed in. This is what heroines were made of. When I thought about telling Abbu about Bhav, I remembered that I was nowhere like Sumayyah bint Khayyat. She sacrificed herself, but would I be able to give up Bhav if that was what was asked? I found myself in a conundrum where being who I aspired to be, this ideal, would require me to let go of the one person who brought me contentment. How did Bhav feel about my beliefs as a Muslim? Could I tell him about this? Would he understand? What would he say?

I decided then that I would tell him, and tell him soon, that I couldn't love him and my God at the same time, and that for him, the case could also be the same for loving me. It was perhaps the first stone to hit the foundation of what we had built. We would have to figure out a way.

After Ramadan, I met Bhav so I could tell him. I was sitting in the passenger's seat of his grey Dodge Neon in the grey parking lot of Caledonia Park in North York, where he often spent time with his friends. Bhav unwrapped his California sandwich, two thick buns, steak in the middle, and brought it to his mouth. I started by telling him that I missed him, then explained what had happened earlier that day, when Ammu shouted at me for entering the kitchen and clumsily breaking her glass plate. From the car CD player, Method Man and Mary J. Blige expressed their love to each other. *You're all I need* is exactly what I thought, too, as I watched Bhav sitting there, eating, listening, absorbing, then forming his reply. "One day we'll have our own kitchen, and we can burn and break whatever we want. That'll be part of the fun of it." I laughed.

We stepped out of the car and climbed the grassy hill next to the lot. Our ankles brushed against green grass culms, their mauve spirelets blinking back up at us. Bhav's tawny linen summer jacket against the sky's scattered cyan hues, wind blowing between his dark-brown locks, landing casually on his forehead. I moved them with my slender fingers then took a deep breath.

"So, I have to talk to you about something," I started. "But first, I want you to know I love you."

"Okay," he replied. "I love you, too."

"As you know, if you haven't noticed, did you know that I am a Muslim girl?" My eyebrows were raised. I did not blink.

Bhav chuckled. "Yes, I do know that. Obviously. What is it?"

"My family would never accept this. Aside from my family, it would be very challenging for us to be together given all the different, and maybe even opposing, rules of our religions."

Bhav was silent, looking at his feet, then back up at my face.

"It could clash, the way we both believe in God, or practise our religion," I said in a soft voice.

A bird whistled before a branch fell.

I remembered then Zakariya al-Qazwini's *The Wonders of Creation*. I pictured Bhav and I standing in this celestial dome of earth on the back of an ox. The ox stood on an enormous fish in a glass bowl that held the ocean. The bowl was placed between an angel's wings. I was reminded in that moment that, in this grander scheme of things, we were just specks. I thought, *What did it matter what we desired, if what we desired caused pain to others in some way, if it created such havoc?* We had to care not just about ourselves but everyone else.

"I'm sorry. It would only work if our love was accepted; otherwise, I would be too conflicted," I confessed.

"How could we make our love be accepted?" Bhav said. "You're the woman I want. I can't stop loving you just like that."

Bhav tilted his face and bit his lip, as if he was trying hard to understand. "And just so you know, if you haven't noticed, did you know I believe in one God, too?"

The amiable winds picked up their pace, eolian tunes humming us awake. If he didn't, he'd be like Shayṭān. It would certainly be harder for me, to be disciplined in my practice. I placed my hands slowly on Bhav's chest. I wanted to lean my head forward and rest it there, but instead I swiftly lurched him away.

"It's more than believing in one God, more than *tawhid*," I replied without elaborating. At the time I thought that no one should ever explain belief until they were asked to, or perhaps inspired to, but without any particular expectation, for I hated when others did that to me. It could have been *dawah*, but how could I have taught Islam or demonstrated it through my behaviour when I myself didn't know everything it entailed? There was a lot more to Islam than what most people knew, including other Muslims.

In response to my prolonged taciturnity, he said, "Everything will be fine. It's all the same God. We will be married soon, one day."

"*Inshallah*," I said.

Then his face lit up. "We could always elope, like they do in those silly Indian movies you make me watch, with your favourite, Shahrukh Khan, whatever his name is."

I pushed him away. "Stop! It's not funny. I am being serious."

I didn't consider elopement because at the time I didn't see myself ever without my family.

Bhav clutched my hands quickly then brought me closer to him again. "Think about it. We will run away."

"Well," I played along, "even if we ever considered it, we have very little money. Where would we go? How would we even afford food?"

"Don't worry," Bhav said, softening his voice then raising it again. "I will sing and play an instrument, maybe a trombone, or maybe the *tabla* to keep this story culturally reflective."

"Well, you do have a soothing voice. Maybe I can dance or say my poetry. We'll need to go somewhere with subway or metro stations where we can perform for money," I said.

"But, well, mmm," Bhav looked around, "we'll be easily found if we run away to a city that has a subway."

"Maybe we can flee and hide in a small town," I suggested, beaming.

"I'll milk cows and become a farmhand, and you can sew clothes," Bhav said.

"Oh, you mean like what they do in Elmira or Ayr, Ontario." I was genuinely excited. "You know though … you're the only real cow around here."

I giggled and then Bhav leaned in to whisper, "You're the only cow I love."

"Are you calling me a god damn cow? What's wrong with you? You never call a woman a cow!" I exclaimed.

To which Bhav cackled, "Cows are sacred in some cultures."

I placed a peck on his cheek. "But in all seriousness, if we did elope, this would be a rather poorly planned plan. We need to be more strategic."

"Well, what if we went somewhere, like Estevan, where I could find work in the Bakken?" Bhav said.

"What's the Bakken?" I asked.

"It's where men go to die," he replied.

"Now why would we want that?" I asked.

Bhav looked at the single leaf that was slowly falling from the nearby tree. "Because you deserve better."

"Better how?" I inquired.

"Better to elope with someone rich. Maybe all those doctors and engineers your family would rather set you up with. They could take care of you better. Yes, better to elope with someone rich," Bhav declared with certainty and a tinge of sadness.

"Rich in love, though?" I raised one of my eyebrows.

"Richly foolish," he said.

"I don't like that plan," I stated, pushing Bhav away. I turned my back to him then stomped across the field.

"Wait, wait," Bhav called out, then ran to catch up to me. He caught my hand with his, ensured they were intertwined. "Okay, fine," he said. "We will stick with the small-town idea, since you like small towns so much."

"Yes," I said, my face glowing again. "Our babies will be named after the towns we hide in."

"There's a town called Drinkwater, Saskatchewan. If we live there, we'll definitely be motivated to stay hydrated."

"We're not going there."

"Why not? What do you have against water? What about Booger Hole in West Virginia?"

"Okay, what the hell? Is there really such a place?"

"Maybe Intercourse, Pennsylvania."

"Okay, we are definitely going to hell."

Bhav and I plunked down on the grass and continued to think of silly town names. He turned his face toward me, staring for a good two minutes. "Your parents would be right, if they were to disagree," he finally said.

"Why? About us? Our differences?"

"About you, overall."

"What do you mean?"

"In any case, you deserve more. You always do."

I rolled over and put my head on Bhav's chest.

"Will you speak with Abbu? Please let me know as soon as you can," I asked. "I have an inkling that I will lose you and —"

Bhav brought his palm over my lips. "I will talk to him. I mean, I'll certainly be scared, nervous. But I have to. I love you, after all. I'd like to do this the proper way."

We lay on the grass that day, wrapped in each other, in both dread but also hope that everything would be okay.

Before Bhav could speak to Abbu, Abbu learned about him when he found one of the Polaroids of Bhav and me on my bedroom floor. Its usual home was between the last two pages of my Moleskine journal, the ones unblemished, preserved for future tales. The Polaroid had a white frame around our supple faces; our bodies were snuggly embraced.

When Abbu found it, he called me calmly into the room. He sat on my lavender bedsheets, and I on the wooden chair across from him, the one that chirred from its right back leg whenever I moved. Rays of sunlight seeped through the window slats and across the chestnut floor. Behind Abbu, a half-open wall closet with overflowing clothes. The pale white walls. I pressed myself into the chair's cross rails.

"Who is he?" Abbu asked.

I looked at the Polaroid in his hand. In it, I had burgundy hair and was wearing a floral peplum shirt. Bhav had on a plaid shirt and backward baseball cap. Glasses resting on his nose. Neither of us were completely smiling.

Abbu started waving the photograph. His hand was gripping the corner so tight it darkened to red. The photograph fluttered back and forth,

"Who is he?" Abbu repeated.

How could I put into words then that Bhav was both peace and dissonance?

∞

One day a boy from the military came to visit his lover, who went to my high school. His name was Wasif and her name was Priya, although at the time I noticed them I didn't know who they were. I saw them at the front entrance, where I was waiting with some friends before the school bell rang. Wasif was wearing camouflage pants, and I'd learn later that he had served in Afghanistan. Priya ran toward him with outstretched arms. He had flowers in his hands for her. His eyes saw only her until he noticed me looking at them, and that was all it took.

Soon after, Wasif tracked down my number by contacting friends of my friends who knew him. I started to receive calls from mysterious telephone numbers. A ring, silent whisper, then dial tone. The calls came late in the evening when Ammu and Abbu were on our corduroy sofa in North York, Abbu reading a book and Ammu watching her latest Hindi soap opera. First Ammu picked up. Nothing, then the dial tone.

"This is strange," she said.

Another call. "Who is this and what do you want?" Abbu shouted.

Then one day I picked up, and the mysterious entity said, "Hi, do you know who this is?"

The voice was nonthreatening, monotone, and frankly, quite plain.

"No, I don't," I replied.

"I saw you that day in the hallway, at the front of the school. I was the one with the roses. I was hoping we could get to know each other."

It was Wasif.

"Um," I said, "okay. Nice to meet you, but I am not interested really in anything."

"Who is it?" Abbu asked.

"No one. Just a friend," I answered, afraid of his reaction if he knew there was boy on the other end of the line. So it continued, almost every day, this stranger calling my family home. When I hung up, he would call again, which would seem further suspicious to Ammu and Abbu.

I decided to talk to him, but in a platonic way, to stop him from phoning again. This didn't work; instead, it encouraged him to keep calling.

Until, one day, Priya found me in the hallway where all the overachievers sat. She moved like a thunderous cloud, slowly and with a certain dimness. Trailing behind her were a handful of girls, all of them also with firm faces.

She hovered over me. I hunched over my notebook, my eyes squinting at the floating algebra equations on the page. I kept my head down and away from Priya's disgruntled face. I peeked at her flaring nose. A petite girl with shoulder-length hair. Suddenly, I remembered that we had already crossed paths. It was a school event I had organized as president of the South Asian Club. The event was about fashion, so we had all been dressed up. Priya in a cream *lengha*, and I believe I was wearing a black-and-gold *gharara*. She hated her plain black heels; I had overheard her say this in the girls' washroom. I went up to her and handed her my gold pair. I asked her what her size was, and she grinned. I had thought then that she was quite beautiful. This stranger was wearing my sandals, and I hers, but on this day, in the present, she seemed unable to travel in my shoes. Priya pounded her fist into the locker I was leaning back on. I managed to keep still.

"My boyfriend tells me you are coming onto him. What kind of a whore are you?"

I looked up, my eyebrows scrunched and my throat dry. I had no idea what she was talking about. I had done no such thing.

"Stay away from him," she threatened.

All my other classmates in the enriched program did not blink. I shrugged my shoulders then looked away.

After this initial threat, it just got worse. Every day, I found Priya almost everywhere: in the hallways, the lunchroom, at the front entrance, and in the parking lot. Her and her crew of other girls, who echoed everything she said.

"Porn star," they yelled out. By this time, I was as confused as ever. I had never watched porn; I didn't really understand what the accusation meant, and how the association could have been made.

Okay, I thought, *how plain stupid.*

After school one day I was in the subway with a bold, intelligent classmate who I admired and was excited to befriend. I loved her attitude and her flair. We were talking about the details of an upcoming assignment when I saw a growing shadow from behind. I didn't know it was Priya running toward me in silence, her pace frantic. As usual, my reaction was measured, until I felt her hands grip my back, grabbing my shirt, pulling me, and my feet slipping backward and closer to the yellow danger line of the subway platform. The train was coming into the station. All I saw was the constant yellow beam of the train headlight in the distance. Was it my lungs or my still-beating heart that was in my throat? With the growing fire in the pit of my stomach, and its smoke starting to cloud my pupils, I shrieked aloud then held my breath, prepared to die and be forgotten — like Islam's veiled Divine Feminine, who removes jealousy and envy from hearts as she belongs to each and every person — all within that split second, when my friend pushed me out of her arms and away from the platform's edge.

My friend stepped toward Priya, who looked utterly disappointed with her slouching shoulders and quivering lip.

"Stay the hell away from her."

"This isn't over," Priya said, then left.

By then I had had enough, of her and this ridiculous rumour that manifested itself in whispers, snickers, and odd looks.

Porn star.

Me?

Porn star.

The fathomlessness of it all, the cartoonish aspect of the lie, the laughable randomness were what kept my anger at bay. I didn't know then that the hate I saw in Priya's eyes that day on the subway platform was a thing that gets women killed, by men and other women who were threatened by men. I guess she had amplified and esteemed me to the level of mistress, even though we were still just teenagers in high school. I didn't know then that she had not only tried to push me over the yellow danger line of the subway platform, but had made the decision that her freedom, her life, meant less to her than my death. That she'd not only wanted to kill me but had tried to kill me. That she'd thought to dispose of me, toss me like a napkin over the subway platform, only because I had looked at somebody. That I'd been standing alone in the mundane hallway of my ordinary high school and that had been enough to justify all manner of spectacular delusion: that I was a demonic mistress, a horny, immoral slut, good enough and shameless enough to make money off it, and do so publicly, a porn star, a traitor, a broken person, someone fallen, disgraced. I grew cynical about my own agency, my capacity for autonomy. Going to school, standing in a hallway, answering the telephone, not answering the telephone: these were enough to make others think they could do what they want with you. Do what they want with me. Kill me.

I had to do something.

"What lies are you making up about me?" I asked Wasif that evening, with neutrality, when he called once again.

"Sorry," he replied. "I was just trying to get her jealous."

"Please don't get me wrapped up in your drama. I have nothing to do with this! And I told you, please stop calling me or I'll have to tell my parents."

"Will you really tell your parents?"

I slammed the phone down. He didn't call again that night.

I tossed in my bed as if ants were crawling all over, and by the time the morning rays rediscovered my face, I'd decided I'd take the approach of a diplomat. I'd consult the school principal, and I'd have to help Priya see reason.

The next morning I found myself on the principal's red barrel chair, facing the girl who'd plagued both my waking and sleeping hours. I took a deep breath and I told her everything. At first, Priya was in denial. She didn't want to listen. "He would never do that to me." Then, there was anger. "I can't believe he lied to me!" Then a form of gratitude perhaps. "Thanks for telling me."

I left somewhat satisfied.

Wasif called me later, enraged. "Tell her you lied about everything you said!"

"And what? Also say I'm a porn star?"

Sunny Leone wasn't in mainstream media then, but I later pondered what she would have thought about such a situation. We kind of look alike, at least that's what some wooers would tell me. I'd cherish the compliment. To be so beautiful and desired by so many. To be so brave as to fashion a life out of your desirability in this world that's already loaded for women.

"I'll fuck up your life," Wasif threatened.

"I'd rather speak the truth than be wrapped up in your messed-up relationship."

And this time, I hung up without worrying for a second.

I didn't know then but what would follow for days, weeks, and months was Wasif calling Abbu and Ammu, especially when I was at school.

"I'm just a concerned Muslim brother," he would say. "Do you know what your daughter has been up to?"

And days later, in our living room, on our brown corduroy sofa, Abbu looked at me with tenderness and said, "This young, concerned man, he just has your best interest at heart. I'm truly grateful he has notified me of your troubles."

I couldn't swallow. It was as if I were back in front of the subway tracks again.

It never ceased to amaze me how a fictitious story can have so much power to shape the trajectory of a life, especially a woman's life. That people are often more interested in a woman's perceived sexuality than her own voice. Why wouldn't anyone ask me for my truth or get to know who I was? The masses of students and even the concerned parents. *You have to be saved.*

"If you don't believe me," Wasif told Abbu one day, "visit the school parking lot during lunch hour, when her lover will be present."

And Abbu did, only to see Bhav there.

After Abbu found the Polaroid, shaking it as if instructed by Outkast, I told him everything about my relationship. Then, a few days after the Polaroid's discovery, Abbu confessed he'd seen me with Bhav during lunch break, sitting in a Dodge Neon, eating a California sandwich, listening to Method Man and Mary J. Blige while discussing who knows what. If he'd only come a bit closer, he'd have heard us discussing our faith in God and plans for marriage.

"Well," Abbu had said, his voice a little softer than usual.

After a minute or two of reserve, he said, "I trust in you, your judgment."

I remembered that Abbu told me often that he was most proud of my intelligence and, furthermore, the softness of my heart, which he warned could also prove to be my greatest weakness.

"My Ammu," he continued; it was what he called me often, "I only ask that you use your *aql*, too. Read and learn about all the world's religions, and human nature. Become knowledgeable, use your cognition, before making any decisions that could twist and turn your life on paths that may not be the best for you, at the end of the day."

Then Abbu got up, made his way to the door, and then turned around and said, "If you do lie to me, it would certainly break my heart."

He took the Polaroid with him.

The time had come. It was more urgent than ever. Bhav needed to call Abbu and express his intentions. I needed him to, being who I was. He loved me, so he would. When Bhav called Abbu, I was in one of my classes. I spent the duration of it imagining the voices on the line oscillating. Abbu's voice calm then rising then completely dead. Questions: "How?" "Who?" "What?" and then "Who do you think you even are?" Would Abbu slam the phone down with a certain passion, or would he listen? I tapped the pencil in my hands on my desk during a calculus lesson — limits, functions, derivatives, integrals all blended into one buzz in my ear. The thumping in my chest was like a wild boar about to run over my very existence. After class, I waited for Bhav in the school parking lot, biting my lip, ferreting for his face. He pulled up, parking on the other end of the lot, not close to the door where all the students usually stood. I passed all the cars and all the eyes, curious or oblivious. This would be the moment that would determine what our future could possibly look like.

I opened his car door and shuffled in. He was looking ahead, hardly taking notice of my entrance, not saying much or even moving.

"Tell me what happened, please," I asked, my voice shrieky. "How do you feel?"

I considered for a moment how fragmented I'd be, misaligned and disorganized, without Bhav's presence.

"Well," Bhav said, "I am relieved. It had to be done, asking for his permission for your hand. But I am no better or worse than before."

"What do you mean?" I asked.

Bhav's voice and lips were flat lines on a heart monitor. However, he tapped his foot on the brake pedal, and his arm resting on the ledge of the car window was more tense than usual.

"What did you say and what did he say?" I asked.

"Well, you know," Bhav started. "I said that I love you and I can't stop, just like he can't stop loving your mother, his wife. And that I was committed to overcoming any challenges with you. I'll do anything."

Bhav took my hand and put it in his. "I tried to convince him. Kept telling him that I loved you, but he said that love was made up."

I gripped Bhav's hand tighter. Abbu had described it as fleeting, based solely on intangible stirrings of the heart and hormones, and nothing grounded. As Bhav told me this, recollections of stories that Ammu had shared arose: Abbu writing poems for Ammu, serenading her, during the first few years of their marriage.

This could have only meant then that true love was limited within the context of dating; in this case, it was just Shaytān's meddling. It was through marriage that you'd keep perspective on a higher purpose, and avoid getting caught up in the workings of the *nafs* — sight short, wavering desire, and a distracted or stubborn mind. Bhav and I, however, didn't believe then that we were *dating*. For us, it was destiny.

"Listen," Bhav said, his whole body turned to me now, "to be honest with you, when I found out you were Muslim, I wasn't necessarily thrilled. I thought there would be more obstacles."

I tightened my grip again.

"I've heard about honour killings," he said, his voice a little sombre. "What if something like that happens to you because I am with you?"

I bit my lip. "Why would you say that? Because I'm Muslim?" I asked. "It could happen to those of other religions and other cultures, too."

I reminded him that men in North America could also kill because they felt honour was at stake. The many murdered women. The incidents of domestic violence across various cultures and religions. His disquietude could have been entirely legitimate, but it periodically stopped my breath, particularly when I wondered, *Does he think of all Muslims a certain way?*

We didn't know then that soon a Sikh man who had stabbed his wife would be convicted of second-degree murder. The man would say her behaviour was a defiance to the Sikh community, for she smoked, drank, and talked with men other than him. We both didn't know then that years later there would be plenty of other cases, and they wouldn't necessarily involve those who identified as Muslims.

"You know that I am not particularly religious, but I see what role religion plays in your life. It keeps you focused. I love that about you," Bhav told me.

I loosened my grip and released my shoulders.

"I love and accept this part of you. Is it the whole you? I don't think so. I don't believe it would ever take over your entire heart."

I sat reserved for a moment. My love for Allah was the entirety of my heart. Bhav, to me, was a manifestation of Allah's blessings. I could never separate the two out, despite feeling the pressure to do so.

"I love Allah, but I love you, too," I replied.

"Then, we will make it," Bhav said.

"Yes, we will," I agreed. "We will figure it out."

I decided I would get a vestige of some sort for Bhav and I that would remind us of each other and carry within it our essence when we were united. Something that would store the immortality of our commitment in a tangible way. With the limited amount of money that I had in my purse, I scoured the malls like a high school student (which I was) except with the strategy and purpose of a corporate professional — Yorkdale, Lawrence Square Plaza, Dufferin Mall — just to find the right ring. Some were quite plain, a silver band made of steel, and others quite fancy, multiple stones that sparkled from miles away. My fingers resting lightly on the glass counters of the jewellery stores, my eyes squinting, as if I were on a mission to ferret out the right diamond, except it wasn't an actual diamond I was searching for. I was searching for distinction. What would be simple enough, but also unique, like Bhav and I? After days, perhaps weeks, I found it: a silver band with gold plated lining, one single stone in the middle. I decided to get a pair. The rings were identical, with no signifier of gender, other than maybe size. I had carvings made in its interior wall that read *Unbreakable*.

I presented the ring to Bhav one day on the bridge at the Getaway. The scattered hues of the sky overhead, both bright and gentle, were like the pastel ribbons of joy on the ring box — acknowledging the happiness Bhav brought into my life.

He was telling me about his latest hockey match, after which I said, "I have something to give you."

He smiled. "What is it?"

With that, I turned my body toward him then went on one knee, pulled the box with the rings from my pocket and presented it to him. "Will you be my Unbreakable?"

Bhav retreated to his own knees, placed his hands on my arms, then pulled me up. "Of course. Of course I will. But please, never fall before me like that again. Your place is high, and it's me that should be at your feet."

I felt prickles on my entire body. It was like the sting of excitement felt touching the thorns of a rose, while anticipating the fragrance to come. I opened the ring box and we then placed the rings on each other's fingers.

"If we were ever separated, somehow apart, maybe we can talk to it, the ring," I told Bhav. "The message will be received, I am sure. A portal for telepathic communication."

Bhav laughed. "Or we can just ask God directly. No third-party messenger."

"Yes, you're right," I replied.

∞

Bhav found out that he had an irregular heartbeat. I visited the doctor's office with him often for his checkups. I sat in the waiting room one day, anxiously clutching a magazine in my hands, and flipped to an article titled "Grave Mistakes Lead to Surprises in Graves." There was a middle-aged blond woman staring vacantly at the white walls, and a bald, bearded man tapping his right foot while humming under his breath. I closed my eyes, trying to drag in my breath, which was escaping me. After about thirty minutes or so, Bhav came out and I stood up. We left the room, the anxiety of the place still following me. Outside, on the sidewalk, I saw some cars pass, some stop, some blocked, all at the mercy of traffic lights. I was three steps behind Bhav as we walked. I caught up and pulled on his arm.

"Tell me," I asked. "What happened?"

"The loud beats I have been hearing, the fluttering, well, I have heart palpitations. It's called a bicuspid aortic valve," Bhav told me as the car swiping past us honked. "The passageway in the valve is narrow, so it can take longer for blood to travel between the heart and the other parts of the body."

I moved in close to Bhav and put my ear on his chest and listened carefully for the lagging beat, then I looked up at him.

"I'll be okay," he said.

Ever since Bhav had spoken to Abbu, he had been more scattered in his thoughts than usual. Each time I had asked him if he was feeling fine, he said, "Yes."

I put my fingers on Bhav's forehead, which often wrinkled up when he was distressed, and then on his furry caterpillar eyebrows. "You're too young for this."

Bhav nodded. "I will eventually have to get surgery to get the blood flowing the right way. But you, you don't have to worry about this. Let's go."

This wouldn't be the last time I worried about Bhav and his state. For, leading up to this visit and after, Bhav would often be anywhere and everywhere but the present. I would ask how he was and he'd say fine, but then I'd see all the bottles from which he drank scattered on the grass of the same park within which we stared into the grand blue sky. And then there was the indignation that he carried under his sleeves and on the edges of his collar, connected like a circuit, that rested dormant but then blew like a fuse at arbitrary moments.

"Why were you late?" he asked one day.

We were planning to see a performance at Hart House Theatre, and I had had tremendous trouble getting out of bed. It was a curse of rumination I battled almost every morning, remembering how our union wouldn't be legitimate until we were wed. Then there was also my melancholia that sometimes visited like an unwanted guest.

"I'm sorry," I said.

Bhav hit the steering wheel with his palm and didn't talk to me for the rest of the day.

On another day, Bhav wrote to say he was upset but then didn't explain. My thoughts whirled: *What could have happened?* I ran back to Caledonia Park. I took the 59 Maple Leaf to Weston Road via Benton and Culford and the Gary Drive bus from Lawrence West Station. The entire way I conjectured what I could have done to push him away.

I found him surrounded, once again, by bottles. It seemed that getting drunk was how he metabolized the situation.

"What are you doing here?" he asked, his voice a little hoarser than usual.

"I wanted to see you. To see if you were okay," I asked, whiffing the rum from two metres away. This was certainly not a scene I would have ever experienced growing up in my own family home, where alcohol was taboo.

Then, Bhav's friend ran up to me and said, "He isn't in the right state of mind. He has been stressed. I think you should leave."

"Why won't he talk to me? Tell me what is wrong!" I cried, with my soaring voice. I wiped my wet face. "Tell me!" I shouted, now at Bhav, who had his back to me.

In that moment, my knees weakened and my hands shook. I wondered how we could suddenly be so separated while standing on the same ground, without there even being much physical distance between us.

I left the park without wanting to, but having to. On the lonely bus ride back, I was determined not to experience such a rupture again. To never do or say anything to hurt Bhav in any way that would create such distance, even while intellectually aware that his behaviour was his, and not necessarily tied to mine. I also wondered if there really was a distance, even while intuitively sensing it. I still believed in him and wanted to be strong for him, as well. For the next day, Bhav didn't remember my pain nor his. A sort of amnesia that left me confused.

I would later learn that Bhav didn't quite know how to put what he felt into words the way I did, or thought I did, and that he wouldn't to prevent any distress. I didn't know then that while being straightjacketed in his own shortcomings, Bhav was still trying to be my hero. And I, I still believed in him.

While Bhav's inner being sometimes sung discordant notes, so did mine, and it started the first time we were intimate. A ruffle of the hair, playful moments packed with joy, notes left in purses and pockets, a spur-of-the-moment peck prolonged. A string of acts that paved the way to alternate realms: half-open eyelids, blinking lights, the gushing in of gasps, sighs like colliding waves, whiffs of cologne, salty sweat sprinkled on the tongue, the tips of my fingers across smooth coarse surfaces, my form fumbling into fissures of places. Magical places, and I thought it could only be a spell that began to compel me this way.

When I looked in the mirror, it was as if the curves on my face altered, reshaping into a woman of smokeless fire that I recognized: the Shayṭān Bride. The crossing of lines on bodies, hearts, and souls bringing pleasure was also the crossing of lines that brought a certain unease.

These forbidden moments — they split me into different parts. The books I read, the shows I watched, what I learned from friends or understood as the *fiqh* of marriage, in Islamic jurisprudence, and the experience of simply loving a person: all of these sometimes clashed. Was it possible to be so many people within one body, or one person with mismatched beliefs and actions? It resulted in a kind of discomfiture that ate away my peace. I thirsted for consistency, an integrity, while navigating girlhood and womanhood when it came to courtship, love, marriage, sex. Who could I talk to — parents, teachers, counselors, imams, or friends? There was no one place to understand all these worlds in a way that was integrated.

So, whenever shame eclipsed pleasure, it left me betrothed to my sin and not my love. Could Bhav have grasped the discomfort from within my spirit or from my consciousness? When his watch got caught in my hair or when the chain around his neck hit my face, and I would shout, "Leave me alone!" Later, I would shudder on the prayer mat, remembering that I was consciously not solving the problem I faced, and I would ask, *Can I even consider myself a Muslim at all?*

I was playing with fire in a slow burning in hell, yet it brought me closer to my faith in ways I had never been before. I became more aware of my *nafs* and this led me to ask questions, perhaps the way Iblis had: Did sinning mean you didn't belong within particular lines of religions or communities, that you should simply leave? Or did it mean the sins you faced were your test? Did good things come more easily to those who obeyed or those who failed, then tried again? For God would never give a person a burden that was more than they could bear. What made a good person? A good woman? Within the dark light, I looked for clarity.

In all this, one thing was clear: what women do with their bodies or what feelings they have cannot be imposed on them, nor can they be taken. Not through a look, nor rational, scientific explanation. Nothing that is *done to* can tamper *with*. As a human, her dignity is an innate right, and what she does with her body is for her to define.

Bhav and I at the time were fighting the fight of our lives: *aqls*, *qalbs*, *ruhs*, and *nafs* behind smoke screens, or feigning retreats in the middle of night combat or some ambush. We only heard the rumbles of passing thoughts with no clear direction and the sound of each other's breathing.

"Please, please can we solve this problem? I can't stay like this," I cried to Bhav one day. "I can't live with myself." Yet, I didn't go on, because he was a non-Muslim after all, and might think I was too anxious. And if he was white, maybe I would have thought he would have said, *Oh, that crazy chick.* But then again, I probably wouldn't have fallen for a man like that at all, irrespective of whatever background he had.

Years later, when I would finally have the ability to articulate such nuanced experiences to Bhav, he would say, "When I met you, I fell for you. When I got to know you, I fell for your heart and mind. I knew for me that you were all I wanted. So, loving you was extremely sacred, I didn't want to hurt you."

"It was sacred for me, too," I replied. "I would have just preferred Allah's blessing."

"I don't think I fully appreciated that you were going to have these conflicting emotions between me and your family and religion. I was only thinking about me and how it was special for me, and that it would be for you, and we would both feel the same together. But it wasn't like that. It was difficult for you. As it always is for a woman, for the first time, for maybe a Muslim woman generally, for a woman like yourself."

Ammu confronted me about the ring on my wedding finger. I was in my bedroom, straightening my hair.

"Why are you always wearing this ring, as if you're married," she asked, but it wasn't a real question. "Is this from that man? You know he is much older than you, and you're not in a place to be getting involved. Why do you keep forgetting who you are?"

I turned my face away from Ammu and remained focused on the device, which was now almost burning my hair.

"Talk to me!" she shrieked.

"Okay, fine, yes, but it means it's serious. We will be married one day, *Inshallah*," I replied.

Ammu pulled the plug of the straightener out of the outlet. She pulled up a chair and sat across from me. I was sitting on the bed. I looked at my reflection in the big mirror in front of me, where I saw Ammu's frigid back and what I thought were flames running through the veins in my face.

"You're out of control. First that boy who called our house telling us things about you, the way you're dressing, and now this man. You've become unrecognizable, as if there's something in you," Ammu cried. "Don't you know, life is not easy for women. People will always say things behind your back. We're trying to help you." She grabbed my hand, preparing to take the ring off my finger.

I couldn't deny that; it was true people always said things, did things, even though they were flawed themselves. Like I was, like we all were. For example, girls at school who continued Priya's rumours when I turned down the Turkish boy who followed me home, brought me chocolate and flowers — then broke his arm hitting a locker and ended up in the hospital because his advances weren't working. It happened a lot. I continued to learn that my desirability, sexuality, was something I had to hide because without having done anything, it made those around me rather uncomfortable. Perhaps others would have thought the attention was a blessing, but I just wanted to become invisible. It was as if young girls, women, had to make themselves smaller than they were. All I wanted then was peace of mind and no further damage to my relationship with my parents. It would only be years later that I'd own these parts of myself and feel joy revelling in my femininity and sensuality. So yes, people always said things, did things. Ammu didn't know I'd already begun experiencing this first hand.

"No, stop." I pulled my hand away. "Please don't take this." I thought about how Ammu herself had agreed to an arranged marriage without knowing Abbu, and that he was about ten years older than her.

Ammu pulled the ring off my finger slyly, leaving my hand dangling in the air.

I screeched inside but said nothing.

"Someone must have cast some type of *nazar* on my jewel of a girl," she said, and left the room.

What I didn't know then was that Ammu might have been worried that my way of expressing womanhood would infringe on her way of expressing womanhood, and therefore her faith, if she didn't fight what she perceived to be a failing of my soul. How this manifested was mostly through the topic of marriage. But Ammu couldn't know the inner makings of my soul, only I could. Nor did I know hers.

For much of my adolescence and beyond it, I felt that being myself meant I was hurting Ammu, but the reason she was hurting wasn't because of me, necessarily. It would be because of something innately gendered, those gendered notions hurting both her and me.

It was true also that in the middle of settlement, immigrant parents like Ammu and Abbu were still making sense of the new society they were in and how they connected to it. Like me, they were sorting out which values were core and which could be considered with more flexibility, or renewed understanding. It wasn't fair for them to be misunderstood, either, or not have a chance to be heard for who they were, the way I also wanted. Immigrants already faced pressure to assimilate. It didn't seem right to dismiss their thoughts, feelings, perspectives, all that made up who they were, reduce their world as *old* and *futile*. Who got to decide which worlds were valuable and which were not? Who defined what was *modern*, anyway?

It would be later that I'd come to understand and feel, like Ammu, the weight of the onus on a woman to be the conduit — to both negotiate and bind the meeting of different worlds, to pass on to future generations, like heirlooms of particular significance, the things considered most precious. Ammu was only fulfilling her duty, however insensitively, and it would only be later that I'd appreciate how deeply love and loss were the same — how the fear of losing what you loved, or continuing to love what you felt you were already losing, was so very painful. The panic this could create.

Ammu felt personally responsible. She would do what she could, not to just save me, but to save what was important. In the years to come, I would feel a similar way.

At the time, the traditional aspect of me had oddly become my greatest rebellion. While most of my friends were busy flirting with boys, preparing for exams, and caught up in other social, friendship entanglements, maybe deep in exploring various hobbies to discover what they liked, who they were, I already had a sense of who I was.

"In you I see potential. Study hard and focus. Better not to spend your talents and time on the wrong people," Abbu had said. Being educated and cultured in literature, arts, and religion were important in our family; the expectation was equal for both men and women. I, too, was inclined, but at the time, I felt it would be equally honourable to be a wife and a mother.

So, when the secret phone I had that I used to call Bhav was found, I was terrified I'd never see him again. I consumed an entire bottle of Tylenol pills, almost losing my kidney and barely making it. When the white man walked in, a psychiatrist, and asked how I was doing, I thought, *How can I even explain without you also wanting to save me in some way? How can you understand this particular grief, which I can't pinpoint to any specific thing and that will most likely stay with me forever?*

I sat on the hospital bed and thought of the Shayṭān Bride. She was standing there, in a milky-white sari. Nothing but the drip attached to my arm, the lights that felt stale against my skin, the buzzing of the television nearby. Was it a dream when I asked her, "What is this immense pain I feel? Is it existential, or is it the fear of losing my beloved? Is it merely Allah testing me to see what faith I truly have?"

She didn't say anything to me, just looked on, her face stoic like mine sometimes was, despite the fire in my body that spun like a tornado, emitting no wind, no smoke.

There could have been so many ways to understand my indulgence in a yearning so deep, and why I attempted to withdraw from life, but all I knew was that this life couldn't be it. Perhaps I had wanted to skip the steps and take the shortcuts, to get to Allah faster, even though suicide was a sin, so I could ask Him what all this was, face to face. I gulped this thought down. *Allah must be testing me. I have to be grateful, and I have to hold on.*

I imagined Parakeet flying in through the window and landing on the Shayṭān Bride's shoulder. I imagined the grand blue sky I looked out into every day.

I bought another pair of rings, more expensive and sturdier. Gave one to Bhav. We were unbreakable, after all.

High school was almost ending. I didn't bother asking to go to prom, to avoid any disagreements. The night before, Bhav came to my window. He threw some sort of rock and I dragged myself off my bed.

I opened my window to see him standing there, whispering loudly, "I'm just here to deliver a message. Can you meet me tomorrow at 4:30 p.m. at the park?"

"Shhh!" I hushed him quiet while rubbing my eyes. "Why? Yes, okay."

"And please bring or wear a red dress," he advised.

"Why?" I almost shouted.

"You'll see. That's all. Get some sleep!"

After Bhav left, I rushed to my closet in the middle of the night to find a dress.

I changed into it the next day, right before 4:30 p.m. It was long and fitted, three-quarter sleeved. I also was wearing red stiletto heels. My hair was down, straightened with some curls at the end. I had red lipstick on, as well.

When I arrived at the park, I spotted Bhav in a tuxedo coming out of a 1989 Oldsmobile Cutlass Cruiser. The vehicle was his father's, but he sometimes brought it out because he knew I loved classic things. The Oldsmobile was decorated with garlands of red roses.

"Welcome to our very own do-it-yourself prom, my special lady in red," Bhav said, extending his arm to grab my hand. "May I have this dance?"

I nodded, excited to finally experience something like this, and with Bhav.

Bhav turned on his boom box to Chris DeBurgh's "Lady in Red." He then gently placed his right hand on my waist. And so we danced, in Caledonia Park by the decorated Oldsmobile, the birds and trees a witness to our secret prom. As we danced, I asked him, "Why this song of all songs? 'Lady in Red'?"

"Well," Bhav replied, twirling me around, then bringing my face back to his, "first of all, you look beautiful in red always. Secondly, you were wearing red the first time I saw you in that hallway. Thirdly, red is for passion, which is what you are in essence. And finally, fourth, this song, well it's about how people often take who they love for granted, and that we should always pay attention."

I remembered then how Bhav noticed almost everything.

"Stop," I blushed. "Stop staring at me so intensely."

He continued piercing his eyes into mine, and somewhere behind the affection lining his pupils I saw a flicker of distress. "It might be my last chance to do so. Actually, any time can be."

"Stop, please don't say things like that." Knowing very well that I, too, felt and thought similar things often.

Bhav spun me again then dipped me, the tail end of my dress touching the cement. I felt my entire being melt in his hands.

Bhrura Madhye / Between the Eyebrows
(ভ্রুর মধ্যে)

It was 2005, the summer after my first year of university. I was enrolled at the University of Toronto. Ammu had just told me that the family would be going on vacation. We'd be visiting Dhaka again.

The night she told me, I looked out of my window into the onyx sky. A flashback of my last visit overcame me with the suddenness of a flying comet. It was six years ago; I had been about thirteen. My family and I had made a trip from Dhaka to Jessore, a small village where Abbu's brother, Shajan, his wife, and daughters were living at the time. Dadi, my paternal grandmother, was also alive and living there. She was a tall woman with sharp cheekbones, peach skin, otherworldly, dressed in widow white. With our family was Safa Fuppu, Abbu's younger sister, and Nusrat, my Boro Chachi's daughter. Boro Chachi was the wife of Abbu's elder brother.

During this visit, I had almost drowned. Safa Fuppu, Nusrat, my younger sister, and I went out to the muddy green pond not too far from Dadi's hut, the one by the family's chicken farm and abundant vegetation. The afternoon was warm. We entered the pond slowly by climbing down a flight of stairs that reached the pond's base. Our *salwars* were raised high up to our knees.

"Come on," Safa Fuppu yelled out to Nusrat and I, who were at the top of the stairs. She was already in the middle of the pond, her head plunging in and out, her lumbar-length hair now floating around her head like a flat crown. Or octopus legs.

"But there are leeches," Nusrat said.

"Yes, and snakes," I added, for I was so afraid of snakes.

"Come on, girls! No need to be scared. I'm here," Safa Fuppu said, laughing.

When Nusrat and I entered the muddy waters, we floated slowly to Safa Fuppu, past the water lilies, web of algae, and reflections of palm trees. The sun above was relentless in how it breathed its hot heavy breath on our faces. The water slithered between and through our fingers and toes.

"The villagers come here with their large silk thread nets to catch tilapia and catla fish," Safa Fuppu explained. "But it's also where people sometimes bathe."

As Safa Fuppu spoke and we watched her dive in and out, as if she was following the U-shaped trail of an oxbow lake, I forgot about the dark creatures under my feet. Instead, I cupped my hands and filled it with the water and threw it on Nusrat's face, who screamed. With that, I suddenly tumbled backward, the back of my head sinking deeper. I jerked it back up, trying to keep the water above my head. Against the tips of my toes rubbed smarmy substances. I cycled my feet under the water as quickly as I could, screaming between my gasps. I felt tiny teeth. Could have been the minnows or a blood-sucking leech.

I struggled to stay afloat and, at times, stopped treading water. I let my legs drop like heavy cargo from a ship. I stopped flapping my arms and brought them closer to my chest. Then I shrieked so loudly that I could have tipped nearby canoes. In the seconds between breathing air and water I looked around for some kind of anchor and only saw floating logs on the other end of the pond, where Safa Fuppu was now swimming. When she saw me, she dived in the water and kicked her feet harder. She was too far away. I looked to my right and there I saw Nusrat floating, also in a blip, tumbling. We were both drowning.

I pushed Nusrat's shoulders down in order to pull myself up, sending both her and I deeper, almost unable to breathe. It was then that I saw Safa Fuppu with the log. She pushed it to us both and we hoisted ourselves onto it.

Later, back in the hut, after we were in dry clothes and Safa Fuppu sauntered in with warm dhal in a cup, I saw that Nusrat had her back turned; she was no longer talking to me. When I asked Safa Fuppu what was wrong, she said, "She's upset that you tried to save yourself first."

"I am sorry," I told Nusrat. But she did not turn around.

I spent much of the next few days immersed in guilt, as the looks of disapproval were sent my way here and there, like letters from old enemies received unexpectedly. At the same time, I was enraged. What had she expected me to do? It was a reflex, an instinct. I was driven to survive; this was strong in me.

The situation left me wondering whether saving yourself from drowning would be the same kind of selfishness as standing up for yourself, advocating for your needs. If such a thing would be considered foolish or headstrong, and to what extent. I wondered, also, *Will Nusrat ever forgive me for this?*

Nusrat did eventually forgive me, it seemed, or at least we chose not to talk about it. Instead, we spent the rest of the weeks taking singing lessons from a well-known actress and singer named Shampa Reza, a friend of her mother, my Boro Chachi, who was once an actress herself. Boro Chachi had eyes that were the arboreal wildcat type, always lined with kohl, paired with a rather contagious smile, a large circular red *bindi*, and terracotta earrings. She was fond of poetry, especially that which could be found in between the notes of songs. Her brother was a famous rock star in the country. She was the quintessential Bengali woman. She had wings on her back that were heavy but redemptive, and a heart that could reach depths of understanding. I observed her keenly and deduced that the space between heaven and hell was a long stretch of grey. That although I felt a deep sense of shame for what I had done, I could forgive myself for simply wanting to survive.

So, when thinking about the Dhaka I visited six years ago, I thought of her, Nusrat, Safa Fuppu, Dadi, and everyone else. Memories of both fear and joy. It had been a magical time overall, all of us generally immersed in whimsies of the heart and nature, music, then later dancing on rooftops in the rain.

Now that I'd be returning to Bangladesh, I wondered what it would be like this time.

Ridoyer Porda /
Veils of the Heart
(হৃদয়ের পর্দা)

A few weeks later, I boarded a plane to Dhaka. After many hours of flying and a layover, we landed at Shahjalal International Airport. When I got off the plane, my nose was plugged by smog, the kind that makes you choke just a little.

As I walked from the plane to the airport door, the sharp sun-rays began melting the cherry balm off my lips. My loose puff-sleeved cotton blouse now clung to my chest. My jeans were stiff against my legs.

In the airport, I moved my head from left to right, searching for a passing breeze, even from an air conditioner, but all I felt were the heavy hot breaths of the men in passing crowds, their leering eyes piercing through my skin, dismembering me bit by bit.

I looked for my suitcase in the baggage claim. It was made of a Tegris material painted a black grey. I saw it on the conveyor belt but couldn't reach it due to the family blocking me: a thin *hijabi* woman who appeared to not have slept for days, her two chubby teenage sons, as energetic as the bounce of their black curls, and her grey-bearded husband limping. They were all waving their hands in the air and shouting at their bags on the conveyor belt, as if their bags had feet to march to them.

Once I found my bag, I pulled it off the conveyor belt, and Ammu, my siblings, and I once again passed in and out of crowds in a kind of osmosis.

As we did, I thought this trip would indeed be long without Abbu. Abbu and I were of a similar temperament, not fans of excessive noise or small talk. Ammu would stretch the hours of our vacation, filling every minute with visits to relatives and heated debates about family dynamics.

We made it to the airport's reception area quickly, and didn't have to wait very long. Boro Mama strode toward us, removing his hands from his pockets to wave them in the air. The last time I saw Boro Mama, we were standing in the same airport, on two different sides of the gate. His eyes pure of surety, as if he were saying, "You'll be something great, I know you will."

The folds around his eyes and speckles of grey in his hair reminded me that he had aged. I hadn't thought about Boro Mama all these years but now I remembered everything: him helping me with my homework, him sipping tea asking me about my progress at school while I sat on the sofa dangling my legs, him bringing me an assortment of toys when I had passed certain tests.

"*As-salam alaykum*, Boro Mama," I said.

I was secretly excited to share with him all that I'd been up to: the many awards I had won during my last graduation, the fact that I had been the valedictorian again, the As I had received in my new enriched academics program, and, of course, my excitement over making it so far in the Royal Canadian Legion public speaking competitions. Yes, I would brag, because he would certainly be proud of these achievements. There were also things I could potentially share but probably wouldn't, such as my playing on the school's volleyball team, as I wasn't quite sure where he stood on sports. However, I definitely wouldn't mention that I had been considering dying my hair another colour after this mahogany brown, or that I was in love. I anticipated that he would be upset that I wasn't going into medicine, although for a time I had been fascinated with the idea of becoming a heart surgeon; that I was instead curious about the mind, storytelling, and world issues, despite deep down secretly wanting to be a writer and an actress. These were the details I preferred to keep hidden.

In the airport, Boro Mama gestured us to move through the aisles and out to the parking garage, where stood his very professional driver wearing a white shirt with a fancy ballpoint pen in the left pocket. On the highway, two wide-open asphalt roads with two or three lanes separated by white paint. Between the two sets of opposing traffic were orange-red *gulmohars*, also known as flame trees. This Dhaka wasn't in my memories. It seemed so modern and so spacious.

It took us about an hour to get to the interior. As we did, the streetlamps and paved roads turned into dirt pathways. I saw cows marching in front of the shiny black Jeep and half-naked children who ran up to the car windows, their soiled hands leaving prints on the glass. The ringing rickshaw bells startled me, their horns melding into the commotion of passing pedestrians and peddlers, that familiar discordant melody. The melody that cradled me at night and woke me in the morning. I remembered it now.

Boro Mama's wife, my Mami, opened the door when we got to the house. Mami looked as she did always, glistening skin, silky black hair in a bun, her two lips the colour of the intoxicating punch they served at high school dances in all the teen shows I watched. She was wearing an orange maxi with white floral print, a cerise *orna* across her chest. She waved a straw broom while shouting at her three young sons, then turned to us and, in a soft voice, said, "*As-salam alaykum*" and "*Kamon acho?*"

Inside, we were taken to a room with two large beds and a ceiling fan that revolved above our heads. One side of the room was attached to an open veranda with a hanging swing. The other to what seemed a dark storage closet and, attached to the storage closet, a bathroom larger than my room in Canada. Across from the two beds was a metal *almari* within which Ammu placed our things.

I plopped my tired body on the bed as Nani tiptoed into the room. Lovely Nani, in a white cotton sari as soft as a pillow, her henna-red hair still vivid. She hugged us all. I smelled rain on her shoulders and thought of the evenings of monsoon season in her white house in Rajshahi. Each time Nani embraced me, each time I smelled the cleansing monsoon rain, I felt belonging. I wondered how much of me though belonged to Dhaka and how much of that sense of belonging was now fraudulent, negated by my life in Toronto. The thought filled me with a nervous grief. Was this still my home?

There was a lapse between the minutes that passed, during which I was simultaneously embodied in these two worlds of mine that I felt were distinctly separate. When the lapse passed, the worlds were together again. So much time had gone by, yet it seemed my old role in the family still existed.

"My second-eldest granddaughter, I am so pleased to see your face, and that you are here," Nani said, beaming. "Wash up soon, everyone, and come to the dining room. You must all be so hungry."

And so we did. Shortly after, all of us other than Mami's three boys were at the table nose-deep in mustard oil from her famous egg curry. There was also an assortment of other colourful dishes. Mami scooped the orange spiced pumpkin mash and vivid red-purple amaranth spinach leaves sautéed and tossed with *panch phoran* into neat portions on our plates. As I asked for a fork, she passed it, saying, "Don't you eat with your hands?"

I shook my head.

That same night, under the whirring of the fan's plastic blades, as I sat on the pillow-top mattress looking through my Moleskine journal pages, Ammu ambled over and said, "This will be a great trip, don't you think? We can maybe have you meet some young men."

I flipped through my journal pages, almost tearing one by accident. "I don't want to," I responded.

"Why not?" she asked, and I sighed, as she knew very well about Bhav by now.

Each time Bhav's name was not spoken or heard, I would feel my chest cave. So, when Ammu swung around and huffed through the room's sliding door, the weight of my chest pulled me down to the cotton-cased pillow and I appeased myself to a deep slumber.

During the next two to three weeks, things were as normal as they could be on a family trip to Bangladesh. There were countless visits from relatives and family friends — some of whom I had previously met and others I had never seen. We sipped *cha* on the balcony, played different boardgames, rode rickshaws to local markets to purchase traditional clothing, sat around in the living room watching *natoks* and Bollywood films, prayed with the family, and later had discussions about politics. I became reacquainted with cousins I had not seen, who were curious about my life in Canada. Sweety Khala's two younger daughters, Nabila and Maryam, took me to their school to show me off to their friends. "Our cousin from Canada, who we told you about," they said, and the other girls ogled with a sort of fascination, as if I were a celebrity living some coveted life, although I wasn't sure why, because their own lives seemed to have no shortage of luxury and comfort compared to the average Canadian — minus, maybe, the access to universal health care.

"What's the secret behind your pretty eyes?" They giggled and rummaged through my makeup bag, looking for some magical Western brand of makeup they thought existed that they hadn't yet discovered, but which I might have had.

"Say *Mashallah*!" I reminded them. "And stop. You two are beautiful." I hugged them close.

During these early weeks, I also spoke more with Boro Mama's sons Shahzad and Shayan, as well as Saad, who was just a toddler then. Although I was older than them, they often teased me and pulled pranks, which I appreciated, for they made me laugh. I sat often on the veranda eating *chanachur* while they played cricket, observing their mischief with each other, which dissipated as soon as Boro Mama entered through the front door. Their smiles would drop to their feet and they would run into their room to get their books.

In between these moments of simplicity and people-watching, Ammu interrupted with her very same question. "So, will you meet anyone?" I ignored it, holding on to my frustration, hoping she'd soon give up her efforts. However, Ammu seemed increasingly worried with each passing day, revealed by the way she paced back and forth.

One day I noticed Shahzad taking a cellphone out of his pocket and putting it on the glass table on the veranda before he took a swing with his cricket bat.

Although I knew this was the son of Boro Mama, which meant whatever I did or said could somehow travel back to his ears, I took a risk.

"Can I ask you for a favour?"

"Yes?" Shahzad answered, swinging his bat, as Shayan prepared to throw the ball.

"Do you think I can text my friend? It's just that, this is going to be one long trip. I just want to say hi, discuss what classes I might consider signing up for when I return."

"Hmmm," Shahzad swung, missing the first time. "I don't know. Baba makes me keep it in his office, and he usually checks my messages. I don't know if it's a good idea."

"I promise I'll delete the message. Just one message, and one response. Please," I begged him quietly.

Shahzad hit the ball a second time and it almost hit the glass table. I ran after the ball and picked it up, then I picked up the phone. I pointed it at his face. "Listen, I will owe you for life. This is really important."

Shahzad looked around. Mami was in the kitchen cooking. "Okay, fine. Go ahead." He nodded.

I smiled then took off my *orna* and wrapped the phone in it. I ran to the bedroom, past Ammu, through the storage closet, and into the bathroom. I let the water run from the tap. I clicked on the icon for text messages and typed in Bhav's phone number with the appropriate area code. I told him that I was now in my uncle's home and that, so far, the trip was going all right, other than the questions about marriage, which were increasing, but that I loved him and couldn't wait to return. I told him not to text beyond one text.

As soon as I finished typing the message, I hit *send* with my perspiring fingers. I went to the veranda where Shahzad was now preparing for his tutoring lesson. I handed him the phone. "Please don't read this. Do you think you can hide this from your father for the next few hours? Give me the phone back in the morning, just to check?"

Shahzad nodded. "Okay, fine." He took the phone and put it in his pocket. As he did, we heard the front door open, and Boro Mama's booming voice, "Shahzad, Shayan, Saad, where are you?"

Shahzad hastily opened up his notebook, and I scurried off the veranda, keeping my eyes on the floor.

That night, sleep did not even visit my eyes. I tossed under the fan blades. I had an inkling that something unpleasant would soon happen. I sat up, waiting for the sun to meet the earth, their union only temporary but at least consistent. I remembered Allah then, and how my thoughts of Him also drifted in and out of my consciousness, and my desire to have Him there permanently. "Allah, please stay with me," I whispered.

As the morning unravelled, I found my way to the veranda. Mami was setting the table, bringing out morning *cha*, *roti*, *paratha*, potatoes, and scrambled eggs. A gentle wind lifted my *orna*, and I breathed in deeply. Boro Mama had already left for work. Soon, in my periphery, I saw Shahzad tripping out of his room in his school uniform. I went to him.

"Do you have it?" I asked, keeping my tone low.

"Yes, here. You have two minutes. The driver is going to pick us up in a few minutes, after breakfast."

I snatched the phone he pulled out from his pocket, and found the corner of a nearby room. I flipped the phone open and scrolled down the text messages to look for Bhav's, and there it was. Bhav reminded me to stay strong, that we would see each other soon, that I just had to make it through this time, that he loved me, too, and thought of me all the time.

The phone almost fell out of my hands. Although his words brought me a certain calm, I couldn't stop fidgeting with the end of my *kameez* with my other hand. *I wish you could see and feel the tension I am sensing. How it is growing*, I thought, rubbing my lips together. I heard the wall clock tick. Jerked back to the present, I pulled my body forward and dragged myself to the breakfast table. Shahzad, Shayan, and Saad were already there. I could see Mami was still bringing out the plates of food, and that Ammu and Nani were also making their way to the table. I sat next to Shahzad and handed him the phone underneath the table.

"Thank you," I said.

"You know I can't do this again," he reminded me with his widened eyes.

"Yes, I understand."

A few days passed. One afternoon, when it was time for *cha* and siesta, Mami was in the kitchen cutting gourd, onions, and *kerala*, and Nani was sitting with her hip-length hair out on the veranda, the scent of *amla* coming through the window crack. I was in the bedroom reading a book. I had just had a disagreement with Ammu the night before. She said I was much too angry and for no reason, and I told her that I felt a similar way about her. We had been two women making sense of their anger. So, this morning I sat reserved, when Boro Mama's silhouette on the other side of the sliding door appeared to grow larger. He stormed in with his face furrowed.

"Come, I would like to talk to you," he said.

My breaths became thin. Although I hadn't spoken to Boro Mama alone in recent years, and for more than five minutes, I knew enough to intuit that his requests for individual meetings signalled something serious. I thought, however, that I could have been mistaken. Perhaps he really just wanted to know how I had been keeping, as such meetings were also quite formal in nature.

I followed him to the other side of the sliding door, into the living room. He sat down on a wooden claret cloth sofa and gestured for me to sit across from him, which I did.

After I left the country, Boro Mama ceased to be in my immediate thoughts, other than the brief moments in the middle of some nights, when Ammu passed the phone to me to say hello. His voice would be faint on the other side, and I'd answer, "yes," "okay," "all right." What could he ask now? Where would we start? There had been a lot that had happened during the years that had passed, but certainly, his sense of authority was still there.

"Your mother told me about the boy in Canada," he said matter-of-factly. The suddenness with which he stated a secret I had hidden for months felt like a dagger being pulled from my gut. When it was revealed, the truth of how much I desired Bhav drained all the blood from my face.

I saw the bobbing heads of his three sons peeking from the veranda window across from us.

"In love at nineteen is infatuation," Boro Mama continued, and I gulped while holding my breath, trying to quiet my heart, tame my expression, not give away my fear. "But you are a sensible young woman. You already know this."

An image of my elder cousin Azeema arose without warning. I recalled her sitting on her bed, surrounded by all the Khalas and Boro Mama with a finger pointed at her face. It was what I had seen the last time I had visited six years ago. Azeema had protested for years, more than the number of fingers on my own hand, to marry Saif, the person she loved, who was now her husband. Regardless of her curfew and the informants that monitored her day and night, Azeema found ways to meet Saif discreetly at college, amid garment sellers in the hubbub of Gausia market, and behind century-old banyan trees that would keep their secrets. Both Azeema and Saif had a large network of friends that worked together to covertly deliver their coded messages to each other, as well as gifts. Saif was indeed a rather intelligent and successful businessman, quite the socialite, too, and of the same cultural background and religion, but Boro Mama wouldn't have it because *love* was not a thing.

"Eccentric," he had said, and now he told me the same thing.

For a moment, a faint inkling of the Shayṭān Bride came and went. For a moment, I wondered about Boro Mama. Hadn't he ever simmered with passion for another until he felt he might explode if he suffered through another lonely hour without them? Hadn't he dreamed of someone's hair, their eyes, thought he heard their voice or had visions of them walking toward him with arms outstretched? Had he ever whispered "I love you" to himself, to an empty bed, to a wall because of the condition of the heart, the way the mind searches for compatibility, compassion, comfort, kindness, companionship? Had he ever closed his eyes to piece together his lover's face to see if the memory itself could invoke the feelings he felt when he was with the person? Had he ever been struck unexpectantly with pangs of visceral sadness while going about his day, reminding him that he was not with the one he wanted? Did all people not have a part of themselves that was like this?

Boro Mama interrupted my thoughts. "First of all, he's Punjabi. Secondly, he's of a different religion. Thirdly, you're only nineteen. I heard you're out of line. Is this why I sent you to Canada? To become so uncultured and disrespectful? You've had exposure, you've had opportunities to better use your brain."

Boro Mama listed on his fingers all the reasons this was trouble. The complexities of an interreligious, intercultural quandary were too difficult to break down, and the possibilities of *zina*, unlawful sexual relations in Islam, were far too great.

How does he perceive me? I thought. A Canadian with minimal understanding of her ethnic and religious identities? Her gender role? Or a Bangladeshi Muslim immigrant who has lost her way? An outright disbeliever or an ill-informed person in a terrible situation?

What I did know, but he didn't know about me, was that I did have dissonance. He didn't know about the countless number of times I found myself asking Allah, sometimes on the *jai-namaz* or mumbled under my breath, to show me the way. To retain the purity of the love I felt, to reconcile it amid the felt divides, within myself and the world within which we were all embedded. Boro Mama didn't know about the *Istikhara* I prayed, often with wavering patience and sometimes anger borne through hefty silence.

As Boro Mama spoke, goosebumps sprouted across my forearms and on the back of my neck. My purple T-shirt and grey jogging pants scratched my skin. Was it the hot climate that suddenly made this clothing uncomfortable, or the aspect of me I was being asked to shed? He spoke as if he had known me forever and was a close friend. In Canada, although I considered the thoughts of those around me, their advice and direction, I aspired to be an independent thinker, and Abbu himself encouraged in me such things, while still desiring between us a deep philosophical and worldview resemblance. I also always tried to speak my truth, and it was usually a natural inclination. I'd do it, of course, with a bit of discretion. Here in Dhaka, remembering Azeema and the stories of other relatives who had similar interactions with Boro Mama, and considering Ammu's strong desire for approval from him, I gulped down my urge to interrupt. He was still my elder, after all, and that much I respected. I had only just returned. The last thing I wanted was to stir up unnecessary trouble.

"She's overcome." Ammu marched in the room with both Mami and Nani.

They looked at each other, nodding their heads. They said something about me mistaking myself as Canadian, but also that being Canadian, I should have far greater sense. Yet, I still didn't know what being Canadian really meant; its multiple meanings presented a sort of double-bind situation, repeated exposure to irreconcilable concurrences, without opportunities to resolve one or the other, or both.

Boro Mama abruptly stood up from the sofa and strode over to Ammu, Mami, and Nani, all of their eyebrows slightly raised. "Did I ask any of you to be here? Come on, please leave. I am speaking to her."

As always, his order was final. He didn't need to say anything else for them to dash away. Nor did he need to say much else for me to plead, "Boro Mama, I'm sorry. His name is Bhav and I love him."

Boro Mama squinted a little but did not blink. It was as if, for an instant, he had thought, *Who is this?* He was motionless, other than his fingers, which tapped against the sofa's arm. I tried to pinpoint where on his face, within each fold, he was storing his temper. Yet, he remained still before asking me to elaborate about Bhav — how I had met him, what he was like, what he himself expected — and I excitedly shared, for I believed Bhav's good character would shine through any disapproval or concern. His thoughtfulness, sense of responsibility, and loyalty, sometimes exceeding his own need to eat or sleep. His sentimentality. I could depend on him.

After listening to me, observing my animated face, and extensive hand gestures, my emboldened eyes and blushed skin, Boro Mama cleared his throat and responded, "Perhaps you need to sleep on it. We'll continue our conversation later."

With that he returned to the dining table, where he pulled out a chair and sat, flipped through the pages of the local paper, then yelled out to the maid to bring him more tea. I saw her then, the maid named Bilkis. She was wearing a cotton black-and-pink floral dress down to her knees, and a red headband. Bilkis stared at me with her big brown eyes from across the room, as if she wanted to say something. I was shuffling toward her slowly when Boro Mama turned from his chair and shouted at her, "Why are you standing there? Go on, get lost."

Bilkis ran away as fast as she could.

I went to bed unsure of what exactly to expect. What does Boro Mama think about all the positives I had listed? Would I get to marry Bhav? Or would he decide otherwise? And if he did, what would he do then?

The conversations continued every day, happening in a similar way, like a repeated waking nightmare. Me mustering all of my bravery and dragging over to the living room hazily, Boro Mama laying out all the pros and cons of my predicament as we sat across from each other at the glass table. The familiarity of his rather judicious approach was striking. We'd done this before my family had emigrated. It was as if Bhav himself were the entire country of Canada. Suddenly, I was that young girl again, sitting next to him as I did my math homework, him leaning in, saying, "Good, good. Carry the one over like this." Him tapping his fingers and feet, then leaving the room shortly after to smoke a cigarette.

As the conversations continued, all other topics of discussion came to a halt. I slowly stopped going out with my family, or stopped feeling as if I were allowed out. There was a zero-in on my responses to Boro Mama's questions. What did she say? How did she react?

"We're all part of something bigger than ourselves," Boro Mama told me on one of the days. "It won't just be you and him, alone. You have to think about the life you'll end up creating for yourself. *Chinta koro.* Do you want your children to be confused? There's so much of your roots you're already forgetting, moving to Canada. Think long-term. Not just with your impulses in the present moment."

To which I replied, "If you meet Bhav, you'll see. His character — Abbu says character matters most, and that's what he has."

And then Boro Mama's lips twitched. "Apart from his lack of education and higher career aspirations, this is religiously wrong. Your fundamentals are wrong."

"In Canada," I began, "there are so many cultures, religions, and backgrounds. Everyone is together, while still practising their beliefs. And I believe this is how it is also in Bangladesh. From what I know, it's also a very diverse place."

To which Boro Mama let out a deep roar of laughter. "Are you that naive? All that is great, but who you are doesn't just disappear; it is always there. Our differences."

I thought then about Yonge and Dundas Square, how it hung in my memory like a watery watercolour, the edges of the different faces dripping into each other. But Boro Mama, he had a point. For in Toronto, ethnic enclaves were many in number, and there were many different reasons for this.

One of the reasons that made sense was that people with shared religions, histories, and languages would be inclined to stay together, especially in new places that didn't yet value them — not entirely. It was a testament to the idea that the essence of people are made of their lands, customs, and beliefs. These things are not so easy to leave behind, even in a new place.

A memory drifted by as I further considered Boro Mama's words: myself as a child with Ammu and Abbu at annual functions organized for and by Rajshahi University alumni in Ontario. Ammu offering her flavourful *kaachi* biriyani, setting it on the table.

Tagore tunes transmitted through *tablas* and harmoniums. *"Amaro porano jaha chay."* Abbu shaking hands with his fellow comrades, his rare throaty lion laughs. The people intoxicated by the nutmeg, cardamom, cinnamon, ginger, and *ghee*, all the laughter merging into one harmonious note.

And it was true, that Canada — touted around the world as democratic, peace loving, and tolerant — also had its own set of challenges. First being swearing to a queen and other practices that marked allegiance to an old world. Even the word *tolerant* itself at first glance seeming to be a liberal and welcoming description of the country, but dig a little deeper and the asymmetry appears: the white, anglophone Canadians do the welcoming, and the brown-skinned immigrants, such as myself, are welcomed. In Canada, racism still existed.

So yes, there was something to be said about differences — how they were perceived, amplified, used to oppress others.

So, I told Boro Mama. "Bhav and I, we are of similar racial roots. We would have many similarities. That should help."

I was optimistic, but Boro Mama's face hardened. He brought his right hand to his chin and said, "Religion, for us, is the most important. Don't you know the lines of South Asia are, to an extent, determined by it?"

The ceiling fan above our heads turned as Boro Mama reminded me about the history that both represented and reinforced differences in beliefs. It took me to the time when I saw Nana's face in a particular photograph. It was the one where he was planted in a chair with brown leather padding, me standing on his lap, almost on my tiptoes to reach one of his wrinkled cheeks with my perfectly puckered lips, through which I freed a smooch. Nana gleefully received the kiss, as if in the front row of a magic show.

Nana had passed away, but he was still alive through his stories. He was as diaphanous as he was opaque: playful and lightweight yet prodigiously stern. Nothing could get through to him when he'd made up his mind. Ammu had told me once about the non-negotiable daily curfew of 6:00 p.m. she and her siblings faced. That Nana would be waiting for her at the door at exactly the time, with a wooden baseball bat or, of lesser punishment, an outstretched hand. The slap on the back of their heads with his heavy palm.

"It would hurt so much," Ammu had explained, rubbing the back of her head. Then, she'd go on to share that Nana was of fine texture, almost workmanship quality, in the way he was built.

"He was the best part of my day. I think I was his favourite." Ammu beamed. "And you, well, he was enthralled with you the most."

Nana was born in Malda and spoke Urdu, Bangla, and Hindi, too. His wife, Nani, was from Murshidabad, the predominantly Muslim, Urdu-speaking town in India. Nana was a political activist who did not support British colonial rule. One of my Khalas told me once that at some point, he had also worked for the same government. So, I wondered whether he was notorious for not only his protests, but something else: Had Nana exposed the ways in which people in power could distance themselves from the oppression they create through layers of paperwork and cryptic language? I knew for certain that Nana was of rebellious spirit, but also that he left newly independent India because his popularity had made him some sort of target.

There were always missing pieces to the fuller story of both my paternal and maternal history. I wondered often if the forgetfulness was self-inflicted and a response to the desire to forget the lifetimes before, or was it just poor memory? I did not know.

What I did know was that Nana and Nani left their home in Murshidabad in newly independent India for East Pakistan, one of the five provinces of the Dominion of Pakistan. This was at a time when over half of Pakistan's population spoke Bangla, and the rest other languages, Urdu not being a major one. Many of the Bangla speakers were in the East Pakistan region. Nana and Nani moved to East Pakistan and eventually settled in the city of Rajshahi, and then Kushtia in later years. Rajshahi sat right on the border with India, and became one of the first places where Muslim *Muhajirs*, or émigrés, settled, often for political reasons. It was world famous for its silks, the reason Europeans had posts there, specifically the Dutch.

Nana brought Ammu and her elder siblings to visit Murshidabad and Malda after Partition. He would paddle the boat himself on the river to Malda, and sometimes he would jump from the boat into the water, and Nani, Ammu, and her siblings would scream. Nana would dive into the water, pop his head out, swim closer to the boat, and rock it back and forth, pretending to be the giant sea serpent Avagrah, found in the waters of Bengal, also known as the Nyan in neighbouring Myanmar. The children would scream and scream until they cried, then Nana would release a bellowing laugh, sending ripples through the water, climb up back onto the boat, and continue paddling away.

Nana's childhood home had vivid green bushes surrounding it. Mango orchards and mulberries and a streak of mahogany across the mid-sky. There were also the Mahananda, Kalindi, and Padma Rivers, how they glistened with speckles of sunshine. At the time when they crossed these waters, there wasn't a need for any passport or signifier of where you were from.

Much has changed since, with modern times came modern borders between the different parts of South Asia — checkpoints, round-the-clock surveillance, and guard dogs. Memories that can never be made or revisited. Flags on both sides of the border changing over the decades — India, Pakistan, Bangladesh.

In 2011, a few years after our visit to Dhaka, a Bangladeshi citizen, a young girl who worked in New Delhi as a maid, would try to cross the India-Bangladesh border, get caught in barbed wire, and be shot to death.

A decade after Partition, Sheikh Mujibur Rahman (co-founder of East Pakistan's Awami League) had an overwhelming democratic success and became the first democratically elected prime minister of Pakistan. It would have been the first time a Pakistani Bengali would have a say and be in power since Partition. However, Zulfikar Ali Bhutto (the leader of the Pakistan People's Party) and President General Yahya Khan refused to accept the results of the democratic election. This led the military government of General Yahya Khan to shoot the first bullets, and the predominantly Bengali citizens of Pakistan responded in resistance — legitimate self-defence on the part of the voters, who were mostly concentrated in the province of East Pakistan.

So, the Liberation War, or *Shadhinota Juddho*, broke out, and Bengali nationalists and rebels sought to pull East Pakistan out of the Dominion of Pakistan. Nana, being multilingual and able to pass for multiple ethnicities, was able to get his entire family, with the help of his son Boro Mama, to safety during these treacherous times.

Embedded within these stories was the story Ammu told me once about the government forces that knocked on Nana and Nani's door. Ammu and her sisters scurried to a room in which they had dug a hole in the ground. They jumped in the hole and Boro Mama moved a board over their heads. The *Razakars, Al-Shams,* and *Al-Badr* were scattered in different parts of the country, always monitoring, making their respective rounds. Ammu and her sisters had to always be on the alert and, as girls, especially discrete.

When the government forces knocked, Nana opened the door and welcomed them in Urdu. He conversed with them for a minute or two. During these moments, Ammu's mouth was dry. She almost shrieked, feeling her heart leap out of her chest, but her sister quickly slapped her mouth shut.

The footsteps grew louder, thudded on the floor above her head. A man's foot missed the spot where Ammu hid, just by an inch. When the government forces went away, Boro Mama removed the board and said, "The men could have taken you away. *Alhumdulillah*, you are safe."

When newly independent India stepped in and helped the Bengali nationalists and rebels, and East Pakistan won the Liberation War to become Bangladesh, this life before Bangladesh became but a secret.

I often asked my family questions about our family that still remained in India and Pakistan, details about the specific political agendas during both Partition and the Liberation War, and their viewpoints. I asked them, too, if what they'd seen ever made them feel ungrounded or suspended, like scattered particles in the air, the way I sometimes felt. I hardly got answers. As a child of diaspora, of communities that themselves went through a lot of internal migration and were subject to varied cultural influences, the concept of one solid place to ascribe all of who you were to seemed like a sort of half-truth, a reduction.

I wondered if being born in a place meant that's where you were from, or whether where you were from was the place where you found the most love. For when I closed my eyes and thought of Bangladesh, I thought primarily of Nani, Nana, Dadi, Dada, and all of the people who loved me in my childhood. When I thought of Canada, I thought mostly of Bhav.

Boro Mama's lips continued to move. I thought, *If warfare and bloodshed over the course of generations has made the battlegrounds layered and fluid, people's identities can be similar.* Whatever deep fears we had about the unknown or the different, which led to ideas or stereotypes that justified the most atrocious of things, in both subtle and drastic ways — well, we didn't have to perpetuate them. That was how I saw it, sitting in Boro Mama's living room, talking to him.

Boro Mama, on the other hand, advised self-preservation and caution, and asked me to consider history and the current state of the world, as well as what was written in religious books. I felt, however, that destiny was amenable, limitations were negotiable, and possibilities were endless. The world was a bowl of fruit you could simply pick from. In my teenage body, I could feel no other way.

A light in a window across the street flicked on, casting shadows across the claret cloth sofa, the glass table before us with *nimki* snacks and two glasses of water, mine untouched. Boro Mama and I sat in silence and took our leave from the conversation soon after.

It was summer. In Toronto, the city would be alive. The streets would be full of people, not looking down or away, as they usually do on winter evenings, but instead looking at each other, soaking up the calm, joyous, ever-present expressions on one another's faces. They'd be sitting on patios, raising their glasses for no reason at all, or trying on vintage clothing in Kensington Market. People on subways and side streets, in front of bright murals, playing tunes on various instruments in a type of vagabond fashion. There would have been all sorts of festivals lined up: Caribana, Pride, Jazz, Afro-Carib, Summerlicious, Cider, just to name a few. There would be wild bergamot and meadow rues in High Park, and ferries doing daily rounds at Harbourfront. People would still be humming to Nelly Furtado's "I'm Like a Bird" or talking about the last season of *Sex and the City* or digesting the newly aired *Grey's Anatomy*.

The sun would be bright — yes, it would be bright. Bright for Canada, at least.

But I was in Dhaka, Bangladesh, sitting in a room full of darkness, in a city where sunlight is a constant. It was almost a month into the trip, and I was now under house arrest in Boro Mama's home, no longer allowed to leave the premises. There were relatives and servants everywhere, and they followed me around asking the same questions. To avoid them I hid in the small storage closet that was a passageway between the bedroom and the bathroom. During the five months I was stuck in the house, that was where I would retreat to.

The closet was the size of two-and-a-half average toilet stalls. It was crowded with dusty suitcases of all sizes, textures, and colours. Dusty suitcases that were sealed shut, the keys missing. Dusty suitcases that held in them lucidity.

The small room was windowless and relatively dim, even in the light of day. My eyes fell mostly to my feet, a few inches from Ammu's barn-red expandable thirty-two-inch luggage and a ninety-five-litre indigo canvas duffel bag. Against the walls were shelves, each loaded with cardboard, metal, and wooden boxes. These boxes were enormous, and I wondered what they contained. I imagined old photographs, thousands of them, with clues of kinships and pedigrees unknown to me.

When Boro Mama wasn't home, all the Khalas who visited and Nani herself would ask the same questions he did the day before, as if hoping I would change my answer or perspective. They wondered why it was that I debated so much, why I wouldn't just accept the advice being offered from the man who influenced most of their family decisions. Yes, I would take advice, but I also had my own mind. I would make my own perspective make sense to them all, win them over somehow. I would not try to run away, nor would I acquiesce. I would make it my goal to explain through logic, the way that they did.

So, when I was back at the living room of horrors with Boro Mama, and he gave me examples of women who had married out of the faith and the problems they had faced, I said sternly and firmly, "Do you think forcing me to see other men, with whom you want to set up my marriage, is any less un-Islamic? I didn't agree. And also, this much I know: Islam doesn't teach force, hate, discrimination, or violence."

I didn't know that I'd have a similar conversation with Abbu a few years later, under very different circumstances. We'd be at a Turkish restaurant, finishing our *kofte* and *bazlama*, moving on to *baklava, kadayif,* and tea. It would be warm, introspective, and I would feel like I was at home in this familiar pensive dialect with Abbu.

"Is it true that East Pakistanis, us Bangladeshis, weren't seen as true Muslims by West Pakistanis? That we were thought to read the Quran in Bangla and that this made us less Muslim? It doesn't make sense. Wasn't the Quran translated into Urdu, too? Even if these things were true, the people were probably just trying to be more inclusive; make faith more accessible," I said.

Abbu looked into the distance and took a deep breath. "Hmm."

I leaned in closely.

"I used to be quite involved with the *Tablighi Jamaat.*"

"What is that?" I asked.

Abbu explained that the *Tablighi Jamaat* is a non-political global missionary movement started in 1927 by Muhammad Ilyas al-Kandhlawi, which had thrived to the present day. Rooted in the *Deobandi* movement in India, its purpose is to revive the Islamic spirit; disentangle Islam from politics, and focus simply on the Quran and *Hadith*.

"What did the *Tablighi Jamaat* believe in?" I probed further.

"We believed in following the path of Allah, especially in times of crises, and we supported everyone in a spiritual journey, including those from West Pakistan."

Abbu went on to share that one of his best friends killed another one of his best friends during the Liberation War, because of misunderstandings related to faith.

"It had nothing to do with religion. Just politics, propaganda. Such a shame."

Prior to the war, Abbu and his two friends spent many days on the emerald fields of Rajshahi University, their noses buried in textbooks under the carnelian sun. They'd frolic down promenades by the lake or sip cups of tea in the nearby coffeehouse, inseparable — that was, until the heat of the war diffused into every village, city, institution, and private circle of the country, leaving all the people much too hot-headed.

I asked Abbu where he stood on the matter, and he said that despite his religious inclinations, one Islamist state would have been a challenge to achieve, given the linguistic, geographic, and religious composition and diversity of the two areas. He understood the blood boil behind a more unified country on the basis of religion, but didn't think it was practical.

I nodded, for I appreciated Abbu's pragmatism. But then I drifted off, thinking about how India functions as an extremely diverse country. Wouldn't it have been possible to include Bengalis in a similar way in Pakistan? They were also Muslim. And why couldn't Bengalis, Indians, and Pakistanis acknowledge they were all once from the same place? Why isn't a shared heritage enough for Bengalis, Indians, and Pakistanis to coalesce around a shared feeling of belonging? Why couldn't they be one while also being the other? Perhaps something like a federation?

I sat quietly and thought.

Abbu observed me, then said, "Don't bother too much with these politics. Focus on *iman* instead. Islam doesn't teach war, nor does it teach genocide or massacre. Self-defence, yes."

Abbu gently picked up his cup and brought it to his lips. His eyes scanned the room, one corner at a time, and then he took a sip.

"Operation Searchlight, that was a whole massacre." He was still shaking his head. He went on to tell me about the December 14 massacre, when *Al-Badr*, an undercover group of *madrasa*, college, and university students who opposed East Pakistani independence, came out and selectively killed Bengali professors, doctors, engineers, and many other intellectuals. The horrific event happened in Dhaka University. Abbu was in Jessore at the time, almost two hundred kilometres away, but the blood spilled across the country and mapped onto his memories. "Killing of mind, of free thought, of great thinkers is a great tragedy," he said. "And for what? That was not Islam."

Yet his tone was neutral. I observed it, curious to understand how he swallowed life like the way I ate my *kadayif* when he had been amid the painful birth pangs that gave way to a most hungry and impoverished nation. I wondered how much pain he must have seen for such tragedy to be less tragic.

"Was it painful?" I had asked. "To remember such things? To see your friends turn the war inward, onto themselves?"

"It happens in war. It was a long time ago."

No, I thought insistently, *Abbu, this is still today.*

I observed the Arabic writing on the restaurant walls and intricate tapestry coloured a rich green and red. My shoulders were heavy but my chest hollow, as if a bullet had made an irrevocable wound. It pained me to think that the faith that had given me the endurance to keep living and breathing could also be used, and again and again, as a tool for massacre. As more time would go on, I'd continue to see this in other Muslim-majority countries around the world, and not just South Asia. I'd see this, too, in other faith contexts.

Abbu sometimes had the ability to read my mind. As we sat there in the restaurant, he went on to say, "In 1971, religious rhetoric was the tool for massacre, and so Bangladesh decided to separate itself from these things. It would be about acceptance of religious diversity, but not necessarily a separation of religion and state."

Later I would learn that Bangladesh added and removed Islam as a state religion a number of times, as if it still struggled with itself and how it should be defined. I would put Bangladesh side by side with Canada. Both countries aren't truly secular, but that doesn't matter, anyway, because secularism itself, like religion, can also be used as a tool for hatred, prejudice, and discrimination.

Back in the living room in Dhaka, I heard Boro Mama's shoe tap the ground as we tackled the topics of national and religious identity, and how the application of faith required true discipline. I saw his lips continue to move, but I didn't really hear him. And then I saw a shadow pass over his face, like an eclipse. Suddenly, for the first time in my life, for the first time in his life, he slapped me.

If I said my heart stopped, would that be a lie? Does the heart actually ever stop when you're afraid? When you're shocked? Does my body have the capacity to disappear from life at will? To pardon itself from existence and halt my blood, devastate my organs, retract backward into whatever darkness I'd inhabited during that long stretch of time before I was born.

His hand left a red imprint across my cheek. Was it his palm or the back of his hand? In the days and weeks to come, I'd no longer be able to tell the difference. When Boro Mama glared at me, it was as if he had seen Medusa: hair of venomous snakes and the look of stone. Or was it the Shayṭān Bride? My eyes seemed to cast a complicated spell upon him. He was ever so desperate to not let it happen.

"Are you really going to be eccentric?" he shouted.

I was determined not to cry but permitted a single eccentric tear to exit my eye.

When he saw my tear, the lines around his mouth loosened, but before I could speak, he said, "I will arrange for you to meet someone, and I don't want to hear you say no."

"No," I whispered under my breath, but he didn't hear me.

In that moment, Bilkis passed us by, her eyes warm with empathy. Boro Mama stormed out of the room. I stood frozen for a minute, then left, too.

Back in the bedroom, I found Ammu, Nani, and Mami whispering on the bed. They looked at my red cheek and asked, "What did you tell him?" I could see then, from the way they looked at me — lips slightly parted, breath halted, hands shaking — that they were scared of Boro Mama, perhaps even more than I had ever been.

I spent most days in the storage closet trying to understand who everyone was, as people were behaving in unpredictable ways, as if I had not known them at all. Could I also say the same about myself? The passing days felt like one long stretched-out hour. Certainly, Bhav would have doubted me in this long silent absence. We never went a day without speaking: did he wonder why I hadn't emailed? Phoned? Mailed a letter? Texted again? Did he think I didn't love him? Did he still love me? I wondered about him, and sometimes talked to him out loud, as if he were there, the way I often spoke with God. What was he thinking? What was he feeling? I held onto the promise ring and closed my eyes, trying to astral project sometimes, across the Indian and Altantic oceans, the Arabian Sea.

Sometimes in the storage closet, I thought about the absurdity of the Radcliffe Line, drawn by the colonial cartographers during Partition, and afterward all the other decisions and events that further divided all the people drinking from the same Ganga River into factions, in the name of religion or whatever else. I thought about how it could have all contributed to the exact moment I was then in, in the storage closet without Bhav. During Partition, it was as if the colonial cartographers drew their lines with their eyes closed, ears shut to the voices on the other side of the margins. People of varying creeds, ethnicities, and tongues living in a similar place, and the complicated history that intertwined them now erased. Perhaps colonizers thought they were doing India a favour, or perhaps they wanted to withdraw sooner than later, for some apparent gain or protection. It probably came down to a thirst for power, whatever flawed mythology they constructed to justify themselves.

Whatever the reason was, there were now these seemingly irrevocable severances. I thought sometimes about the violence on India's West side. The women who screamed when their clothes were torn off and they were made to march naked, who were soon after gang raped and murdered by enemy soldiers. The wife of the railway porter, whose hands were chopped off, her body thrown into fire and then a well, along with her two daughters and a son. The chopped breasts of women of enemy states, torn labia dripping what was called polluted blood. There were also the Hindu families who threw their daughters into wells so the Muslim men couldn't touch them. The feet of rioters kicking remnants of the *shikharas*, the spires of temples placed at the centre of the universe, the axis of the world. Golden Mount Meru. The feet of rioters picking up fragments of the *garbhagriha*, the temple's womb chamber, to inspect them and then throw them away again. The feet of the rioters kicking the crushed-dome multi-patterned rooftops of mosques, the vaults of heaven. The feet of the rioters picking up fragments of the *mihrab*, doorways layered with tiles and the inked strings of Arabic letters joined together. The *mihrab* broken, the direction to Mecca lost. The feet of rioters rushing forward and backward in crowds, their bodies swaying with sounds of people's anguish, the moans, screams, and blood dripping from swords.

I thought also about the violence on the East side. In mother Bengal, the riots during Partition and the decades after. The 1946 Calcutta Killings and Noakhali riots. Hindus and Sikhs and Muslims who ended up dead. Hindus and Sikhs who felt unsafe in East Bengal, and Muslims who felt unsafe in the West. Abduction, death, mass rape. Ethnic cleansing. I looked at my feet, now shaking. By them I imagined the bodies of women raped, abandoned, and killed, corpses covered in rotten filth. Their bodies washed over with the echoes of voices of both strangers and kin. It was always the women who got the brunt of it, their bodies the battleground for all the sins.

Despite having been born three generations after familial exposure to many of these atrocities, the screams of these women were still with me.

I thought then that a new renaissance needed to be birthed, where the people of diaspora could help mend these previous India-Pakistan-Bangladesh atrocities based on religious, linguistic, and ethnic divides, so the next hundred years could be different.

All the generations that would come after could be haunted less by beliefs that travelled across seas and influenced the kindness that people had or didn't have for each other of the same brown skin. They'd be more conscious of the ways colonization was still bleeding into their everyday.

I thought also about the greater Muslim *ummah*, the ways Muslims across the globe were tied together by faith, a faith which was under intense scrutiny by those who feared it, and which supposedly formed the bedrock of communities that continued to discriminate amongst themselves. The alienation, the segregation.

What a shit show, I thought. I usually refrained from profanity but was now unable to help it. *How are we supposed to fix this?*

I wondered about Abbu. How was he keeping?

We didn't have many other relatives visiting the residence, especially those from Abbu's side of the family. One day I heard Boro Chachi would be visiting, Abbu's elder brother's wife, the Chachi with the arboreal wildcat eyes. She would be bringing her daughter Nusrat along, the one I almost drowned out of reflex during my last visit, as well as her son Manshoor, who was about my age. At first Boro Mama advised Boro Chachi that it was probably not a good idea to visit, as there were some important matters being dealt with, but Boro Chachi persisted, saying she had missed me and the rest of the family. It was odd that I hadn't visited her, for usually I'd love spending time with these family members, who were more on the artistic side.

So, Boro Chachi was invited, and as she entered, Mami greeted her and her children with a plate of cake *rusks* and tea. They all sat on the claret cloth sofa. I was next door in the storage closet, scribbling in my journal. When I heard Boro Chachi's voice through the walls, I was instantly calmed. She would surely understand my passion, as well as the injustice of the situation. I jerked up and went to the bedroom door, preparing to open it and meet them, when Nani, who was on the bed, called me from the *jai-namaz*.

"Sit here," she instructed.

I trudged to the bed, fighting the urge to run out the door to Boro Chachi and tell her everything.

"I need to know," she said, "how intimate you've been. And remember, you cannot lie." She pointed to the prayer mat, which I took a seat on.

"Tell me," she asked again, shaking my arms.

I stayed quiet, looking down at the green fibre of the *jai-namaz*, which reminded me of the greenery Paradise was supposed to have. I trembled. Nani replied, "Child, your nonresponse says it all."

I felt strange, sitting on a prayer mat with a third party, face to face with the shame I already felt. At the same time, I held firmly onto the remembrance of my *niyat* and Bhav's.

"Nani, it's not what you think. Yes, I know Allah will not be pleased with me, but I do believe Allah knows that Bhav loves me and I him. We intend to be together forever, I promise."

Now, I was holding onto Nani's ankles, my head on her feet.

"Again, with this love. Your ideals are too high. A man's true commitment shows after he has married his wife. One day as an older woman, when the rush of your hormones has diminished, when you see the world for what it really is, when there are a few wrinkles on your face, you will sit like me, telling your daughters the same thing."

"No, Nani, no!" I cried, still gently pulling on her feet. "I'm sorry."

Before Nani could respond, Mami entered. She opened her mouth to say something, froze looking at us, then continued. "You can go and meet Boro Chachi now."

"Go," Nani instructed me.

I got up from the bed and she added, "I'm only telling you for your own good. I hope you learn, my child. Listen to your Boro Mama, do what he says, or you'll be cast out. You still have time to ask him for forgiveness."

I left the room with Mami, eager to see Boro Chachi's familiar face. In the living room Boro Chachi dipped a cake *rusk* in her tea. When she saw me walking in, her eyes widened. She put her cup down then got up to give me a hug. Her soft cotton sari felt good against my skin. Nusrat and Manshoor also stood up and shuffled over to me. They both looked like they did the last time I visited, except a little more mature. Manshoor had grown his hair out just a little bit, had stubble on his face, and wore his usual goofy smile. Nusrat now wore glasses, appearing timid, but in reality she was always saucier than expected. They hugged me. All the physical contact was exhilarating and uncomfortable at the same time. It was as if I had forgotten what a hug was supposed to feel like, what genuine affection was supposed to feel like.

Nusrat and Manshoor sat down. They were beaming as they sipped their tea, eager to converse.

"You are so thin, and you seem so tired. Sit down," Boro Chachi said. "Where is everyone else?"

"They've gone out to the market. They'll be back soon," Mami replied.

"Okay, well, why haven't you visited? We've hardly seen you and your family this time." Boro Chachi leaned in. I fought the urge to open my mouth, the urge to do whatever it took, just to get someone to appease Boro Mama, to stop everything.

As I was about to respond, Mami squinted at me and Nani appeared, and so I said, "I don't know. You'll have to ask Ammu."

"Okay, that's fine," Boro Chachi continued. She offered me some cake *rusk*, which I refused. Nusrat and Manshoor asked me questions about life in Canada, how I was keeping, all while Mami stood over us, just watching. Nani was now sitting beside me, also carefully observing. I forced a smile. I asked them questions, too, about their lives. I thought then how often people did this in regular life, presenting one way on the outside while battling something else inside. Eccedentesiast.

As we spoke, I heard the doorbell ring. Mami went to answer it, leaving us for a moment.

"I have to go to the bathroom," I said. "I'll be back." They nodded that it was fine. I went through the hallway and the bedroom and then closed the bathroom door behind me. I splashed a handful of water on my face. I needed a way to tell Boro Chachi, Nusrat, and Manshoor what was happening. They would most likely advocate for me. Boro Chachi especially appreciated understanding the interior worlds of her children. Could she do the same for me, too?

As I wiped my face with a *ghamcha*, leaving the bathroom and entering the bedroom, I saw Manshoor standing there.

"Hi. I just came to get you. I think they are serving some lunch," he said.

The beating of my heart reverberated in my ears, drowning out every other sound. The thought came to me as clear as could be: I would tell Manshoor everything in the two minutes I now had with him. But like a pendulum, my trust swayed back and forth. My doubt remained. I took the risk, anyway. *Should I tell him?* I did.

"Manshoor, I have to tell you something. I only have two minutes."

He scrunched his eyebrows in bewilderment. "Okay."

I ran into the storage closet and pulled out my journal from under some clothing. I ripped out a blank page, took a pen, and scribbled down Bhav's name, phone number, and email. I returned to Manshoor and handed him the piece of paper.

"All you need to know now is I am trapped here. I'm being asked to meet with men here who are interested in marriage. I don't want this. This number is Bhav's number. He is the man I love. The man I want to marry. I need to find my way back to him. Will you please help me? Will you get in touch with him?

Just tell him that I haven't been able to contact him because things here are getting worse. Okay?" It was the fastest I'd ever spoken in my life.

Manshoor stood there quietly holding the paper.

I told him about the endless circular conversations, how my actions were monitored, and that I couldn't go anywhere. How nervous I was that if I said or did anything oppositional, I could be stuck here for longer.

"Are you both coming?" I heard Nani shout, and then, shortly after, Ammu's voice. She must have just returned from the market.

"Please," I repeated, my eyes frantic and voice now raspy.

Manshoor seemed tormented. I could see his hands were trembling. "How could they do this to you? This is violence. This isn't right."

"What?" Mami appeared and he quickly stuffed the paper in his pocket. We both exchanged looks with each other to confirm our arrangement. We left the room.

Manshoor sent Bhav an email soon after:

From: ██████████████████████████
██████████

Sent: September 1, 2005 9:51 AM

To: ██████████████████████████
██████████

Subject: about ....your love......... ██████

hi this is ██████. cosine and friend. she is in a lot of troble. she is

being forced to get married. i can read her heart. she will die without u.

so think fast and take a discision. u know what i am saying. it is about what will be your steps when she returns to canada. she may not be able to return canada as single. cause her elders have gone mad. they are pushing her harder and harder.

I would have to wait until I could talk to Manshoor again to know Bhav's response.

One day, in Boro Mama's home, while I was under house arrest, some relatives were invited over.

"They're here to visit the family. I trust you won't share what we've talked about. They don't need to hear it," he said.

Mami entered and handed me a golden peach sari.

I nodded, as by this time I was getting tired.

I draped my body with the sari. Its patterns were so intricate, threads that were seamlessly interwoven. It had lace and sequins, too. The cloth settled on my hips and draped across my breasts, free-falling down my back with the gentle push of gravity. Wearing it usually brought about a certain sensuality, an inexplicable wildness, but it now felt like a trap.

When I entered the living room wearing it, I saw the handful of guests strolling in: some ladies and some men, all middle-aged or older, none my age. They smiled at me from afar, as I shuffled back into the bedroom, dreading the small talk expected of me, which I didn't feel competent to deliver considering the state of things.

Soon after, Sweety Khala and Gollapi Khala, who was the eldest of Ammu and her sisters, traipsed in with Ammu and handed me a floral-patterned tray. *Nimkis*, nut mix, samosas, pitas, with *doodh cha*.

Ammu pulled up the sari *anchal* that fell from my chest. "Be mindful of your *lajja, haya,* and your humility, especially around guests," she said.

As I made my way into the living room, I got a closer look at the men and women on the sofa. There was a man with a blunt brown moustache and scrawny arms. There was another man who had a white beard, petite frame, and kind eyes. I also saw a woman with a chestnut bob, and another with her hair in a small bun and a cotton sari with wrinkles. I speculated what the lives of these people were beyond their demeanour and physical characteristics.

I saw the ladies on the sofa were, in comparison to the men that sat next to them, very quiet. I was in awe when they finally spoke, how they shaped their sentences, about topics that ranged from domestic duties to politics to history.

I brought the floral tray with snacks to the men and women; my eyes were weary. I almost tripped over my hem. As I got closer, I considered asking these people for help. What would I say? *Hello, I'm hiding in a storage closet because my uncle doesn't like my handsome Toronto boyfriend, my future husband — who also happens to be Sikh, but we're going to find a way.* Would they help me? Who was I to them? They answered to Boro Mama. Instead, I said my *salams* and put down the tray, just as I had been instructed.

Boro Mama stood up to greet me. He held a lit cigarette in his left hand that he brought periodically to his purple-tinted lips. He went for daily jogs, and got frequent checkups. He watched what he ate, and made sure he meditated. However, smoking was something that was hard for him to give up. I thought he would at least understand then that habits die hard, whether it be cigarettes or a lover's presence.

Just the other day he had Bilkis bring me a plate of yellow turmeric-coated *kabuli chana.* He had bent down so we were eye level, picked up my hand, and said, "These are not normal circumstances, but you have to eat. You have to take care of your health." He had said this to me with eyes that looked like hibiscus China rose flowers, ferocious yellow petals with a tender pink in the middle; a little off, kind of sick. I speculated whether he himself had been deteriorating the way I felt myself to be.

Boro Mama gave me a weak nod and I stood there in the living room staring at his guests. He sat down. The sunlight burst in from the surrounding windows.

"Sit down, sit down," said the man with the blunt brown moustache and scrawny arms stretched across the back fold of the sofa.

The man with the white beard looked at me as if he had known me forever.

I accidentally sat down on my *anchal*, shifted my body side to side to move it, and then brought its tail end to my lap.

I heard then one of the men say, "Essentially, they're scapegoating Muslims." I heard the tapping of feet on the floor. "But you have to admit that Saudi Arabia doesn't help."

"This is more about resources than anything else," I heard the woman sitting next to me remark. Her chestnut curls grazed the top of her silky white sari. The maroon shade on her lips matched the pashmina wrapped around her slender arms.

She smiled at me, revealing perfect ivory teeth. Her elegance attracted me. Slowly, memories of my teenage life began to rise with the smoke above my head. I watched the conversation.

I learned that Boro Mama had requested my passport from Ammu. I heard it from Shahzad one day. He said he saw his father open their bedroom *almari* and store it there, in some kind of case with a lock.

"Do you know why?" I asked him.

"Well, obviously," he whispered. He was in the storage closet with me, looking around as he spoke. "I think he is serious. I don't think he will let you leave. I have to go."

"Thanks for telling me," I said.

Shahzad was in his early teens and preparing for exams. He hoped to move to London or maybe Australia, anywhere that would allow for him to pursue his father's aspirations. He didn't express much, but I could tell by the way he studied my face that he was genuinely concerned. He left to continue working on his assignment.

I thought about my own siblings, too, who were also quite young and who followed Ammu around without getting much involved. And I, as the elder sister, didn't talk to them much either about any of what was happening, for a number for reasons, although I was sure they already knew. One being that I could easily be seen as influencing them, and it was important to me that they make their own judgments and decisions. If I did have the Shaytān in me, like what was thought, then it would be better for me to stay away. It was a distance I harboured out of a desire to protect, although this in itself had its own consequences. If they were to somehow support me, I knew they would also be subject to criticism. I hoped and prayed that they'd not let any of it cloud their hearts.

I sat down and started free writing whatever came, an exercise that allows me to see my thoughts as they appear on paper and examine them with greater clarity. This time, however, I could only muster a single thought that circled again and again and again like a neurotic messenger bird. I wrote *find me*. Then, it came to me: I would need to figure out a way to get Bhav to find me. He was the only one who would listen. He could come and get me out of this place. How could it happen? I gripped my pen and started to jot down the logical steps.

Step one: I inform him of the plan and give him the address using Shahzad's phone.

Step two: He books a flight to Dhaka. Takes a rickshaw to get here.

Step three: He somehow distracts the gate guard or waits for him to fall asleep, which would be highly likely during late afternoon. Then he would enter the veranda from the outside and wait behind one of the rose bushes.

Step four: I find a way to the same veranda from the inside of the house when everyone is napping.

Step five: We reunite …

I erased step five. I would have to enlist the help of either Shahzad or Bilkis to retrieve my passport. That step would need to be completed before I could meet Bhav outside on the veranda. The time between my retrieval of the passport and our reunion would be critical.

Yes, I thought, *this is the solution.* If I were to escape a different way, the chances of a broad public announcement about my character, my family, or Islam would go out. An escape without commotion would break fewer hearts.

I gripped my pen tightly and pushed it into the paper. I decided I would write Bhav a letter that could become an email. In it, I pleaded for him to come to Dhaka and get me out. I told him it was the only way to prevent any kind of public shame. I told him that everyone's *intentions* were good. They were just trying to fulfill their duty as elders, but struggling to find the right way. They were only trying to impart the knowledge they had, things about the world they had deduced. That being said, it wasn't right, what was happening. I carried the note in my bra, for the moment to share it could be almost anytime.

I smiled at my plan, at my letter, and then I burst out laughing, remembering all the conversations Bhav and I had about eloping. Perhaps we would live in a small town after all, milking cows and sewing clothes.

It was then in my reminiscing that I heard a muffled voice that sounded strangely familiar. I looked around the storage closet, wondering if someone was there, but no. I stood up and opened the door, walked into the empty bedroom, and peeked through the crack between the sliding door that led to the living room. Manshoor was standing near the front door, his face half covered by a tall living-room plant. Ammu was talking to him. I saw her fully, her hands swivelling in the air as if she was trying to explain something. I listened in.

"I just want to say hello to her," Manshoor stated.

"She is busy right now. It is best you come another time," I heard Ammu say, trying to get him to leave.

I felt my heart pump with vigour. Had Bhav replied to his message? What did Bhav say?

I also remembered the message that was in my bra. I had to give it to him so I could again communicate with Bhav.

"Well, at least give her this," Manshoor said, handing Ammu a book.

I almost tripped running out of the bedroom, across the living room, and toward the front door to get Manshoor to stay. But by the time I got there, he was gone.

Ammu turned from the front door to me and handed me the book. I am not sure, but if my memory serves me right, it was a translation of Tagore's *Nastanirh*, or *The Broken Nest*, which is about a woman coming to use her own voice during a time when women were encouraged to pursue intellectual and artistic freedom but only within the domestic sphere.

"You don't have time for this. Always buried under books. It's time for you to consider becoming someone's wife, or a mother to children," she told me.

All of what she said I desired, just not like this. I took the book and walked away. It was true that I was not in the right mind to read. Why would Manshoor give me this in my current state? I plunked myself on the floor in the storage closet and flipped through the book's pages. There it was, a small slip of paper, so seemingly insignificant that I didn't even realize I'd been expecting it until I received it. I unfolded the note hastily. Inside it said, *I told him. He loves you. Stay strong. Say no.*

Comfort billowed over me. "*Alhumdulillah,*" I cried. It was the first time in a few days I had felt more inclined than not to pray, and so I did.

On the *jai-namaz* I put my two palms up to the sky. I didn't, however, ask for anything other than *the right thing to happen. What was meant to be.* And for Allah to know *our love is now and will forever be,* Inshallah, *pure.*

A couple of days had passed. I had not seen Manshoor again. I waited patiently, staring at the white walls, sometimes imagining on them grand scenes of reunion, Bhav and I. I hummed to the tune of Daniel Bedingfield's "If You're Not the One," which was our song.

How would it feel to not only be reunited with Bhav, but the sun, sky, soil, all my books, my friends? Would I ever get to enjoy all those pleasures I took for granted before?

I also thought a lot of Abbu and the suffering he was enduring, all alone.

In the storage closet, as I stared at my now protruding veins, I pondered mortality.

Manshoor arrived without warning. Ammu was out with Sweety Khala, and Nani and Mami were home. Mami wasn't one to confront, reject, or debate, so she let him in. He sat on the claret cloth sofa. As I walked out to greet him, Nani followed me. When Mami saw Nani take a seat, she left to get everyone some *doodh cha.*

The conversation began with the usual pleasantries.

"You should come back another time when everyone else is home," Nani told him. "This is not a good time."

"Oh, that's okay," Manshoor said. "I was just in the area and wanted to say my *salams*."

Nani asked him about his mother, his sister, and his two brothers. She asked him about his studies, and covered all the other formalities. I sat there quietly, looking at my feet, for I didn't want to give any kind of sign that Manshoor had been helping me.

When Nani got up, as if to take her leave and therefore imply Manshoor should take his, I broke my stillness and said, "I have that book you lent me. I don't think I will be able to read it, but thank you. I will get it, one second."

With that I scurried into the storage closet where I pulled *Nastanirh* from my suitcase, and then my letter — or email-to-be — for Bhav from my bra. I folded the piece of paper to the smallest size and stuffed it in between pages of the book just as Manshoor had.

When I came out of the storage closet, I saw Nani was on the bed praying. I passed her, avoiding the top of the mat, and made my way through the sliding doors. Mami was now saying her good-byes to Manshoor. I handed Manshoor my book with the note.

"*As-salam alaykum*, see you again, *Inshallah. Khuda hafiz*," Manshoor said to both Mami and I and then left.

When Mami looked at me, my eyes were lowered. When I turned my back to her, I let out a deep breath. I hoped the message would reach Bhav soon.

I would find out later that when Bhav received my message from Manshoor, he thought the idea of coming to Bangladesh to take me away from my family was absurd. At the same time, he considered it as a last resort. He spent nights awake, distraught, pacing back and forth. Bhav, who often let his thought threads overlap, twist, and tangle when stressed, was also being asked to make critical decisions and take action.

Not being able to rescue and protect the woman he loved was a humiliation of the highest order, cauterized to the point where there would be no pain left to bear, just the omnipresent truth that she could never genuinely be his if there was nothing left that he could do.

The helplessness would be an unspeakable shame, never leaving his psyche and growing instead like a slowly spreading disease, a tender haunting that would travel to the bones of his being. It would be something for which he could possibly consider death by his own hands. Which he did.

He would then do whatever he could, but at the same time allow the choice to be hers — mine — with whatever clarity I had.

I didn't see Manshoor again for a while. One day Ammu entered the storage closet with a reddened face.

"Your Boro Chachi keeps calling to ask about you. Did you tell her or Manshoor or Nusrat something?" she questioned.

I shook my head. Yes, I was lying, but I had to.

"Well, they won't be visiting anymore. The doors are closed until we figure things out."

One day Sweety Khala told me that I'd get to stay at her place for a night. She wanted to give Mami a break from constantly looking over me as if I were a child. I nodded, as I wanted very much to leave Boro Mama's home, even if it was for a short while. At the same time, I knew not much would be different. If anything, it could actually be worse. I went, anyway.

The driver took me to her flat late in the afternoon. I spent most of the time lying on a bed and staring at the ceiling with her daughters, Nabila and Maryam, who had been ordered to monitor me. They were to keep track of when I entered the balcony or how long I stayed in the bathroom. If they didn't report any mysterious behaviour, they would meet the end of Sweety Khala's broomstick and no phone privileges. At least, that is what Maryam told me.

"Let's play a game," Maryam said. She jumped up from the bed, ran out of the room, then came back with a piece of neon-pink paper and a pen in her hand.

Both Nabila and I pulled our bodies up from the bed and sat upright.

"What is it? What is it?" Nabila shouted with her thumb still in her mouth.

Maryam plopped next to us and began folding the piece of paper in her lap. She handled it like origami, smoothening and caressing with undivided attention. Nabila and I watched her, curious. She folded the pink paper into triangular petals. She had created a fortune teller. She took the pen and began writing on the petals, single letters of the alphabet, but she wouldn't let me see which. She turned her back to Nabila and I as she did this, and we tried to peer over her shoulder.

Sweety Khala's maid, who had two pigtails and wore a seafoam-coloured dress, walked in with a pile of *salwar kameezes*, pillowcases, and dresses in her hands. She dropped them on the chair and hobbled over to us.

Finally, after about five minutes, Maryam turned to us three, presenting her fortune teller and saying, "Aha!"

I had seen a similar contraption before, in elementary school, and wondered if Maryam would be playing the game I had played, where we could ask questions and receive answers.

I placed a strand of my hair behind my ear and fixed my *orna*. I shuffled closer to her. "What are we going to try and predict?"

"Well," Maryam began, "we're going to find out the first letter of the name of the person you are going to marry. Will it be *B* or something else?"

As ridiculous I thought the notion, I was also desperate. Anything, anyone, whatever it took to give me some hope. "Okay, let's do it," I said.

Maryam got on her knees on the bed, as if to tower over us a little bit. "Oh, Allah, tell us, what is the first letter of the name of the man Sumaiya will marry?" She leaned in close to me and asked for a number. I told her three, as that was my favourite.

We all held our breaths as Maryam opened and sealed the petal lips. Finally, she opened one of the flaps to reveal the answer.

I closed my eyes, holding an image of the letter *B* somewhere between my temples and the middle of my forehead, where futures are shown.

Maryam cleared her throat, "Oh, an *S*!"

Nabila and Maryam jumped up and down on the bed, and the maid squinted, then went back to her pile of clothes on the nearby chair.

This isn't a joke! I wanted to shout to my two cousins, but I didn't. I wondered then how they, despite being so young, could react like this, at this moment, as if it were all normal. And then I heard procession music and lots of mirth. The rickshaws were louder than usual. I hauled myself off the bed and crept to the balcony, almost toppling over on the way. From the balcony I saw a *bosti*, a row of slum shelters.

The rooftops of the shelters were covered in blue, orange, and red lights, and there were rows of women carrying large pots on their hips. There were a few men and little boys and girls twirling around in circles. It looked like a celebration of some sort; I looked on until this was confirmed. It was a wedding. A bride with a red *Kumkum bindi* in the middle of her forehead and smaller white *bindis* around it. The *Kumkum bindi* is worn by Hindu brides and signifies not only that a woman is married, but also *Shakti*, the feminine aspect of the divine in Hinduism — the creative force that moves the universe but which can also destroy. The bride had *altha* on the tips of her fingers and the base of her feet, the way Muslim brides also wore *altha*, as well as *Odissi* classical dancers. She beamed, losing reservation and swaying her hips to the procession beat. *Such joy*, I thought, and as I did, an idea came to me.

When I looked back at Nabila and Maryam, I realized they were now only two inches away. Their hands on their hips, they stood there scanning me.

"Maryam, can I ask you something?" I lowered my tone, which was already soft to begin with. I ushered her back to the bed where I sat her down. "I believe you have a phone."

"Yes," Maryam replied. "Why?"

The maid was now putting up the mosquito net tent, tucking in its ends under the bed mattress.

"Girls, come eat!" Sweety Khala shouted from the kitchen.

"Can I use it?" I asked. "Just once, tonight?"

"I'm not allowed to," Maryam answered. She snuck a look at Nabila, who was sprawled out on the bed.

"If you let me use your phone, I'll let you have absolutely everything in my makeup bag."

To which both Nabila and Maryam jerked up.

"Really?" Nabila asked. She was swaying her arms around as if to draw away the mosquitoes. The mosquito net almost came down.

"Yes, I promise you."

"Eh, Maryam, just give it to her." Nabila gestured to Maryam, clapping her hands.

Maryam squinted. "Okay, but no one here can back bite and tell anyone that I did this." She pointed at me, Nabila, and the maid who was now picking up Maryam's dresses from the floor.

We all said *promise* at the same time, other than the maid.

"Eh, girl," Maryam yelled at the maid. "Will you tell?"

The maid shook her head. Her bemused eyes suggested she had no idea what on earth we were talking about , but nonetheless she'd be loyal.

"Shh, keep your voice down," I told Maryam. "Also, she is harmless. Let's not yell unnecessarily. Thank you so much. And if you ever visit Canada, you can have every single makeup product I own."

Maryam grinned.

Later that night, when everyone was asleep, I texted Bhav. The date on the phone read September 27, 2005 — it had been about two months since I last saw him. In my text, I told him that I still hoped he could come to Dhaka to get me. I asked him also to call Mrs. Seidu, who I thought could perhaps help by contacting Abbu and having a talk with him. I didn't have her number, so I asked Bhav to track it down. Told him to not text back after I myself stopped texting, for I was still being monitored and the stakes of being found out were far too high. I told Bhav I loved him. That I was scared. That I wasn't exactly ready to give up yet. I would find a way that had the least amount of damage and pain for everyone involved.

I erased all my texts.

The next morning Sweety Khala found out that I had used the phone. Someone must have told her. But she couldn't retrieve any messages, so she had nothing to tell Boro Mama. When she asked me, I remained quiet. I never found out who had squealed.

Atyanta Cene Aparicita Byakti /
Familiar Stranger
অত্যন্ত চেনা অপরিচিত ব্যক্তি

There was a caramel-skinned lizard with bulging black eyes watching me record what I was observing as I sat on the cement bathroom floor, the door locked and my back against it. My journal was in my lap with its tattered edges, a slender silver pen between my thumb and index finger.

I was startled by a series of knocks — anxious and demanding — so I hid my journal under my fuchsia *orna*. When I opened the door, Boro Mama stood there with a smirk on his face.

"Please get dressed," he said. "We're leaving."

"Where? Where are we going?" In my mind I was shouting as I asked the question, but in reality, I was merely whispering. Only a few days before I last texted Bhav, some cousins shared rumblings that my family would consider potentially moving back to Dhaka if I remained so rebellious. Only a few days after I last texted Bhav, I learned that Boro Mama was considering leaving me in a village if I didn't acquiesce sooner rather than later.

"I'm taking you to meet someone," Boro Mama revealed.

"Who?" I asked.

"A relative," Boro Mama said, clearing his throat.

I imagined natural light wrapping my body in a sweet caress. My spine — twisted from sitting for prolonged periods of time in the storage closet, hunched over my knees and frequently immobile — unwinding itself at the call of the sun. The sun's rays tracing my face. I thought also about the forced smiles and pleasantries, which required willpower that I was still trying to reserve for my escape.

So I asked, "Can I just stay here? I'm not well."

"Get dressed," Boro Mama replied, ignoring my question. "Bilkis, can you find her a proper outfit?"

Perhaps I could have protested further, but I didn't.

Boro Mama had multiple cars, but the one I remember taking was a black Jeep. As I stepped outside of the house the flying dust grains in the air hit my face, and it was a sort of reminder that I was indeed still alive. The light rays I craved smothered me all at once. I squinted at the surrounding buildings, which seemed to twirl, and I peeked through the front gate to see the hot-pink roofs of tent stalls, where snacks and cigarettes were being sold. I battled to keep my body upright and not fall unconscious. I didn't even notice the driver, who appeared at my side and then helped me up into the Jeep. The front gates opened, and we were on our way. I looked out the Jeep's windows, desperate to climb out. Not to run away exactly, for there was nowhere to run. To go for a walk. On my own. Alone. Free.

The restaurant we arrived at was an upgraded Pizza Pizza. At the entrance were big glass doors. Looking through them, I saw women with kohl-lined eyes, peach cheeks, bright lipstick. I touched my own face; I had forgotten the feeling of painting my lips or nails, tracing a wing at the end of my eyelids.

The glass doors were opened by two service men, who gestured for us to enter. On the other side a man was waiting. My eyes moved to him immediately. He was handsome. Tall. Something about his body language indicated he was gentle, open, kind. He was ten inches taller than me, rather soft-featured, wearing a light-blue collared shirt, black dress pants, and shiny black dress shoes. His hair was combed back, not pretentiously, just casually, slightly tousled. On his face, a semi-smile, high cheekbones, long eyelashes that flickered like a burning candle on a bedside dresser while pages of a good book are turned.

Who is he? I wondered, but not enough to pay attention further. I was already tired and a little overwhelmed by all the sights and sounds I was absorbing in one day.

Boro Mama opened his arms as if to invite the man in for a hug.

"Meet Shoaib," he said, turning to me.

"*As-salam alaykum*," Shoaib said to me in a deep, sonorous voice.

"*Wa alaikum salam*," I muttered.

The heels of the men's polished dress shoes clacked on the marble tiles. I looked around and noticed that in the upgraded Pizza Pizza, people ate pizza with cutlery, in their finest attire, while being eagerly attended to by servers with a time-honed perceptiveness. It was so different from what I'd seen just moments ago while sitting in the Jeep: slums upon slums and skinny children asking for money. The striking contrast between the rich and the poor left me with a somersaulting stomach.

As I waded through these reflections, I noticed in my periphery that Shoaib kept occasionally turning his face toward me, catching my eyes momentarily, then looking down, then back up at Boro Mama again.

So, I focused my attention on him, how his voice was genial, his shoulders leaning, his grin appeasing, as if he was politely trying to make a space big enough for Boro Mama's grand ideas so that he could speak at length. Although we said not much to each other, I deduced that Shoaib had about him a certain modesty. A certain tact that differed from all the other boys my age, who were careless with their words and far too influenced by each other; of no distinction or ability to stand apart on one's own. Shoaib was most likely a handful of years older than I, and moved with an easy gracefulness as if he never thought about where he was going but was always content when he arrived. This began to feel comforting. I admired it almost, that kind of uncomplicated enlightenment. All this I deduced without knowing anything about him.

I continued watching Boro Mama and Shoaib converse but didn't follow the conversation myself. I didn't hold onto any detail, just remembered the impression Shoaib had left and, of course, the absurdity of the restaurant I was in. I got the sense we weren't staying for long, as we hadn't taken a seat.

So, I stood there, my heels clicking nervously against the floor as the achromatic uniforms of the servers blended into the glittery saris of women and the short shiny skirts made of leather, worn by the young well-off girls — most likely from the rich, liberal part of the city, called Gulshan. The cackling at the tables, once whispers, had now increased tenfold, and deciphering the threads of logic in all the conversation around me left me utterly exhausted.

As Boro Mama and Shoaib continued talking with each other, a thought sauntered into my mind: I could get up and just run. In my fantasy of the escape, I stood up, took off my pointy-heeled sandals, held them in my hands, and then mustered all my strength to shout, "Burn, you lousy liars!" I took a hard look at the faces of Boro Mama and Shoaib. The silver trays in the hands of the servers fell with ringing clangs. The forks hit the plates, the plates shattering into sharp triangles that broke into smaller pieces as I ran. The heavy earrings slapped against the faces of the rich ladies. A piece of pizza crust fell out of a woman's mouth, another fainted, another said, "Why I never," in a British accent for some reason, and the bald man at the corner table, shocked to see me bolting past him, began to choke on the knife in his hands, pushing his belly into the table, causing the knife to shoot out of his throat and into Boro Mama's heart.

"Well, we will talk again, *Inshallah*," Boro Mama said to Shoaib. My escape fantasy dissipated. He said goodbye to Shoaib, who said his *salam* to me and left.

Boro Mama then escorted me to his Jeep. I climbed into the back seat, trying to remember how it felt in my imagination just a minute before, to leave. Like an expanding balloon in my chest lifting me up, a lightness. During the ride back to his home, I said not much, just wringed my hands wondering what the purpose of the visit had been and what could unfold.

On the way from the Jeep to the front doors, I straggled behind Boro Mama. I noticed a slight bounce in the way he moved.

Once inside, I scurried off to the bedroom, where I was surprised to find Ammu, my Mami, and my two other Khalas, Sweety and Gollapi, gathered.

"How was your meeting?" Sweety Khala asked.

I said nothing, just continued to the *almari* to find something else to wear.

The ladies left me alone to change. I saw the outlines of their figures on the other side of the bedroom's sliding door. It seemed they were chatting with Boro Mama, and although I was curious what about, I remained focused on changing.

Soon after, Bilkis knocked on the door to inform me that lunch was being prepared. Having meals together was a tradition followed strictly in Boro Mama's home.

Before I could leave the room, however, Nani, Mami, and my two Khalas walked hastily past Bilkis, pushing her aside and eyeing me with curious anticipation. They asked me directly and while smiling, "What did you think of the man you met today?"

"I don't know ..." I answered earnestly. "I didn't pay attention."

"Wasn't he so polite? Well mannered?" Gollapi Khala asked.

By now, the ladies had guided me to the bed. I felt my shoulders knot as they circled around me. I sighed, looking at Gollapi Khala's serious face. She usually had her hair back in a bun, which brought further attention to the beauty mark underneath her bottom lip that was just like the one I myself had. She was far more reserved than Sweety Khala, but no less fierce.

To her question, I answered, "He seems shy, but in a good way." I wasn't sure what they were trying to get at.

My response brought a glow about everyone's face, and I thought I should have perhaps bit my tongue.

"How am I related to him?" I asked.

Ammu and Boro Mama then walked in and, upon seeing us all on the bed, he stated "I'd like to speak with her alone," with a sternness that resisted questioning.

The women exchanged glances, got up, and made their way out of the room. When they left, he closed the sliding door, and took a few steps toward me.

"What did you think of the man you met today?" he asked, squinting his eyes just a bit. I was so tired from earlier that I just nodded.

He then went on to lay out some facts he thought it important for me to know: that Shoaib was an only child and therefore prized, that he was the head of a well-known company and therefore hardworking, that he tended to many family responsibilities, including taking care of his father, who wasn't well, and therefore he was compassionate and responsible, and, finally, that others had known him to be rather romantic. Also, he'd already expressed his fondness of me.

"I can tell," Shoaib had said, apparently, "that she is the kind of woman I've been waiting for my whole life."

Boro Mama's hardened expression broke into a self-satisfied smirk as he told me these things, then threw his arms into the air. "Shoaib is a good man."

I knew what was going on.

"How am I related to him?" I asked.

"You're not related," Boro Mama finally answered.

An urge to throw up.

"I wanted you to meet him because I do believe that he would be a great partner for you," he said.

My face and shoulders drooped as I responded. "But I told you about Bhav. He is the one."

I heard Boro Mama grit his teeth. To my repeated words he repeated, "Okay, let it be for now, but I do want you to think about it." We were still going in circles.

I hadn't spoken to Abbu for weeks. When we finally spoke, it was only for a couple of minutes. I wondered if he knew the truth or if they'd twisted everything I said. Boro Mama stood over me as I mumbled to Abbu, my voice quavering and body trembling.

"They …" I tried to tell him that each day I was sinking more and more into a deep blankness that I imagined as a patch of wet sand at the bottom of my brain; the harder I fought, the more buried I became, until I was fully submerged in what can only be described as a radical emptiness.

But I couldn't explain as clearly as I wanted, and he responded, "Being there will be good for you. Have you been watching the news? How they've invaded Iraq? The things people are saying about Muslims here? It's really a terrible thing. People are dying. Stay there and learn a little more about who you are and where you came from."

And I thought, *There is still some sort of misunderstanding.*

Soon, words of persuasion became injuries on my physical body. Tightened grips and the force of hard surfaces against my skin, harm by the same person I had once considered a friend. I was learning, as a nineteen-year-old, what I could have never ever fathomed: that harm wasn't just at the hands of strangers, but family, friends, close colleagues, acquaintances, lovers. This couldn't keep on forever. Something had to break.

I had been waiting for Shahzad all afternoon, but it seemed he had been at school longer than usual. I'd convinced him the day before to let me use his cellphone just one more time. He had been avoiding me — I could tell because he no longer played cricket at his usual spot, and he would hardly look me in the eye or speak to me for longer than a minute. I couldn't tell if it was because he couldn't tolerate what he was seeing or if he just feared for his own well-being, the whip of his father's belt. But that day I had found him alone and pleaded to use his phone, almost falling to my knees, and I suppose it was the healing scar on my forehead that might have changed his mind. He agreed to let me use his cellphone again.

So, I waited. Where was he? I needed to tell Bhav that things were getting even worse, and it was time to take action — but exactly what kind of action I still wasn't sure. I wouldn't budge on my duty to my parents, given everything I'd seen them sacrifice to give me an abundant future. I had already violated my loyalty to them by continually choosing Bhav. To leave drastically would only hurt them in a worse way, potentially breaking them psychologically, or even spiritually.

Shahzad finally ambled in. I saw he was carrying more books in his hands than usual. I turned my neck to the left then right, and saw that no one was around other than the driver who had escorted Shahzad in. The driver, whose properness reminded me of men on Bay Street in Toronto's financial district, nodded to me and Shahzad then left.

I ran to Shahzad. "Will you still help me?"

"Yes," he whispered, avoiding eye contact. "But after this, never again. My dad scolded me yesterday, asking if I had released any information to you or if you'd asked me anything. I think he's catching on."

"Okay," I said, trembling slightly. Bilkis told me the other day that she had heard some Khalas telling Ammu they would sever their relationships with her if I did not do what I was told, because I was a terrible influence on their daughters and I was creating too much mayhem and distress. This threat of estrangement was enough to worsen Ammu's breathing at night and prevent her sleep. I thought then how lonely Ammu and Abbu sometimes seemed in Canada, but when they called their relatives here in Dhaka they were always giddy and eager to plan the days of their future. I did not want to take this away from them.

Shahzad pulled out the phone and I took it from his hands. With that, I ran to the bathroom, the one with the perceptive lizard who witnessed everything that went on within those four walls, and I typed away. I told Bhav the truth. Then I gave Shahzad his phone back right away and thanked him.

A few days later Sweety Khala dragged me to meet one of her relatives. Everyone else was out, and so she was given the duty of supervising me. We were in the middle of Dhanmondi, on the rooftop of a building, in the middle of which Sweety Khala and another lady were having tea. I shifted away from them, my pale legs and arms swinging, moving, stretching farther, instead of sitting. The experience of sitting. The joy of sitting. The terrible act of sitting. In the storage closet. Now I was moving as if my body didn't belong to me. I looked back over my shoulder to catch Sweety's harsh glare, as if she was warning me, "Don't you try anything!"

I walked away from her as she continued to chat with the lady about the latest *anarkali* dress she had purchased for Maryam to attend some other woman's wedding.

Underneath the fossil-grey cement of the rooftop were the faint sounds of muffled voices. Above me, the late-afternoon sun hid behind a cloud in a smoky grey sky, as if it was too embarrassed to see me this way.

I wobbled over to the edge of the roof, which was without fencing. When I got to it, I looked straight down to see cars squeezing through narrow tube-like streets. There were a few men just standing around chatting and smoking, some in striped or checkered *lungis*, others in trousers. From the roof, their faces appeared as circular brown smudges.

I saw the circles of smoke from their cigarettes, heard their hoots. Their heads bobbed up and down. Some periodically re-tied their *lungis*. Scratching their heads. Patting each other on the back. Whatever they were doing, they were free.

I wondered how my death would look to them, if I stepped onto the air beyond the edge of the roof. I imagined myself then like Parakeet, with my shamrock wings spread, my striking red beak. I brought my arms from my side up to my shoulders, my neck pulled back to take in the light, my eyes closed, my one leg forward, just slightly over the edge. *If I jumped, would I fly or would I splatter?* All my organs released from the structure within which they were contained. I wondered how it would feel to be free from systems all together. To not worry about identity or school or books or friends or love or marriage or money. To never have to answer to anyone again.

Would the men down on the ground gasp and stare? Maybe run for help?

Would the gruesomeness of it impact the rest of their lives? What would the local headline be?

Bideshi Girl Falls to Her Death After Committing Grave Sin

Girl Dies to Save Family Name

Girl Dies for Lover and Disgraces Family

Possessed Girl Breaks Her Bones

Girl Kills Herself After Demonstrating a Pattern of Behaviour that Includes Making Questionable Choices: Lying, Promiscuity and Betraying Her Family, Her Culture, Her Homeland, Her God

Girl's Death Due to Mysterious Circumstances

The horn of an oncoming scooter. I opened my eyes. The tips of my toes curling over the edge of roof. I stepped back and away. Sweety Khala was behind me with her arms crossed over her chest.

"What are you doing? Come, let's go." She grabbed my arm and pulled me toward her, ushered me down the stairs.

On the ride back to Boro Mama's home, the buildings beyond the car window blurred into vapour. "It's too foggy," I mumbled. "People's messy minds."

"What are you saying?" Sweety Khala asked, unfolding a *jamdani* sari the lady had gifted her to investigate the designs in its interior.

I stayed quiet. Later she informed the others that it was indeed quite possible that my mind had been overcome by some malignant force, given the way I was behaving, which was disturbed.

Sayatanera Badhu / The Shayṭān Bride (Part Two)

(শয়তানরে বধূ)

I heard them speaking about a woman in the city who was tampered with by a jinni and now remained in a state of paralysis. Like me, this woman often sat in an unhinged marble state, staring at the walls counting one, two, three, four o'clock. Numb, pale, and unmoving, often silent, was how she passed the day.

It was during one of these days, while sitting in the storage closet eavesdropping on a conversation between Ammu and Sweety Khala, that I learned about this woman. I listened through the open crack of the closet door, which I had left ajar. They were sitting on the bed.

Ammu and Sweety Khala discussed the many hypotheses of how she ended up where she was, unmarried beyond marriageable age. A family falderal and disgrace. Nani and Bilkis joined later, listening in.

They discussed that her paralysis came about the morning after an evening when she had gone out for a stroll. During this evening, she looked particularly beautiful. Her black waist-length hair was down, fluttering over her breasts, resting in her curves, grazing her bottom. The full moon above her head followed her as she drifted by mango and *boroi* trees, rusty red-bricked buildings, *gandharaj* bushes, and a stray Labrador retriever of hickory shade barking incessantly, as if to warn her. There was a palpable pulse through the veins of the earth as she made her way over upturned roots, ancient moss, and thick mud.

"It was deep into the evening, around sunset during *maghrib* prayer. There were no human witnesses to bear sight of what really happened. Most people were indoors praying, preparing for dinner, or spending time with their families," Sweety Khala said. "This is when the jinni saw her."

She went on to explain that the jinni was hiding behind a stout tree, the bark covered in moist sapwood that smelled of jasmine and lemon blossoms.

Yes, only during maghrib, I thought, because like *fajr, maghrib* is a threshold between night and day, when the pathway between the observable human world and invisible world of jinns and angels opens and the unseen can appear more easily to the human eye.

"The jinni saw her and raped her. She couldn't say no. It was a jinni after all," Sweety Khala continued. "A jinni's lust would overpower any twitch of resistance."

Yes, that was probably true, for I thought Shayṭān could roll the world between his hands like a rubber ball; why wouldn't he be able to touch this woman the same way?

"Well, I think she agreed to the jinni's advances. Some people say he came in the form of a beautiful man," Ammu added.

"That's possible," Sweety Khala replied.

Apparently, the man was smooth-skinned, broad-built, tall, with eyes the shade of a smoky quartz, calling to her and her lust.

In that moment, the woman had been compelled away from her faith, as if she dissolved her family and her God and was drawn into a place within her own body where the Shayṭān was waiting for her.

"You see, it would be different if they were married. Marriage happens between jinns and humans. But some jinns, they consummate with you then go away, and you're left longing for them forever. Making love to a jinni is dangerous," Nani shared. "*Ekdom shorbonash!*"

"Or maybe the jinni is in her," Sweety Khala chimed in again. "The jinni could have just made a home for himself in her body."

Whether or not the woman was raped by the jinni, or fell in love with him in human form, or was simply possessed, it intrigued me that this woman was now in such a state, where she just stared at walls for days. Hardly moving or speaking. I considered that it could have just been a mental health issue. However, I also believed in jinns, so I parked my thoughts and I listened.

"If there isn't a jinni involved, then it's probably because of the evil eye. Nazar, *ovishap*," Ammu said. "The woman is beautiful, how she looks and her heart. Maybe this made lots of people jealous."

According to the concept of nazar, a person could give another a quick glare — unintentional or intentional — during a moment when his or her heart espoused so much jealousy that ill-wishing was inevitable. This would leave the person receiving the glare cursed, unable to flourish in specific areas of their lives.

A person who had the intention to harm another could blow ill wishes onto a strand of hair or piece of food before consumption. The target would then be cursed, trapped within an inescapable metaphysical knot that would manifest either in an emotional or physical circumstance in the human world. Although these theories sounded metaphorical or otherworldly, the impacts on the afflicted person's life were real. At least, this is what I had heard.

"Actually, she's a *petni*. Yes, she must be that," Nani deduced.

A *petni* is a female ghost from the Hindu world, who had died unmarried and haunted people on earth to seek revenge.

"No, no, not possible. Listen, I know the real truth." Sweety Khala's voice increased in both tone and pitch. "We all know she met some human man and they had intercourse. It was *zina*."

Sweety Khala was never shy to utter words considered provocative. Ammu, on the other hand, covered her mouth, and Nani just smiled.

"I still think she's possessed by a jinni because she doesn't move on. The jinni made her do it; otherwise, who would be so stupid?" Sweety Khala asked.

I listened carefully. I gathered that someone or something had blocked her desire for marriage and so she was now destined to be a spinster, losing the opportunity to fulfill a role within a family and a broader community. A social recluse.

"What about the suitors they brought in?" Bilkis asked, then lowered her chin.

"They come and go. She says no to everyone," Nani explained.

"Did they try to fix her?" Ammu asked.

"Yes, Zam Zam water, the *ta'wiz*, even the *Huzoor* came in. They also beat her, left her alone for months, but nothing," Sweety Khala explained.

I heard that the woman's parents had also cleansed the home where their daughter stayed, removed the photographs and any kind of decoration, then burned incense. Everyone in the home tried to ensure purity of their body and environment. When the exorcist arrived, he asked some questions to the dormant jinni. "What kind of being are you? What is your intention?"

Apparently, he had asked her to lie down. He then put his hand on her head, preparing to cure her inflicted heart or *qalb*. "*Bismillah*," he began.

When the exorcist, who they referred to as *Huzoor*, started reciting the Quran, his voice was low at first, and then it rose, the strings of sounds. While the rest of the city slept, the melodic sounds floated against the harsh snores.

I wondered if she had been awake or sleeping like me.

"She still hasn't been cured," Sweety Khala said.

"What did her mother and father do?" Bilkis asked, also deeply intrigued.

"Well, what can they do? The mother is still seeking a cure, but the father, well, he has withdrawn. It makes no sense. Why would she not want to be a wife or a mother? The way she stares — you should see her face — definitely the possession of a jinni that led her to fall for the mysterious man. And now he is gone!" Sweety Khala explained.

As I followed the discussion, I thought it all sounded so familiar to the description of the women whom I had heard about when I was younger. When my Khalas, cousins, neighbours, and domestic help had brought them up in the past, it seemed their distinguishable trait was their audacity, which landed them in trouble. They could not find a way out of it afterward. This left the people saying, "Well, she is at fault. She deserved it. She did not know her place. It's how the world and God takes justice."

These women were spoken about matter-of-factly, as if their pain couldn't be identified with, was not relatable in any way.

Those who told the story always seemed so proud of themselves for having avoided a similar fate. I questioned if they would ever consider that perhaps these women were just living their lives, and that even if they were troubled or conflicted, they needed to fight their own inner *jihad* in order to decide for themselves. Or perhaps there were other circumstances of which we were not aware. How could anyone know what was really in her heart or mind if they just judged based on what they heard? People were not asking the right questions, but they were quick to shame.

I sat quietly with my thoughts. I did believe there could have been tampering of jinns, because in Islam they did exist, but nothing excused force, slander, or physical torture by the hands of humans, before, after, during, or without a jinni involvement.

So, as I heard this story about this particular woman, I deduced that she could be one of them; she could be a Shayṭān Bride.

Footsteps grew louder. Ammu and Sweety Khala were on the other side of the storage closet. The door swung fully open.

"Come, we are going to visit someone and you can come," Ammu said.

I wondered for a moment if she could have been talking about the tall man whom I had met in the restaurant. Since that day, he had sneaked into my mind, making a couple of appearances. In my recollections, he'd sporadically give me a sideways glance, with the grace of a feather quill caressing textured scroll paper. He'd have broad shoulders and a thick neck, which I assumed would smell of vanilla and a little bit of musk. I pondered what types of books he read, what kinds of thoughts he had.

Would I mind seeing him again? No, I didn't think that I would. But I did have bigger things to worry about, like getting out of the country somehow.

Whoever it was that we were going to see, this time I nodded to the idea of visiting them. I was desperate for another chance to see the sun.

Outside, we walked down the gravel roads to a destination that still remained unknown. It had been days since I last left Boro Mama's home. The route was rather circuitous, and I, with wobbly legs that compelled me to sit, was also constricted in the chest. I navigated the twists and turns with no regard for the rickshaws that darted past me with ringing bells, or cars that sideswiped my starved body.

As I struggled to keep to Ammu and Sweety Khala's trail, I was startled by the mumbles under their breaths about the flat in Dhanmondi that was apparently haunted. I heard them say something like "Whoever visits there hears strange sounds and feels a strange presence."

Soon we were in front of a gated, brown-brick building. Its guard snored soundly on a white plastic chair.

"Hey!" Sweety Khala yelled. "Open the gate!"

The gate guard jerked awake and let us in. We climbed up cement stairs until we reached the third floor. Sweety Khala knocked on 3A, and a short woman in a fern-green cotton sari opened the door with a limp smile. She recognized Sweety Khala, who introduced Ammu and I.

A couple of seconds later, we were seated on a taupe sofa, being served coffee and samosas that I refused. My appetite had been gone for a while.

I scanned the room: one wooden *almari*, white lace curtains, a lonely *tabla* tucked away in a corner, and Bollywood tunes on a loop on a television set in the adjacent room.

The door of the room in front of me had been left ajar. A crack. I squinted. Through the crack I saw a bed, blue-and-white checkered print bedding, and the slender figure of a woman. She was sitting. I could only make out her back. Two pale arms, motionless, dangling from her body.

I thought, *Could this be the woman Ammu and Sweety Khala had been talking about? Could she be a Shaytān Bride?*

I longed to see the young woman's face, read her eyes for something like sisterhood or kindredness, but she was turned away from me.

I hadn't been paying attention to what Ammu and Sweety Khala had been saying. I had just been staring. So, when they abruptly stood up and walked over to the open door, the one I had been peering into, my pulse quickened. They told me to stay put on the sofa with the aunty, who was now offering me samosa again. I pushed away the plate and kept my eyes ahead.

Ammu and Sweety Khala entered the room where the woman was. They closed the door behind them.

The lady with the fern-green cotton sari remained sitting with me. She must have been the mother of the young woman in the room.

"So, how old are you again?" she asked me.

I told her nineteen.

"How do you like it here in Dhaka?" she asked.

"It's fine," I answered. Phlegm foamed somewhere at the base of my throat and my chest tightened a little.

She nodded, her eyes down at her feet. "My daughter is very sick," she whispered.

"What happened to her?" I asked.

"I don't know," she answered.

"Has she seen a doctor?" I inquired.

"She doesn't want to get married," the lady said, ignoring my question.

"Her sickness has to do with marriage?" I asked.

She looked up at me, silent for a couple of minutes.

"Maybe she likes to be alone. Or maybe she loves someone else," I said. "Has she ever been in love before? She might be longing for her lover."

"She has only been sick. It's a sickness," the lady said, her tone rising and nose scrunching a little bit.

I remembered then the story of Zulaykha, the beautiful married woman who tried to seduce Prophet Yusuf. He resisted her advances, but she persisted. When her husband caught her he said *inna kaydakunna*, meaning a type of female cunning or temptation. The words soon began to travel through the lands as if they were handed down from God Himself. Many even claimed that *kayd* was worse than the con of the Shayṭān. However, the way Zulaykha's love for Prophet Yusuf had pierced through the veil of her heart was not something she was judged for by Allah, just the people who spoke ill of her and through rumours. So later, when she invited other women over for a feast and Prophet Yusuf walked in to introduce himself, all the women could not take their eyes off him. They cut themselves unintentionally with the knives they were using to cut the fruit in their hands, as they themselves were so mesmerized by Prophet Yusuf's face.

It is okay for women to long for a man or whomever she desires, I thought. *How can desire be a sickness? Is it only supposed to belong to men? God made Adam in His image, did he not? Al-husn. So, all people must be desirable in some way.*

"Tell me something; how is it like in Canada? Do women get married often and early?" The lady interrupted my thoughts.

"Well, it depends on the person," I told her. "People are generally free to marry who they choose."

As soon as I said it, I felt my words as a partial truth; evangelicals with supervised courtships, women in Yorkville fulfilling the obligations of their aristocracy, women alone in kitchens secretly eating chocolate, drinking beer, popping Xanax because they don't want to have sex with the man they settled for. In the context of Islamic marriages, practising Muslim women unable to find practising Muslim men, so they remained single despite wanting to be married, or Muslim women who lived secret lives with lovers whom their families would never accept. All the ways marriage is legislated by circumstance and issues that arise across faiths.

"Do they get sick like this? Are they always in battle?" she asked.

I thought then about the women who held pregnancy tests in their hands wondering if they wanted children at all but felt they had to. The women who tried for years but were unable. Women who loved women. Women who wanted to leave but couldn't.

"It seems she doesn't have the energy for life. She lives only with the company of her bed," the lady said.

"Maybe she's sad," I suggested "When I'm sad I don't want to get out of bed, either. Maybe she's really, really sad. Heartbroken."

I sat with my statement for a moment. It hit me that perhaps depression in this context could have been perceived as a type of isolation, a separation from one's God or the social fabric within which one was immersed. I thought perhaps I had been a little too daring in revealing my thoughts to this lady, not only because I knew not much of adult life in Dhaka but because the intersection between beliefs and mental health was complex. Also, word could easily travel to Boro Mama about what I had shared, and who knew how he would react.

The door flew open. Ammu and Sweety Khala rushed out.

The lady stood up. Both Ammu and Sweety Khala hugged her.

"It is unfortunate, *vhabi*," Ammu said to the lady, "to see your beautiful daughter like this. *Inshallah* she will get better."

Later in the night, while lying on the bed, again I watched the fan blades above my head rotate in unison, forming perfect round circles. The wind was making a musical note that did little to soothe. I sank deeper into the dark with each rotation of the blades; the streak of light pouring in through the window blinds kept me grasping onto the edges of my consciousness. And then, finally, I fell asleep.

As I drifted off to sleep I imagined the young woman again. I was in that same room she was in before. I ambled over to her standing figure, until we were side by side. I heard her breathe, in and out, steady. From the corner of my eye, I tried to make out her face, but it wasn't until I took that extra step forward and to the right that I saw it. Heart-shaped face, a small dimple on her left cheek. Iris the colour of hazelnut wood, cornea pearl white. A nose not too straight or thin, lips full, supple, ruddy. She dragged these eyes of hers across my face, her head slowly rising up as she did. She grimaced. Upsurge of laughter.

I looked down at her body. She was naked. On her wrist there was a series of intricate blue veins in a vile winding trail. I followed them up her thin arms to her collarbone, which pulled on the surrounding skin like an anchor. She had perfectly round nipples, a small brown beauty mark under the right one. From her abdomen and the small pouch around it, she pulled through an inhale then released the air through her mouth, as if she was releasing life itself. It was a breath of fire, *agni-prasana*. She was alive. To this I also smiled. I placed my hands on the dips between her waist and hips. My hands fit the concaves effortlessly. Then we both started laughing. Her hot breath in my mouth and mine in hers. We dived into the brown of each other's eyes as if looking away itself could result in some death. So, in our locked gaze, we saw all the embarrassing romantic, sexual desire and all the ridiculous absurdity of the heart, the passion, the longing, the ego — the entire world. How beautiful, when she respired. I reached out to touch her face until black enveloped the back of my eyelids — my eyes opened. I was awake. I could not move my body for a few minutes, yet my senses were perked: I heard feet walking and knobs turning, and may have seen a flickering light in the distance. Behind my head I felt warm, rising air, and a weight on my chest as if someone was there, sitting on top of it, their legs wrapping and holding me in place, stuck. I mumbled *Ayatul Kursi* under my breath, my voice rising with each sentence:

"*Allahu laaa ilaaha illaa huwal haiyul qai-yoom*
laa taakhuzuhoo sinatunw wa laa nawm
lahoo maa fissamaawaati wa maa fil ard
man zallazee yashfa'u indahooo illaa be iznih
ya'lamu maa baina aideehim wa maa khalfahum
wa laa yuheetoona beshai 'immin 'ilmihee illa be maa shaaaa
wasi'a kursiyyuhus samaa waati wal arda wa la ya'ooduho hifzuhumaa
wa huwal aliyyul 'azeem."

As the sensations passed and I twitched, the eeriness of the woman dissipated with her. I only realized then that she was just a regular woman.

Ammu told me about the young woman's life. I learned that she had fallen in love with a rural man she couldn't be with. He loved her, too, but some city dwellers believed they didn't belong together.

Days, months, and years passed of their secret meetings and their protests to be together. When Ammu shared this, I imagined the young woman and her secret lover meeting at Lalbagh Fort, their agreed-upon place. This was a Mughal complex that stood before the Buriganga River, its construction started by Prince Muhammad Azam, son of Emperor Aurangzeb. I imagined them both strolling in the complex discreetly, drifting in and out of crowds.

They'd both find their way to the rooftop garden, where they'd stand parallel to each other, keeping their gaze ahead but their elbows grazing, until they could no longer resist. The young woman would remove her black sunglasses and pull back the scarf on her head to reveal the deep kohl that would draw him in. Once she smiled, he would perhaps reach out his hand, and she'd hold it. They stroll through the grounds, past the old mosque with the three domes and the *Diwani-i-Am*. Although historically it was a place of loss, unfulfilled dreams, and beauty in ruins, this young woman and her lover only felt hope.

"You see, the people had heard that the man asked her to elope one day, but she couldn't do it then, and rightly so, as there was a lot to consider." A disembodied voice floated as I continued to envisage the lovers. It was Ammu's. She shook me by the shoulders.

She continued to tell me that the man had disappeared, and the woman's voice disappeared along with him. A few years later, her lover returned, married to another woman with a child in her belly. He had moved on.

I asked Ammu if the woman felt regret, and Ammu said, "Do you want to end up like these women? Do you want this fate? There is only sadness and risk."

Distrust lingered in the air.

"What happened that day when you met with her?" I asked. I had been wanting to know this for a few days now.

"Nothing. I asked her questions. Told her she still had a chance at life," Ammu explained.

"And then?"

"She's too far gone. There was no response. Poor girl. I pity her. It's better you stay away from her or don't even ask — it's still possible there's a jinni in her."

I thought about the young woman and others like her every day. She was the woman who had to decide between doing what she was told to do or staying true to what she wanted for herself, both of which came with consequences. So, she stayed in stasis. In her radical stillness, she had a type of agency; she resisted. In her situation, could inertia have been a type of freedom, an assertion of will? Or perhaps she was paralyzed from all that had happened to her, the friction of society against her bones. I still have not heard her speak, however, so there will always be holes in this story as I tell it.

Obhishonkot / Fork in the Road
(অভিসংকট)

It was still late September 2005.

"So, what will you do?" Boro Mama paced back and forth.

By this time, I barely spoke, as my available willpower was dwindling. I was still trying to reserve whatever I had left for whatever I was going to do.

"Are you going to do it?" he asked.

I stayed quiet. By then, it actually hurt to talk.

"The man who visited us weeks ago, the small man with the white beard, that was Shoaib's father and he is not well," he spilled.

Aha, I thought. He had treated me with a familiarity I didn't understand then but did now.

"Given his health, he wants his son to marry sooner rather than later."

I had also learned, and this was worse, that my own brother, who was just twelve, had been admitted to the local hospital because he was not well. He did not take to the climate or the food in Bangladesh, where he had not been born. So, he was now connected to saline drips and would be for days. I was not allowed to visit him at all. Abbu was also not well, a condition I had no details about. Only Boro Mama knew the details about all of these sicknesses and, like a doctor coveting and selectively releasing information, he kept them all to himself.

"Given that your brother is not well, your family will have to go back. However, since your issue is not resolved, we'll just have to keep you here," he said.

More than ever I felt the urgency to do something — but what?

"Worst comes to worst, maybe you can stay in a village. No access to technology. Maybe you can finally clear your head and think."

My legs shook. Still, I said nothing; I simply had no strength. Why waste words on one who couldn't hear them?

"I will look very bad if you don't meet Shoaib at least one more time. Just save my face, do this for me once. Then we can talk about your final decision."

"Okay."

I watched the passing rickshaw wheels turn. Shoaib stood at the front gates of Boro Mama's place. He was in an off-white half-sleeved shirt and beige pants.

I wondered what Bhav would think of me being in this position.

I thought about the discomfort he might feel, like that which I would have if he started seeing other people.

"*As-salam alaykum.*" Shoaib greeted me in a manner that made me think that I had felt him at the scene even before he had even arrived.

"*Wa alaikum salam,*" I responded, looking around. "I heard your father is not well. How is he now?"

He pointed to an incoming cluster of rickshaws ringing their bells all at once.

"Yes, he is still bedridden. We are not sure what it is, but *Inshallah* he will get better."

Shoaib called over a rickshaw depicting a serene white Taj Mahal nested between petals of a pink lotus flower. When we climbed onto our seats, I noticed its rumal was painted a cherry red, like my lips. I love makeup. As much as I'd been begrudgingly coerced into meeting Shoaib, I'd enjoyed the process of getting ready. I missed the creativity.

Sensing Shoaib's leg from the side of mine, I tucked in my lavender *orna* to my side. Shoaib gracefully shifted away an inch to establish a respectful gap between us.

The wheels began to roll over rocks and squeeze past men with large pots of fish or vegetables for sale balanced on their heads. Shoaib fixed the cuffs of his shirt and repositioned the pen in his front left pocket. The *rickshawala* pedalling us to our destination was wearing a white sleeveless shirt that was drenched in sweat and a turquoise *lungi*. He pushed the wheels for about ten minutes or so, until they rolled, then halted, then squeezed in between other wheels of cars, scooters, and other rickshaws in the middle of the jammed road. We were bombarded by two young boys, a young girl, and their mother. They were barefoot and wearing tattered clothing. They circled around the rickshaw. Shoaib felt his pant pocket for his wallet, found and opened it to give each family member one hundred taka. The children's mother mumbled a prayer, blew it toward our faces like fairy dust, and went away.

Shoaib smiled at me then looked ahead. We rolled over pebbles and potholes, past more groups of beggars, sideswiping cars, and residents. Eventually we turned down a series of emptier narrow streets, and then onto wider busy ones again.

During the thirty-minute ride, Shoaib asked me about my life in Canada. "How is it like?"

"Fine," I answered.

I could have told him then about my typical day, filling my backpack with books, making my way down to the University of Toronto buildings in Queen's Park, usually Convocation Hall, where I'd be one in a crowd of young aspirers. I could have detailed my friends, enemies, and acquaintances, their personalities, appearances, concerns, and complexities, how we passed our time, all of the places downtown: bookstores, cafes, theatres, parks. I could have told him then about Bhav, but instead I asked, "How do you spend your time in Dhaka?"

"Well, work and friends. Of course, taking care of my parents, as well." He went on to tell me about the thriving city; its recent developments and promises for the future. "Maybe you didn't learn this in Canada, but Bangladesh has always been seen as a rather failing country. After its independence, it was left in shambles, not that it wasn't suffering before, either, but we're moving along, we're moving along. Beneath our feet are the lives lost; they don't give us sadness, only strength. There is so much more to this place."

I remember looking around and feeling somewhat the same, as if I'd never left the place at all. As if Canada was like a lightning bolt that came and passed.

"Are you okay?" he asked, noticing me in a bit of a daze.

"Yes."

The rickshaw toppled slightly as we entered Sher-E Bangla Nagar, one of the neighbourhoods in Dhaka, where they have government offices, banks, shops, and financial institutions. It was also where the prime minister lived. In this area was the National Assembly Complex, or Jatiya Sangsad Bhaban, seat of the national parliament. I was struck by the simple geometry, circles, triangles, squares, and half-circles, the ease with which they were held together in one frame, red-bricked and from afar, the perfectly sized windows and solid but hollow columns, reflecting light in the most intriguing ways.

"Beautiful, isn't it?" Shoaib asked me. "You should see it at night, with lights. It sits near a stretch of water, sparkling like the sky above it. It's quite magical."

I watched Shoaib peer up at the sky as if he were paying a certain homage to something intangible. "It was designed by an American. It is about governing in a way that is aligned with the universe."

I smiled. Toronto, in comparison, was grey and hard and severe. The buildings seemed indifferent, even for objects. Godless. It wasn't common that thoughts about the universe, of something bigger than oneself, influenced the designing of structures or when materializing the aspirations of a space. This was something I often craved.

Shoaib studied me further, his eyes fixed on mine, then said, the same way you point out an interesting vintage car or a public restroom, "Quick, look, there. Our wedding will be held there, in the parliament building. On November ninth. You'll see the insides, don't worry. It will be grand."

Startled, I furrowed my brow and shook my head. Shoaib asked, "Are you all right? Shall I stop the driver and get some water? Perhaps a shawl of some sort?"

I hadn't agreed to anything. It flabbergasted me how quickly the situation had arrived. As if I'd been sleeping the whole way.

When the rickshaw stopped and I stood up to come down, Shoaib jumped out and eagerly ran around to my side to extend his hand to help me out. How strange it was, that I suddenly felt like the wife of this stranger?

What am I doing? I wondered.

Shoaib guided me to the entrance of the restaurant, bordered with flowers, *ghasful*, jasmine, *bonak*, and *udla*. The karaoke box inside blasted. The lead singer with long red hair, wearing oxidized jewellery and a black-and-silver *salwar kameez* began to sing.

"This beautiful song." Shoaib pointed to the ceiling and subtly nodded his head to the rhythm. He pulled out the chair at the table we had walked to and gestured for me to sit down. "It's called '*Dukhini Duhkho Koro Na*' by James or Nagar Baul. A lot of Bengali music is inspired by Sufism, mysticism, and folklore. Isn't it nice?"

"It's a lovely song. What does it mean?" I asked him, as I still didn't understand all the dialects or more difficult Bangla words.

"It's about going outside, dancing with joy, seeing the rainbow, and visiting the garden of dreams under the newly risen sun. Not lamenting or remaining in melancholy."

I skimmed the room, then Shoaib's placid expression as he flipped through pages of the menu in front of him. I wasn't sure how I was even conversing, physically moving, interacting after what I had just been told. I had learned that November 9, 2005, would be my wedding when my ecstatic groom told me with eyes softened by a certain rosy fondness.

We sat across from each other, and Shoaib shared with me snippets of his life: his aspirations as a businessman, what he loved most and least about the busy city, more about his father and his noble mother.

"You do a lot, caring about the well-being of others," I told him, realizing as I said it that this was the same reason that I'd fallen for Bhav.

He responded, "When it comes to the people you love, your commitment must not be waves at the shore, but rather the depth of the middle of the sea."

As he spoke, I had begun to believe we had met before somehow, sat across from each other in this very same restaurant. I thought I would hate this person, but no, I appreciated his company. Things had been chaotic, people duplicitous. He reminded me of normality.

I considered then that if I hadn't left at age six, I would likely be here in this restaurant every other day. I imagined that if I had never left here, I would perhaps be catching a rickshaw every morning to travel to college, later meeting some girlfriends at the Dhaka Café or maybe Dhanmondi mall, laughing for hours over *chaat papri*. Or going to *dawats* in *salwar kameezes, shararas, ghagras, lenghas*, or saris. Being taken to the latest spots by drivers and attending week-long weddings. And, of course, the serene *adhan* during Ramadans and shorter workdays for proper fasting. And during *Eid*, the endless feasting.

If I had never left here, I would perhaps have pursued becoming a university professor, taught literature, got involved in politics or volunteered at a local charity, sung different songs, danced differently, and taken to playing the harmonium even more seriously. Perhaps I'd consider pursuing a career in the arts, although Boro Mama probably wouldn't have it. There was much to do in this city. It had so much potential. Why had I insisted on keeping my eyes closed, as if all of Dhaka was simply an extension of Boro Mama? As if I already knew all there was to know?

A whole life I never had floated before me like a passing balloon and I, reaching for its string. After I left Dhaka as a young child, I never once thought about coming back and making it a permanent home, as if it was where I belonged. Here I was now, recalling all that was once familiar and that never had the chance to mean something more to me.

When I returned to Boro Mama's home that night, lying under the spinning blades of the fan, I realized my thoughts often spun the same way: Could I marry this man? Was it good for me? Would this person bring back the parts of myself I had forgotten in Canada? Or help me discover perhaps who I was further? Was what Boro Mama demanded actually really good for me?

In the dark, with my eyes half-closed, I told myself, *Okay, Sumaiya, let's be rational about this. Let's lay out the pros and cons.* I considered all of my options. If I said yes to Shoaib then this house arrest would be lifted, everyone would be pleased, I wouldn't be considered a terrible person, and I'd eventually be able to go back to Canada, possibly. Although I wouldn't know when. I would probably have had a few children by then.

Did I trust Shoaib? He seemed a gentle soul. Although, in passing moments, I asked myself if I had just been projecting onto him what I needed, which was a safe harbour. Or was he really as wonderful as he seemed? I trusted that he was. I would give him the benefit of the doubt. Sweety Khala reminded me that the case could just be one of Bollywood's *Hum Dil De Chuke Sanam*, a film where Aishwarya Rai's character marries a man grudgingly after being forbidden to marry the one she truly wants. At first, she ignores her new husband and feels in her heart only anger, sadness, and longing for the past. Over time, however, her new husband wins her over with his kind spirit.

"See, stories like that are more realistic," Sweety Khala said.

Wasn't it possible that a relationship could blossom in deep and intimate ways with someone after marriage? *After all, all love affairs that began with chemistry eventually fizzled out, anyway, if not tended to, or became more friendly and compassionate over time.* This is what Abbu had told me, and also what I had suspected from my very limited experience.

I would have to be willing to let Bhav go, but I didn't know if I could truly get over him. It was possible I could be haunted by our memories, especially if I ended up quite unhappy with Shoaib. It was truly a gamble.

After this I considered what would happen if I said no. It was highly possible that I would end up in a village, or even just continuing to spend my days in this storage closet, but for how long? I did not know. *If I stop existing outwardly, will I stop existing inwardly?* My being would probably disintegrate. If I was left in a village, never to see a city again, my fate could be like the woman who sat staring at the walls all day. What would happen to my dreams? My ambitions? The ice-skating rink, libraries, open-air pedestrian malls, plazas, and boutique shops, navigating complicated transit networks while holding an overpriced coffee in one hand, museums, themed restaurants, television? Clean water. Toilets. My friends.

And then there was the option I had been considering for the past couple of weeks: find a way to give Boro Mama's address to Bhav, so he could come or inform the government authorities. This option also had its consequences. The people I loved most I would probably never see again, and without them I wasn't sure I could be who I was in my entirety.

But then again, if I said yes, would I really want my family in my life? Would my resentment grow and prevent that? Would it even matter to them? I would be married, and they would go on about their lives and not care if I hated them.

And there was the question of human rights, ethics, right and wrong. Safety. In any case, force was not acceptable. I wondered, *What would Allah think of this?* I did care more about what Allah would say than *log kya kahenge, shomaj ki bolbe* (what the people/society would say).

And there I was, back in my circular pattern, because that's all I could do, be in my head. I wasn't sure if I could truly feel my body, anymore; wasn't sure that it could guide me intuitively. Each option led to the same sensation: numbness.

I drifted off to sleep, then woke up a couple of hours later in a sweat. The room was pitch-black. The large window next to me, open. I looked outside at the blemished moon, wondering if Bhav had looked at it the day before. I thought for a minute that it still wasn't too late to climb out and escape, but I knew I certainly wouldn't get too far. I looked down at my hands and brought them to my face. The bones were protruding. The hair on my scalp was also longer.

I got off the bed and stumbled over into the smaller storage closet. I sat on the cold floor and took a deep breath.

"I'm so sorry," I whispered, to no one in particular, to no one.

I thought Bhav should know that I was coming to accept him as irreconcilably lost from me, and myself as someone else, someone new — whatever it was, there was a difference.

I put my hands on my stomach and curled my body inward, trying to comfort my own being.

I coddled my body with the following thoughts: The intimacy shared when someone paints your henna. The warmth of a bathtub. Taking a nap after a long day. Bubbles. Flowers. The colour red. The sound of the waves of Lake Superior. The feeling of the easygoing five o'clock sunshine on your skin. Walking through a forest when it's quiet and no one is around. Snow.

And then Bhav. I brought my fingers to my face and dropped my head into them. I wept.

"Are you okay?" A soft-spoken voice.

I tilted my face up. It was Bilkis, standing at the door in small, holey pink shorts and a worn white shirt. A pink polka-dot bow on the side of her head. The bottom and sides of her feet seemed crusty and dry. My feet were in the same condition. She cautiously moved nearer to me and then actually sat next to me. We both had our knees up to our chest, breathing in the dust resting on the edges of the closed trunks and luggage.

"Don't cry," Bilkis said.

She leaned her body into mine and I loosened my arms from around my knees. I leaned into her, also. The warmth of her calming my volatile nerves. We held each other.

"It's okay. It's okay," she said. "You're hurting a lot. I see that you're so sad."

For the first time on the trip I felt seen. "I, I just want to go home," I stuttered.

Bilkis nodded. She said, "*Inshallah*. Whatever Allah wills. But I'm sure Allah sees your pain and knows your heart." Bilkis took the edge of her blotted shirt and brought it to wipe the tears on my face. "I see it, too, it's pure. You're a good person. You don't deserve this."

From that night on, Bilkis came to my room at night. She did what others didn't: she listened. When there wasn't anyone to recognize me, she pointed to my face. "I know you," she said. We spoke with each other.

One day Ammu, Nani, and Boro Mama stampeded into the bedroom while I was getting some clothing from the *almari*. I almost dropped the file of folded maxis I had in my hand.

"Give it to us," Boro Mama ordered.

I gulped, concerned that they were talking about my journal. "What?"

"Don't act *boca*," Nani warned. "You know what we are talking about."

Suddenly, I felt as if I was at the end of a tunnel, only picking up very faint sounds. Where did I want to be? Up in the moon somewhere, stargazing.

Boro Mama grabbed my wrist and I shifted away, squirming.

"Your ring," Nani said, chewing her *paan*.

"Why?" I asked, trying hard to be neutral. The ring was the only thing I had, other than my journal, that reminded me of Bhav and of my past self. If it was taken, I could slowly fade away.

My feigned nonchalance did not deter them.

Nani opened her palm and said, "Put it here."

I could tell that if I didn't, Boro Mama would take it by force.

"What are you going to do with it?" I asked.

"Give it to the *Huzoor*," Ammu finally answered.

"But why?" I still wasn't sure what the exorcist had to do with my ring.

"To get rid of jinns, *sihr*, whatever is making you so stubborn," Nani taunted.

I realized then that they were all quite scared.

"No," I shouted firmly. "Not this. You've already taken everything else."

"Give it to us," Nani demanded with equal force.

Boro Mama let go of my wrist, "Oh, she will give it to us, and if she doesn't —"

I looked him in the eye this time. I did not blink. I would not lose this last bit of myself that I had left.

Boro Mama swiftly grabbed my wrist again, and this time snatched my ring from my wedding finger, all within seconds. When I realized it was gone, I had to almost grab his arm to centre myself. Everything was spinning.

Then they left.

∞

The very next morning when I woke up, there was a circle of people around me: Gollapi Khala, Sweety Khala, Mami, Nani, Ammu. They were leaning in as if to investigate my body and face.

"Get up. Why are you sleeping so much? Get up," Sweety Khala ordered. I pulled myself up, still lightheaded. Bilkis strolled in with a glass of water in her hands. Behind her, on the other side of the door in the living room, was a man with a full white beard. He had on a matching white *taqiyah* hat and *thobe*. I saw him give something to Boro Mama and then he left.

I wondered who he was and why it was that I was suddenly surrounded.

I would learn later that my ring had been given to this exorcist for cleansing and keeping. It was thought to hold the curse that kept me from complying. The man had also brought another *ta'wiz* for me, because I had misplaced mine, and a scroll of some sort with some printed *surahs*.

At this point, it didn't even matter to me anymore who he was and what he had done or would do. The imprint of my missing ring on my finger reminded me that now, in this battle, it would be that much harder to say *no*.

It was the birthday of Prophet Mohammed (May Peace Be Upon Him); it was *Mawlid*. The claret cloth sofa was moved out of Boro Mama's living room. The maids laid out large white cotton sheets on the Persian rug. On the sheets sat a handful of guests, including local *maulana*. They were wearing white cotton *kurta* pyjamas and matching hats. Their heads were swaying in unison while their fingers counted *tasbih* beads. Sandalwood smoke spread as they recited the Quran. Women in the kitchen scooped biriyani into Styrofoam containers for the poor. Boro Mama got me from the storage closet, asked me to get washed up and sit next to him. He said it was important for me to be there. So I sat there by him, inhaling incense, losing myself to the melodic sounds. Mending, mending, mending, in a rhythmic motion.

That night I slept in peace until the morning when I felt pins and needles in my arms and legs.

My first instinct was to look for my journal so I could capture what I was feeling. I went to the storage closet and tossed the bags over each other, knocking down stacks of folded clothing. I couldn't find it. The door hinge squeaked.

"What is this nonsense?" Boro Mama asked. He had my journal in his hands and was standing at the door entrance.

I froze.

"I thought you were coming to your senses, but this, this is … absurdity."

It was as if I was standing there naked.

He fumed out of the closet, but I didn't follow him. I imagined he would put the journal in the case where he kept my passport, the one I had been informed about. The case he kept locked in his bedroom *almari*. That would be the last I'd see of my journal and shards of the previous me captured in its pages.

Later, when Boro Mama noticed my lethargic posture, lying there waiting for the moments to be gone, he said in the tone of a commanding officer, "There's no time for distractions or sentimentality. I have bumped up your wedding date. It will be on October thirty-first."

Halloween seems fitting, I thought. Halloween is the time for masks, presenting one thing but being something else underneath.

Boro Mama had violated my privacy by accessing, dissecting, misconstruing, and then sharing with others what I had written. The sacred act of writing, both during this dark time and in general in my life, was an extension and expression of my spiritual self, especially when I couldn't find myself at all in murky, muddy tenebrosity, pain, rage, sin. Where imagination and reality became one to present to us different possibilities. By snatching my means to access my truth, he had acted as God, leaving me spiritually hijacked and almost psychologically annihilated. I didn't know then that in the future, I'd continue writing and face similar exploitation again — raw words that connected to my flesh would be stolen, packaged, and shared between hands without my consent, as if I was being trafficked. To me, the offence would always be considered grave, especially in a world that doesn't always accept people for being who they are, that kills people for being who they are, so writing and art are survival. Self-expression being the highest form of actualization, the means through which we retain our humanity. As Boro Mama stood before me, I remembered that the pain was not only mine; it was also a collective one, experienced by women and other minority communities throughout history who have been burned at the stake, raped, and buried alive for simply expressing themselves.

That was all the confirmation I needed that this man would never change his mind, nor would he soften. Such grave actions could only be taken by hearts that were a little hardened. All my efforts had been frivolous. I imagined that if he had known about Bhav before the plane landed here in Dhaka, he would have perhaps still planned my wedding in a similar way, without me having known anything. And then I would have asked myself, *What kind of titillating exaggerations has he concocted in his melodramatic fantasies of my life in a country he's never visited? In my relationship with a man that he's never met?* I could so perfectly picture him, telephone between his ear and his shoulder, picking at his nails, casually telling Ammu, not explaining, in that vile, gentle tone he could summon to pad his authoritarian objectives so that unreasonable requests suddenly became the only logical thing to do. Of course, Ammu weakened to him. He was the reason the family was alive, why they had survived the war, how they had thrived despite everything. He was her brother.

Like the Darvaza crater, the fire in me rose, and this time I felt it almost engulfing my flesh — smouldering rage. Not like the one a few weeks earlier when I had screamed, then shouted at the top of my lungs, *leave me alone!* and physically pushed everyone away with whatever strength I had, or almost stopped eating altogether so my hunger could wake me up, or barricaded the storage room closet with suitcases upon suitcases, remaining behind them for days so I didn't have to show the world what I had become. It was a rage that even went beyond my close attempt to jump off the rooftop in Dhanmondi. The growing fire would destroy everything in its way.

I had eyed the phone in Boro Mama's bedroom for days. In the earlier months I did not even think to try using it. *It's too out in the open,* I thought. His bedroom was next to the kitchen, where Mami usually was during the day with the maids. The maids often dropped by, both expectedly and spontaneously. I knew they would be there once in the morning, once in the afternoon, and once during the evening, to ensure the room was clean. Bucket of water, a *ghamcha* in their hands, soap bubbles, the hems of their saris lifted high and tucked in to their petticoats while they squatted on the floor and scrubbed. Although Boro Mama would usually leave very early in the morning, almost right after sunrise, he would sometimes return without much advance notice in the middle of the morning and then again predictably for afternoon siesta. I observed also that Shahzad, Shayan, and Saad sometimes would retrieve toys or books they had left in there. If guests were expected or the man selling saris from his basket dropped by, Mami could visit the room to change or clothes or get her wallet.

There were too many possibilities. Furthermore, I had no idea if the phone could call long distance. It was also a rotary phone, which I had never used before.

I tried once or twice to feign getting a glass of water from the kitchen. On my way, I would make a quick turn and swoop into Boro Mama's room. The first time I did that, Mami was in the bathroom, the bucket inside filling up with warm water she had brought herself from the kitchen. I had reached for the phone, and while I did, heard her squeal from the bathroom. The water must have been too warm or maybe she had met the perspicacious lizard. The sound was enough, however, to have me running out the door.

The second time I tried, I got as far as dialing Bhav's number. Yes, I discovered long-distance calls were possible. Before the phone could ring twice, I heard Boro Mama entering through the front doors. "Bilkis!" he called out, and it was almost as if he was standing next to me. I almost dropped the handset from my hands. I covered my mouth and tiptoed out, sliding into the veranda. As soon as I did, I saw him march right into the room. He had missed me by maybe half a minute.

But I found a way. I called Bhav when Boro Mama was at work, Mami with the maids in the kitchen, and her three boys in the veranda in the middle of math lessons. Ammu was somewhere in Lalmatia, meeting with my other Khalas. I tiptoed into the room, my golden anklets jingling. I bit my lip and moved a wisp of hair from across my face to better see. I picked up the indigo *orna* falling from my chest and wrapped it around my neck. Boro Mama and Mami's colossal *almari* had, on its surface, a mirror. I glanced at my reflection. I was like a bending willow. My two arms outstretched, loosely hanging mahogany locks that were now fading back to dark brown, my toes trespassing. There was a bed to my right, draped in a rich green sheet, custard blankets folded on top. An ash-wood desk with stacks of paper, files, and pens. I walked toward the marble night table in the corner. A lamp. Beside it, the beige rotary phone. I picked up the handset, brought it to my ear, looked around one more time, dialed Bhav's number.

I turned the dial with one hand, the other holding up the hefty handset.

"Hello?" Bhav answered.

"It's me," I whispered.

"Where are you? I've been worried. I thought you'd get back to —"

"I don't have much time," I interrupted.

I heard footsteps.

I crouched down with the handset, my nose at the edge of the bed next to the night table. What Boro Mama would do if he caught me.

The footsteps subsided. I got up again.

"I — I am stuck here, with no way out. I can't come back unless I marry this man, Shoaib. If I don't say yes, then I might be dropped off somewhere in a village. All I need you to know —" My words tumbled out, each letter almost knocking the one before it, like bowling balls.

"What?" Bhav asked. "This will all blow over. They must be pulling your leg. They can't leave you in a … a … village." In the background somebody opened a can of soda, as if Bhav had just answered a normal phone call.

I twirled the phone cord between my left fingers, looking around the room. I could feel a hard bump along my neck; my tendons protruding as if trying to walk out of my skin.

"I need you to believe me, please. At first, I didn't believe it, either, but a part of me tells me this is more possible than not," I told him.

Two or three seconds passed while I grit my teeth. One more and I would've slammed the handset down.

"I'll call the police. I'll call —" Bhav stated.

"No. You don't do anything like that. Promise me that you won't," I pleaded.

"Why not? Are you hearing yourself?" Bhav asked. "You really don't sound like yourself. Are you physically okay?"

The footsteps were getting louder. I heard Mami scold a maid.

"I'm okay. The wedding has been pushed up. It will now be on October thirty-first."

"Wedding? What? There's already a wedding? Wait. Why do you have to get married on Halloween? Listen," Bhav said, "this goat herder they are setting you up with probably just wants a green card."

I tugged the cord so tightly the phone almost toppled over the edge of the table. It wasn't as if my family had set me up with just any Muslim man from Bangladesh. They weren't idiots. I heard some pots fall in the nearby kitchen. I swivelled my body to the wall thinking the maids were going to pass by.

I did this all while telling Bhav, "Shoaib is a really kind man. Why would you say that?" My voice was rising.

I didn't expect myself to be so suddenly incensed.

His breaths thinned out and I thought I heard him swear.

"Shoaib? You don't sound like yourself. You can't get married. Please don't. You're not in your right mind."

I wanted to tell him then about all the things I had seen, in both waking life and my dreams. I wanted to tell him that some things were making sense and others not, that I was now questioning where I was and had been before, as if I was pulling myself from the inside out to inspect more thoroughly my origin, how this all started. *Why am I here?* Maybe I hadn't been in my right mind my whole time in Canada — could that be possible?

"I only have maybe thirty more seconds. I can't risk it. If anyone finds out, I'll have to face the consequences."

"I'm going to call the High Commission of Canada just to ask what happens if …"

"No," I warned him. "I don't want to hurt anyone here. Please don't."

"And what about hurting me? Or yourself?"

Through Boro Mama's bedroom window, the sky appeared ashy like crushed bones.

"I still love you," I said. "Don't forget."

I put the handset down. Footsteps. Someone walked in. I turned around, a hurried swivel that threw me off balance. It was Bilkis in a frilly russet frock, a large cockroach in her hand. "The boys," she cried. "They planted this in my things."

"That's terrible," I said, letting out a drawn-out sigh of relief, perhaps confusing her a little, as she continued to peer at me with her large brown eyes.

"Let's go. Let's go over there," I said. I tapped her on the back. Ushered her out of the room. Held her other hand as I took her to where I was staying.

I sat her on my bed. "They're just silly boys who love to pull pranks. The other day, the little one was tugging on my skirt, trying to pull it off me. He chased me all over the house! It's probably just the age. They want to tease girls."

I told her maybe we could put the cockroaches in glass jars. A suggestion we both giggled at.

After Bilkis left, I pondered the exchange Bhav and I had. Why had I really called him? To give him an update or get his help? I felt guilty about what I had done and how my loyalty was continuing to split. If I had been able to remain on the phone for longer, I would have told Bhav, I was sure, that I was sorry I couldn't talk to him for longer. I had been desperate to call him but was starting to feel as if I had nothing more to say. His voice had been a little muffled, a little distant. How was he keeping? I wondered about his mother. How was her health? And what about his friends? It was right what he had observed: that I was changing. It had been almost four months.

The next day Sweety Khala, Gollapi Khala, and Ammu dragged me to the jewellery store in an effort to seduce me with gold, diamonds, and pearls, to get me to change my mind and just marry Shoaib. Regardless of whether or not I'd acquiesce, they'd still make the purchase, for they were planning a wedding to which I had not said yes.

In the store, they each pointed to various earrings, necklaces, *tikkas*, and bangles hanging on the walls. The patient shopkeeper brought them all down and spread them across the glass counter. Sweety Khala picked up the pair of three-layered gold *jhumkis* and pushed the sharp end of one through the hole in my ear.

"Ouch," I said.

"*Mashallah*," she said.

Then Gollapi Khala picked up a matching gold *ratan chur*, and put my wrist through it.

"Beautiful," she said.

Ammu and my Khalas continued layering me, and when I caught my reflection in the store mirror I thought, *Mughal royalty*.

"Gold brings good fortune," Gollapi Khala said. She picked up a large gold nose ring and placed it against my nose. "And this *nath*, for example, helps a woman give birth."

I examined myself in the mirror. I was totally draped in gold from head to toe.

I jerked back and shook my head. "No."

My Khalas ordered the storekeeper to package the purchased jewellery in the red velvet boxes, which they placed securely in their purses. We squeezed through the crowds with pickpockets, the ones who walked with arms hidden or stretched, looking to steal purses or grope breasts.

We got onto the main road, climbed onto the green-and-yellow scooter, and drove off.

When we arrived at Boro Mama's house and entered the bedroom, we found the bed covered in boxes and boxes of presents.

"These are from Shoaib's family," Boro Mama said, when he saw us staggering in. "They've really given a lot. I hope that you'll confirm that you agree to the wedding."

I looked at all the gifts on the bed — the shirts, lace lingerie, shining watches, and six or more silk, *katan*, and cotton saris.

Boro Mama presented me with a small cardboard box. "Another gift from Shoaib. It's a phone. He would like to get to know you better."

I stared at the phone in his hands. I could use it to get out, but would I, anyway?

"You haven't been arguing, you've been more receptive. I think you may actually be coming to your senses." Boro Mama smiled, then handed me the cardboard box. "I am going to trust you and give this to you. You can use it, but only to contact Shoaib. Can I trust you? Tell me, will you misuse this?"

I examined the cardboard box, then took it.

Shoaib called me later that evening to say he'd purchased a ring. "I hope you like the diamond. An elegant one, like you."

I was quiet.

"What about all the gifts? Are they to your liking?" Shoaib asked.

I slid my fingers over the silky camisole spread out on the bed. I closed my eyes and tried to imagine myself on the night of the impending wedding. Behind closed doors, the delicate bed and hard floor covered in thick, velvet petals of a thousand red roses. My hennaed hands adorned in diamond *kundan* rings sinking into the pillow. A candle burning, bringing into perspective Shoaib's dim eyes and the sharp line from his ear to his lip. Shoaib and I sitting on the edge of the bed, considering the possibilities of becoming each other's beloved. Shoaib leaning in his sweet, beautiful face, his expression full of love directed toward me, and I, compelled toward him, in my purest heart and unambiguous mind and body so hot and electric — until, suddenly, a vision of Bhav.

Shoaib and I were at Dhanmondi Lake. The pathways were lined with young lovers. In their hands, they held cones made of newspaper that were filled with salted peanuts from nearby vendors. The couples who were less shy held hands. A little boy galloped past us with a purple kite. The breeze pushed against our cheeks tenderly. It lifted my red *orna* in the air, as if to give a sign.

I thought, *This has gone too far.* I would tell Shoaib then that I had been coerced, despite what revealing this would do to Boro Mama's reputation. There was no other way. I would also tell him about Bhav. This was the least I could do with whatever agency I had or integrity I could practise.

"I have something to say." I stopped in the middle of our stroll.

Shoaib leaned in, and I told him everything that had happened since I had stepped off the plane. A girl with pigtails hopscotched nearby. A man with a glossy bald head pulled the strings of his guitar.

Shoaib strolled out a few metres ahead of me then turned back with open arms and said, "Well, I don't know what to say. What is happening to you isn't right. I had no idea. I won't agree to anything that you've been forced to do. I will leave it up to you."

When I caught up to him, I saw that his shoulders were caving in a little more than usual. His voice became faint. The wind sighed. The purple kite above our heads deflated, fell into the muddy lake. A few of the passersby ran to the edge of the water and pointed at the kite. As the folks debated the most effective way to retrieve it, Shoaib and I left the commotion, heading toward the gate.

"Shoaib is conflicted about the wedding," Boro Mama snarled at me. "What the hell did you say?"

I replied, "I had to tell him the truth. I felt bad for him. He needed to know the entirety of how I felt."

Boro Mama's eyes seethed. "How shameless could you be?"

If I feel shame, it should be in front of Allah, not these other people, and not you. It's individual. My shame is not a tool, I thought, *to be used by other people.*

I could tell he was upset that I was continuing to question the situation, but in Islam there was such a thing as blameworthy modesty. Being meek wasn't encouraged when it came to calling out tyranny or injustice, even in religion.

"Well then," he continued. "Your wedding date has been set. It's too late."

I learned that my henna patterns had already been chosen, my wedding sari ordered. Ammu had been examining the jewellery patterns of the gold received from Shoaib's family. The wedding invitations had been crafted on special handmade paper, delivered to the guests. The caterers had been chosen, as had the decorations and the flowers.

And then the weight drilled me into the earth. It was a lot of people. It would be a scandal if I left.

∞

Boro Mama, along with everyone else, had been busy preparing for the wedding. By now, I had quietened again, and therefore they must have assumed I was fine. I had not heard from or seen Shoaib since I told him the truth. It seemed he was still going along with the wedding because the frenetic wedding activities had not stopped.

It was all so strange.

I needed to tell Bhav about the developments so he at least knew what was happening, and I decided I'd use the phone Shoaib had given me to do it. I'd have to figure out how to get it to make long-distance calls. Boro Mama must have forgotten about the phone, for he hadn't mentioned it. The rules of the phone were that it stayed with Nani for the most part, locked up in her *almari*, the key tied to the tail end of her white sari. She would only give it to me if I had a call planned with Shoaib, and oftentimes the calls would be supervised. My relatives would usually gather around in excitement, offering suggestions for how to flirt. How strange it was that this happened, as if the wedding weren't a lie or that I trusted them. After any of these calls, I'd have to return the phone.

One evening I told Nani, "Nani, I haven't heard from Shoaib for some time. I need to know how he is finding the wedding planning."

Nani was preoccupied, spreading slaked lime on her betel leaf, which she pulled out from her *paan dan* silverware. "Okay, take the key."

After removing the key from her sari *anchal* I dashed to the *almari*, but with contained enthusiasm as I didn't want Nani to get too suspicious. The *almari* used to remain open but now it was always locked. I opened the *almari* door and raised myself on my toes, brought my arms over my head to retrieve the phone hiding under some Kashmir shawls made of *shahtoosh* wool. Small black flip phone. I returned the key to Nani and then plopped onto the bed, spreading a bright red-and-orange *kantha* quilt over my head. This quilt had been handstitched by Bengali women with little money, looking to feed their families. They had repurposed discarded scraps of cloth into something beautiful and with a practical purpose.

Nani chortled, shoved a *paan* in her mouth, then began rearranging her aesthetic *paan* display. Under the *kantha* quilt, I fiddled with the phone, trying to determine whether it was or was not capable of outgoing or incoming international calls. I found out that it wasn't. However, it seemed I could send texts to Canada.

I texted Bhav for the first time using this phone and said something like, "I told Shoaib everything. It is still unsettled."

Before I received his reply, I saw that Shoaib had texted.

"Thanks for being honest with me. I thought about it, and I still want to marry you, if you change your mind."

So it seemed he had known that Boro Mama was still proceeding with the plans and he didn't have any objection. I wondered what Boro Mama's reply had been when Shoaib told him he knew the pressure I was under.

I thought then, *Do I even know Shoaib at all?* I was hiding under the *kantha* quilt in the dark, the phone light illuminating my face. Was I supposed to take Shoaib's inability to see the coercion in this situation as a grand romantic gesture? That he would love me despite my many shortcomings including my heart belonging to another man? Why was he so eager to be with me specifically? I wondered if he, too, had received mixed messages about consent while growing up. Still, I was upset that he was making it harder, because it took strength to say *no* and I would have to say *no* to him again and again, like the chorus of a pop song destroyed by its own popularity.

There was confusion.

And then I got Bhav's text, which said, "Let me call the High Commission of Canada, please. You don't have time. You could be taken the next day."

Before receiving Shoaib's text and then Bhav's reply, there was a vacuum, within which everything moved fast and then remained still. I responded to neither man. I put the phone away.

How did it feel to not have a father during this very critical time, especially when Abbu had been around for most of my life? *What would he do if he were here?* They'd kept him far for a reason. Had he stayed far out of respect for the family? Or was it that he couldn't stand to watch me as the unwilling bride? Was the reason it was so hard to watch out of loyalty to me or the family or Islam? If he couldn't understand, I'd have to move forward by myself. I was the arbiter of my fate. The question was: Did I believe in myself — that I could handle whatever consequences I'd have to face?

I decided to go along with the wedding. Yes, that was my decision. It came down to simple utilitarianism: do what results in the greatest good for the greatest number of people. In Islam, this would perhaps translate to decisions that brought most harmony, co-operation over competition at the expense of your own desires. For, as it says in Quranic verse 216 in Surah Al-Baqarah, a statement along the lines of "But it is possible that ye dislike a thing which is good for you, and that ye love a thing which is bad for you. But Allah knoweth and ye know not." This decision wouldn't feel so good in the present, but perhaps it would be the most reasonable and rewarding long-term. Otherwise, why else would I be presented with such a situation? To act on my free will or to learn how to better recognize and accept that which was predestined, that which was good for me — what was being asked of me — I could not tell. Perhaps now that I was almost an adult, and no longer a child, I'd have to continue to make more decisions like this, where I'd have to work harder to distinguish what was noble, or pure. For it was in puberty and beyond that we became more susceptible to the Shaytān's influence.

So, I spit out the words, "Yes. Although I truly don't want to. But I will do it for you."

Boro Mama threw his hands in the air, roaring with glee. Everyone else, all my Khalas and Ammu, too, jumped around like firecrackers.

"There is so much to do!" Ammu exclaimed. "We will dress you up as the most beautiful bride. It is my dream to see you this way."

As Ammu wrapped me in her embrace, I had the cold chill of that day when I fell on the Dhaka street as a child, chasing after the rickshaw she was on. The sadness usually preserved for the finality of death and grief. It felt like the confirmation of losing her already, although she believed that she had just gained me.

The joy in her eyes and the sadness in mine. How did I come from her because she could not feel the tender pain in my tone? Then I remembered that her ideas differed, about how to love me, what was best for me, how we could connect. At least then, at that time, when I was that age.

As everyone went on, making arrangements, ironing out details, I dragged my body to the bathroom and shut the door behind me. I slammed my back against it. Across from me, the lizard watched, amazed.

"Well, what am I supposed to do?" I asked it. I wished so much for this lizard to talk back, provide a granule of wisdom or a sign. But it just stared. A rush of sorrow made its way through my body. I exhaled deeply to make room for it. I was lonely, despite having satisfied everybody else. I would have to bear with this loneliness, perhaps for a very long time.

∞

I asked Nani to give me the phone Shoaib had given me.

Sometimes I took this phone and made excuses to leave the room with it. It was then I would send a text to Bhav, which I would delete quickly after. Praying and hoping he wouldn't reply when the phone was in hands other than mine.

On the days closer to my wedding, October 31, 2005, I texted Bhav to tell him what was happening and that I was sorry.

"I asked the High Commission of Canada what they need to get you out of there," Bhav replied.

Bhav was still trying. He still had hope, but I had made my decision.

"Just your consent. I have the number. I can call them. You just give them your consent and they will come get you — if you can provide the address."

And then, as much as I didn't want to revert back to a state of ambivalence, where I chose not to act as a way of resisting and of believing a better resolution would present itself, something inside of me, a small shrill of a voice, compelled me to type the address I had seen on some envelopes on Boro Mama's study desk.

I couldn't see Bhav's face while I typed, but I imagined his squinting, his faraway look, vision scattered. He had lines on his forehead when he was bothered. For I had betrayed him, hadn't I? Bhav could never give up on me. Could I give up on him?

"But listen, they need evidence that you gave your consent to be taken out of there."

I stayed silent, just listened.

"The white people might just see me as the crazy brown-boy stalker who is trying to get back a girlfriend that dumped him," Bhav continued. "They need to hear from you."

I thought about the many women who didn't even have this option at all. How would anyone know about them? What about the women who had no one to call?

"Don't contact them," I repeated in my texts.

"I won't do anything that you don't want, but I also know you are not completely yourself."

"I know," I replied. My solemn demeanour and my solemn voice, as if I was at a funeral. "I need to think about it again." There were so many different parts of me now, old ones dying and new ones taking over.

"Whatever you choose, I'm here for you," Bhav assured me.

"They will take me to the beauty parlour on the morning of my wedding to get ready. I will try to call you before they move me from this house. Once they do, there will be no way for me to contact you anymore."

"Sumaiya, tell me, what do you want?" Bhav texted me one last time.

It was as if my head was in the middle of two cymbals. I closed my eyes, then opened them, speaking with a clarity that hurt, "Tell them," I wrote. "Tell them."

The window curtains fluttered.

"It might be too late, but tell them. Please find a way. Regardless of anything, one thing is for sure. This is not safe, and Allah, Allah would never want this. In my heart, I know it. The way it's all happening goes against my principles."

I fumbled with the phone. Out of breath and head pounding. I hastily erased all our texts before I went to sleep, and I was glad I did, because the next day Boro Mama took the phone from me.

"It's better you don't have this now. You're getting married, anyway."

He marched away, signalling his determination through the ebb of his stride. With him my portal to the world outside. To

Canada. To Toronto. Who I'd been about four months ago. Bhav was gone. I was gone.

Would there be a way out? Would it be too late now?

From: ███████████████████████
███████████████

Sent: October 30, 2005, 11:57 PM

To: DHAKA (G)

Subject: Please

This is ██████████████, I opened a case for Sumaiya Matin, DOB ██████████████. I don't know what else I can do, the numbers I gave her are not working, I even tried to forward some messages of sumaiya's to ████ and it didn't work. I'm begging you guys to please just go the addresses I provided and talk to her, and then you'll see. I understand your positions but this is her life, they will kill her if she doesn't marry. Please I'm begging you guys to just go to the house at noon and talk to her. I can pay you guys to go to that house [h]ow much it doesn't matter to me email me back and I'll give you my visa number, I don't care, just please go to that house and talk to her. She never got received a phone call from you guys, she's going to die and all you guys have to do is just go and talk to her. Please just go and talk to her ... tomorrow at noon.

Bibaher Din / Wedding Day
(বিবাহের দিন)

It was October 31, 2005, the morning of my wedding day.

I woke up to a flurry of activity. Ammu and Nani were laying out, on the bed, the maroon *katan* bridal sari with *zardozi* embroidery, gold threads with stones attached, handstitched in the shape of paisley. The type of embroidery that once embellished the royals of India. The sari shone and I rubbed my eyes. My stomach grumbled and I thought, *I have to call Bhav.*

I pulled myself off the bed with my hennaed hands, designs that looked like tapestried arches and pearls. Although I didn't have an actual *mehndi* ceremony, just a few days ago my skin had been rubbed with turmeric from head to toe. My bare arms were now a golden oak; in just a few hours I would have Ammu's heirloom bracelet on one of them.

I tiptoed out of the room. Ammu and Nani were feeling the soft fabric with their fingertips and discussing the silver plate that Shoaib would be presenting me with the next day before the *Boubath* or *Walima* event. It would hold more gifts. After which I'd have to move into Shoaib's home, at least for a little while.

I shuddered at this thought.

I didn't brush my teeth or wash my face. Everyone else was too busy to notice. I staggered past the excited people discussing their outfits and makeup, past the maids cleaning the place for all the future guests, past the *hijras* outside our door who had heard there would be a wedding and were demanding money, past the living room where Boro Mama and I had all our conversations, his multiple attempts to persuade me that he was right and I wrong. Everyone continued to make orders, count *shondesh* sweets in boxes, and fold glitzy garments. Ammu and Nani were arranging my wedding trousseau, as in about an hour I would be going to the beauty parlour to get my bridal makeup done.

At the entrance of Boro Mama's bedroom, I looked side to side, to ensure no one was around. I darted in, went straight to the phone. Picked up the handset and dialed Bhav's number.

"Thank God," Bhav exclaimed when he heard my faint voice. "I have been waiting by my phone for hours."

"Bhav," I uttered his name as if I was already mourning. I said, "I love you, I always wi—"

"I found a way," Bhav interrupted. "It hit me after we last spoke. I don't know why I hadn't thought of it before. I forwarded all of our text messages to the High Commission. It's all they needed to see to assume consent," he explained.

I could feel my heart lifting from within the shell of my body.

"They are going to try and be there by eleven thirty a.m.," he stated. "All you have to do is take the longest shower you have ever taken in your goddamn life."

"Okay," I told him.

"But after they come, the final decision is yours. You asked me to inform them, but whether you decide to leave, we'll leave it in your hands."

"I love you," I told him. "Whether we are together or not. I always will."

I put the handset down as I heard Ammu call my name.

"Get ready," she yelled. "The driver will be here soon to take all the women to the parlour."

I lifted each leg, put them one in front of the other, trying to stay upright. *Allah, I need you. Allah, please don't leave me*, I prayed under my breath.

I turned on the tap. Before I took off my clothes, Bilkis walked in with a bucket of warm water in her hands.

"For you, *Apu*," she put the bucket down next to my feet. "Are you okay? You'll be fine, wherever you are. I know it."

I gave Bilkis a hug. "Thank you, for everything. You'll always be with me."

When Bilkis left, I started peeling off each piece of clothing as slowly as I could. As I did, I imagined the vibrancy of the maroon *Katan* sari that would be draped over me, the gold bangles, and stacked gold necklaces, my hair with copious amounts of hairspray poofed and uplifted, whitish pink flower garlands inserted. I imagined the white powder applied to my face to make my skin lighter, the deep kohl lines bordering my eyes, and the blush dabbed on my cheeks. I imagined my wedding hall in Jatiya Sangsad Bhaban. I hadn't seen the interior at all, but I had been told that there would be a red carpet leading to a grand stage on which Shoaib and I would sit. Surrounding us would be white drapes falling like the garbs of *nawabs* and *maharajas*, and hanging from them red and white roses to signal unity and new beginnings. Every inch of the hall walls covered in fairy lights. The tables for the over five hundred guests, or maybe a thousand, draped in tablecloths made of silk. To the side, by the stage, would be a grand glass table with a colossal whole lamb roast. This is where the close family members of the bride and groom would sit. The roast would be served with plain white *pulau*, peas, onions, green chilies sprinkled on top, as well as *borhani*, the yogourt drink blended with mint leaves. I imagined also faces that I did not know, dressed in their best, greeting me with curiosity and offering blessings. Laughter, chatter, music playing. A chaotic cacophony of scents and sounds, devoid of meaning for me then, all fleeting.

We were to skip all the other cultural wedding rituals, and perhaps many of the guests would be confused as to why: the *paan-chini*, *mehndi*, *gaye golud* or *haldi*, and even the *bou bhat* or *walima*, if necessary. It was important for Boro Mama that the focus be on the *nikkah*. I myself didn't understand why under such a circumstance guests needed to be involved at all, or there even needed to be decorations.

"Because," Nani said, "you only get married once. You are the second-eldest daughter, and our most prized. We wouldn't take this opportunity away from you."

I would have appreciated this deeply if this was a wedding of my choice, but it wasn't. I would be showered with fineries that millions of women all over the world only dream of. Yet, right there and then, it was not something I wanted or even felt worthy of. In that moment, I'd consider anything more appealing than waiting to be disrobed in a five-star suite after all the guests had left. I wondered how was it that love in seclusion, although sinful, felt somehow more convivial than a consummation that everyone would be aware of? I wanted the legitimacy of a socially recognized union with a one true love, but not like this, not at all. After all the merrymaking was done, after all the merrymakers were gone, after the ladies' *Gopi* foundation melted off with their sweat and the young women exchanged phone numbers with young men to whom they'd never reply, after some uncles shared a smoke, and after the low-wage servers and cleaners took home their pay to feed their hungry families, I would just be left there with a marriage contract I had not wanted to sign.

I didn't understand then the logic of it all. *Nani*, I wanted to say, *I don't love this man.* That love and running away for it, giving my life for it, was more appealing than feeling like a queen of a *nawab* and receiving all these gifts, dressing up and looking beautiful, being catered to hand and foot. None of it mattered, when my heart called out only for him and what was right.

If Bhav wasn't there, and the situation wasn't forced, and it was a simple arranged marriage, yes, I could have considered it. There was very much a difference, although most people outside of the culture didn't necessarily realize that.

Arranged marriages aren't necessarily forced marriages. Most marriages are at the very least encouraged by external forces, but a forced arranged marriage is tantamount to legalized rape. Whether rich or poor, it didn't matter on which strata one found themselves, this type of rape could be condoned, although it was not permitted in the religion. In the Quran it says, "You who have believed, it is not lawful for you to inherit women by compulsion."

∞

From the window of the bathroom, I heard the faint sounds of a car horn. Confusion in the voices of the gate guards. "*Ki hochay?*" "Who are they?"

One, two ... I counted at the back of my mind. "We're here from the High Commission of Canada. We'd like to speak to ..." *Three.*

Was it happening? Was it real? The passageways to my lungs were closing. Stifled.

I wiped myself with the taffy-pink towel, along the side of my neck, my collarbones, under my breasts, and across my navel. The terrycloth and its interlaced loops of thread soaking.

I walked over to the mirror, wiped my right hand over the mist, to better see my face. The cavities of my eyes smudged with lead, as if I hadn't slept for weeks. My cheeks were pinched in. If I were to stay longer I would shrink to the point of evaporating like water.

It was then that I thought I saw her behind me. The Shayṭān Bride. Nervous, wilting, lost, but then, as she raised her chin, a sly smirk, as if she knew what would happen next.

The commotion outside was getting louder. Boro Mama was on the other side of the bathroom window; I could hear him talking to the guards and High Commission of Canada officials. I heard English, spoken by a man and then a woman.

"We have an important matter to talk to you about," the man told Boro Mama.

"This is the wrong address that you have. I think what you're looking for is just there, down the street." Boro Mama tried to redirect them, and I listened in, muttering *La ilaha illa Allah Muhammed asul Allah* over and over again. If the officials left, I would have no option left. I would certainly be stuck in Bangladesh. I would certainly have to go through with the wedding. The only way out would be something like sinful suicide.

Still the officials persisted, and I let out a deep breath. "Thank you, Allah," I cried.

"I am sorry, you can't come in." Boro Mama resisted.

"Sir, we have been ordered. Here is our identification. If you do not comply, there will be a problem," I heard the woman repeat firmly a few times.

Suddenly, Boro Mama's voice, which all this time sounded like heavy drums, was now a faint echo from the top of a mountain. I imagined his own panic, how he must have felt to not know what was going on exactly. Especially since he was so used to having absolute control in every situation.

I held my breath as the exchange continued. I even pinched myself. During these days I often felt an uncanny sense of being moved without my knowing, as if there were invisible strings attached to my limbs. Was this really happening? Would it be strange to say that I believe I watched myself like the bathroom lizard, just to make it easier for me to endure what would come next? My skin scaly and stiff, and from my quick lizard eyes seeing the Shayṭān Bride in the mist, strutting out the door to face the commotion, a foreshadowing perhaps of what I should do next. The mist cleared wherever she stepped, as if there was a light emitting from her forehead, showing her the way. An inner knowing.

I heard the shuffle of footsteps. I heard the voices on the other side of my window fade away.

I pulled a *shalwar kameez* over myself. When I opened the bathroom door, I found Ammu and Sweety Khala standing there. Their eyebrows curved and foreheads scrunched. Confusion.

"What did you do?"

"Nothing," I replied.

They motioned me to the living room. I straggled toward it and they followed. When I entered, I saw a white woman and a white man sitting on two stools across from Boro Mama and Nani on the claret cloth sofa. Boro Mama was fidgeting with his fingers. He usually sat against the couch, his broad shoulders spread across the back, his right leg up and over his left one, forming a rigid square that mirrored the rigidness of his jaw. Now, both his legs were on the floor and he was hunched over.

Nani, lovely Nani, appeared confused. Nani, who made mango *achar* for me because I loved it so much. Lovely Nani, who massaged my scalp with coconut oil so I would have soft, silky hair like hers. Fair, petite, with long hennaed hair and keen eyes, caregiver of seven. Nani sat beside Boro Mama, looking at the floor, her hands neatly folded in her lap.

The white woman had moss-coloured eyes and blond hair scooped up in a ponytail. The white man's eyes were a pecan shade. He was bearded, medium build, a little undistinguished, but in a comforting way. They sat fairly still, serious but approachable, both in casual shirts, as if they were ordering coffee in a Starbucks, ready to divulge the events of their day to a friend.

I imagined they'd possibly say something like — especially in the context of the ongoing War on Terror launched by the United States of America — "Today I rescued some Muslim girl from a forced marriage. You know how they are." As if I were only *Muslim girl* and not Sumaiya Matin. As if every girl of the faith was beholden to my story. As if we weren't capable of uniqueness and complexity and individuality, and also as if all our practices could be reduced to uncontextualized notions of consent, as if our men were worse than other men and our women more eager to submit and therefore stupid and deserving. They would not see Shoaib or Bhav. They probably would not understand that it *wasn't about saving other cultures or religions from themselves*, for that would perpetuate the impacts of the damage that had already been caused by colonization and imperialism many years ago. They would not understand the complexity of the war, of love, of family, of tradition — of the complicated history and the beautiful loyalty that had sprung forth between Ammu, Abbu, and, yes, even Boro Mama.

So, the closer I got to Boro Mama, Nani, and the two officials, the more the ground seemed to shake. I would be careful to refrain from stoking the flame of "Canada rescues Muslim girl, again," as it was indeed complicated. I would also be honest.

Ammu and Sweety Khala followed my trail. I eventually sat adjacent to Nani and Boro Mama on the sofa, across from the officials on the stools. Ammu and Sweety Khala scurried closer to Nani, somewhat behind her in the shadows. They remained standing.

The two officials asked to speak to me alone. They directed Boro Mama to provide them my passport and he left the room to retrieve it. As I observed him dragging his feet, I thought about all the times I had to drag my own to meet him in this very living room. Bilkis watched from the other side of the veranda. Her big brown eyes and tumbleweed hair against the backdrop of vivid green bushes, glowing yellow *radhachura* flowers on the branches. Nani, Ammu, and Sweety Khala scampered to the bedroom, where my bridal trousseau filled with dresses, perfumes, shiny stilettos, jewellery, and purses remained open. There were also half-assembled flower garlands lying around.

When they entered the bedroom, I could see their silhouettes on the sliding door from the living room where I was still sitting.

I heard them mumble:

"What is she doing?"

"Who are they?"

"The audacity she has."

"Who made the phone call?"

"I didn't realize she had ..."

When the officials and I were alone, they introduced themselves: Jessica and Mark.

"We received information that you may not be safe. Are you okay?" Jessica asked.

I opened my mouth to say "I'm fine" but then stopped myself.

I sat to think but couldn't focus on anything important, my mind wandering into a strange fantasy-like waking dream.

In my waking dream, it is still October 31st, but no longer the morning; the sun has taken its leave. All Hallow's Eve. I'm at my wedding in the Canadian outdoors, on a cliff somewhere, a luxurious orange carpet unrolled to the edge. The wind blows a white ribbon in my face. When I peer downward, I see that I'm wearing some sort of tacky, borderline-medieval white lace 1980s wedding dress with rebellious poufy shoulders and all kinds of gaudy bows and embellishments. The dress sucks my waist in. It exposes my collarbone and a little bit of my breasts with its plunging neckline. I am covered in blood. The blood is coming from my lips, which are partially covered by a thin mesh veil. The blood is sliding down the exposed part of my neck and chest and drips into the frills, expanding into tremendous deep red stains that remind me of pupils dilating.

I am holding a bouquet of red roses in my hand. I touch the top of my head and feel two horns there. I think I maybe have a tail but I'm not sure. When I look around, I see skeletons, werewolves, vampires, mummies, ghosts that just look like people with sheets over their heads and big black holes for eyes, all bobbing their heads and raising their arms to the "Monster Mash." Many of the guests are zombies in saris, *lenghas*, hijabs, *abayas*, *kurtas*, and *sherwanis*; orange-blooded with greyish-greenish skin, bouncing in circles around small bonfires. Other guests are wearing masks as if attending a masquerade ball, carrying plastic bags with red candy apples, sponge toffee, candy corn, and gummy bears, which they are stuffing into their mouths. Under the full moon the after party has already begun without the wedding having happened. I am struck by the chaos, unpredictability, and mystery.

I search among the crowd for the groom I will be marrying, but only spot black cats, jack-o'-lanterns, witches on flying brooms, and then the Viking from Jungle, who is holding a shovel, preparing, it seems, to dig up some burial ground. And then, from a distance, a hologram of Boro Mama made of red, green, and blue light. He is wearing a wizard's hat. His face is large and hovering over the scene — the dancing, the monsters, the candy — repeating "*Good, good,*" over and over again.

From behind the hologram emerges Shoaib, then Bhav, and Wasif (the boy who called Abbu to inform him of my scandalous behaviour), all three cloaked and masked like bandits, swirling like dervishes in unison as they approach me, chanting in low desirous incantations, as if preparing to make me either their wife or sacrifice; there is no way for me to be sure. Shared, taken, given, as a type of reincarnation. Behind them, the silhouette of a womanly figure, just out of view. I experience it all with a mixture of uneasiness and fascination, All Hallows Eve with the lingering remains of Samhain, my heart beating fast. Then, in the mayhem of the celebration, emerge Jessica and Mark, wearing soldiers' uniforms, both holding a rifle in one hand and a Bible in the other.

"Stop!" Mark yells. "The power of Christ compels you! The power of Christ compels you!"

"We're here to find the weapons of mass destruction," Jessica adds as a troop of goblins skip past her, gnashing their teeth hungrily.

"Are you okay?" Mark startled me out of my fantasy and back to the present reality.

"Yes?" Jessica prodded from the stool in Boro Mama's living room.

"What is happening here?" Mark inquired.

I gulped, then told them both.

"I didn't know this would happen. I thought it would just be a family vacation. It certainly felt that way when it started, but then it just escalated," I explained, everything pouring out all at once.

"The man, Shoaib, he is incredibly nice, but I cannot do this to him, or myself. My heart only has one person, and not only that — this is not okay. I know Allah wouldn't want this," I continued.

Jessica and Mark continued to listen, nodding their heads.

"Take as much time as you need to tell us what you want to say. We are here for you," Jessica reassured me.

So, I told them everything: what life was in Canada, what life was here since I had landed in July, what my predicament was, how confused I felt. How incredible it felt to finally speak to someone outside of my own head or the pages of my journal, or other than maybe Manshoor or Bilkis, who were the only people who actually listened.

"Where is your dad?" Mark asked.

I told them he was in Canada and that I had been told recently that he was not well.

"Abbu would never let them do this to me if he was here." I told them. "I am not sure he knows what has been going on. I want to talk to him."

"We can do that for you." Mark handed me a phone. "Do you want to go ahead with this marriage, or do you want to go back to Canada? Or just leave the premises? We can help you. This phone, you can use it to call anyone you need to, to make the decision."

"I don't know," I responded. "This is my family, and without them I wouldn't be me."

I continued speaking to them as if I was speaking to myself. Disentangling thought by thought. Both the officials nodded in unison, searching my face patiently for end-resolve.

"On the other hand, I know deep down that this is not safe, this situation that I'm in. It wouldn't be fair to the man they're hoping I'll marry. I don't love him, although they have said I'll grow to love him. Although I wonder, what is love? Shoaib does seem like a nice man, and his father is sick. I feel terrible. Apparently, all his father wants is for his son to marry me. Apparently, it's his deathbed wish."

The reels of my mind conjured Shoaib's face. Shoaib, almost ten years older than I, unaware that when I said I was not ready to be married I meant that I wasn't going to marry him.

"What would you like to do?"

I was snapped back to the present moment by Jessica searching my face.

I wanted so much to show her the radical emptiness I felt.

"I don't know. I have to think."

"Take all the time you need," said Mark. "Can we tell you what we see?"

I nodded.

"When you speak, it's almost as if there are two people. One that is very confident, knows who she is, what she wants. The other one is very much concerned about the expectations she is supposed to fulfill, to the point of maybe even forgetting herself," Mark told me.

The tone of Mark's voice irked me at first, as I didn't want him to attribute *good* or *bad* to any of these parts he saw; it was far more complicated. *They aren't just cultural expectations. They are my own expectations. What if it is really within our communities that we discover our truest selves? What if I remember myself best through the roles I play within my culture, within the society I am in? How clear are the lines anyway between our environments and ourselves as a separate being?* It was tricky. There were many ways to look at it. What was important to me was that I needed to be able to choose. *It's just the price of my choices — should they be so hefty?*

Yet, I didn't go on to explain. Instead, I took the phone from them and decided I would call a few people, including Bhav and Shoaib.

Boro Mama was asked to come back in to dial in Shoaib's number. He explained quickly to Shoaib what was happening. Then he handed me the phone.

"How could you do this? I was falling in love with you," Shoaib said when I put the phone to my ear. "I thought you were willing to leave the past behind and start a new life with me. I would give you everything," Shoaib went on. His voice was quavering, and I could tell he was being sincere. He was indeed quite hurt. He had certainly got attached, and fast. Somehow I had, too, to a certain extent. The rhythm of his breathing, which was slower than usual, sped up, indicating that he might have been crying. I couldn't tell whether I felt empathy then or embarrassment for his wounded-ness. I just felt the hardness of my own heart; I had to do this to act in accordance with my own principles.

"I think you already knew. I had told you. It just wouldn't be right, not even for you, if I went through with this," I replied. "You aren't my soulmate."

"We already sent out invitations. My father might have a stroke just hearing that he'll have to face all these guests, and all these costs."

This did leave my stomach in knots, but I had to allow myself to ignore it.

"Please forgive me," I said. I hung up the phone on the man who would never be my husband. I had believed at first that love was servitude, but I was learning that, even more so, it was about being true, especially to oneself.

I shuddered as I handed the phone back to Boro Mama to finish the conversation with Shoaib. He took it from me, saying nothing, only fidgeting with the device in his hands.

I waited for him to finish his conversation. I stood in the living room closer to the veranda, where Bilkis was still observing. Jessica and Mark were still seated on the stools in the middle of the room. Boro Mama paced back and forth as he spoke with Shoaib. I heard only fragments of their conversations. I could tell he was trying to appease Shoaib, console him.

When the call ended, Boro Mama handed the phone back to me and I called Bhav. He answered as if he had just won the lottery. "Thank God they got you in time."

I described the scene to him. He did not have much to say other than, "I love you," and, "This is your decision," and, "I am glad you are safe."

I also called one of my friends in Canada, who said similar things.

After my phone calls, when I looked above my head and said, *Alhumdulillah*, it came to me: if I remove all the noise, there remains one thing, and one thing only: my safety. If after all of this I stayed, my safety would possibly be even more compromised. I deduced this after considering and adding up all the past behaviours of everyone and then predicting what their next response would most likely be.

"I would like to leave the premises," I finally declared. "I will decide later what I want to do, for now I don't feel safe. I want to leave."

Jessica and Mark nodded from their stools. They both stood up, almost at the same time. Jessica walked over to me. "Are you ready?" She scanned my eyes.

"Yes," I avowed.

"Let's go," she said, and gestured me forward.

As I plodded to the door with her by my side, I looked back over my shoulder and saw Ammu, Sweety Khala, Boro Mama, and Nani all now in the living room. Mark was explaining the next steps to everyone.

"Where is she going?" Boro Mama's tone was surprisingly controlled. "How can we contact her?"

"We will inform you," Mark told them.

Before I exited, Nani ran over to me and lowered herself to my feet. She held my ankles, titling her pleading face up toward me. I remembered then that I was at her feet a few weeks earlier, also begging for her to believe in me. It pained me to see this inversion, because Nani was my elder, from my line of ancestors. I respected her.

"Please don't do this to us. Tell them to leave. We'll stop the wedding." She sobbed, her tears snaking down the soft arch below my ankle.

I loved Nani more than words could describe, but trust, trust is like a fallen leaf — once it falls it cannot be reattached. I thought, *I must wait.* Abbu had always reminded me that *sabr*, patience, was key.

A part of me floated in the air, watching this: me angling my body away as Nani tugged on me gently. I didn't know then that only a few years later, she would pass. I'd never see her again. This is the last memory I have of her. I never got to say goodbye.

During this time Mark had retrieved my passport from Boro Mama. He and Jessica were now both at the door, waiting for me. I walked past Nani, and then Ammu and Sweety Khala, too, who were huddled in a corner whimpering. I tried not to look at them, for I'd drown in their tears the way I almost drowned in the Jessore pond during my last visit to the country. I walked past Boro Mama, too, who looked away.

I left the place, the Shayṭān Bride.

I sat in the back of a Jeep with the two officials. We were on our way to a nearby hotel, where I would stay until I decided what I would do next. I closed my eyes; on the back of my eyelids I saw brown hands distributing red-and-white wedding invitation cards, trays of *kachi* biriyani, Jatiya Sangsad Bhaban draped in colourful red, green, and gold lights, and expansive blue skies, Abbu on his bed beside his phone waiting to hear from me, television screens going haywire and bursting into flames, my grandmother still pleading at my feet, my forehead touching the *jai-namaz* in prostration, news footage of planes crashing into the Twin Towers, the feet of people kicking debris of temples, gurudwaras, and mosques.

I was going to go to the hotel and sort it all out. I was only nineteen.

When I got to the hotel room, I placed a bedsheet on the ground. I didn't have a prayer mat so it would have to do. I didn't know which way the *Kaaba* was, either, so I guessed.

Afterward, I paced the small room back and forth, it's plain white wallpaper and the white sheet on the twin-size bed blankly failing to establish a mood. The carpet was a standard grey and its padding underneath my bare feet was coarse. The window was sealed shut. There was also a circular wooden table on which was some food in a Styrofoam container. I wasn't sure what it was, but I didn't care to look. My mind was on the telephone on the nightstand.

My thoughts alternated like my feet as I pressed them on the floor, plodding toward the phone. I picked up the handset, heavy in my hand, wondering who I should call first: Abbu or Bhav. The last Bhav heard of me was when I confirmed with him over the phone that the officials had come. He had no idea what I'd decided to do, where I was. *He must be in distress*, I thought.

Bhav answered "Are you okay? Safe?" His voice was as soft as the pillowcase I ran my other hand over.

"Yes," I answered, then shared all the details of the past two to three hours.

"What would you like to do? I am here to support you in any way you need. You can come back and stay with me. We could get an apartment, or we can stay at my brother's until we figure things out. I can work extra hours. You will be okay."

Usually, when Bhav made plans or gave advice I would lean in and listen. Ascertain his propositions. Now, as much as his presence on the other end of the line brought me great comfort, his voice began to fade out slowly as I heard only mine. *Um, Sumaiya, you just almost got married earlier today. Like, maybe you should pause on big romantic decisions for now? How about sleep? Don't you miss that?*

"I don't know if I am ready to just move in with you," I told Bhav, as we weren't even married.

I asked him how he was, and then I told him I'd call him back.

I put the handset down. I had salty tears in my mouth. Slowly, and like a much older woman, I bent down to sit on the bed, reaching my hands out and feeling for the nearby table in case I fell. The hard edge of the soft mattress, the flocculent duvet, and the empty air around me. I lightly plopped myself down onto the cushioning.

The pillow morphed to the shape of my skull. My cumbersome eyelids protested for sleep.

After a minute or two I picked up my heavy arms and brought them to the phone. I picked up the handset and dialed home. After so many months, I would finally call Abbu directly. He would finally know the facts, not hyper-exaggerated or minimized recounts of truth.

"Hello," he answered.

I paused. Abbu sounded confused, as if he were at the edge of the earth and in need of further direction.

"It's me," I replied.

"My precious, how are you?" This question gained other questions: "Where are you? What is happening? When will you come home? Please, come home now. I want to see you."

I just listened to him repeat "Please come home," which he did a few times, as if to fill up the space between us.

I pulled on my hair strand.

"You can trust me," he replied.

How must it have felt as a father to be deprived of an opportunity to guide his daughter? As I listened to Abbu's voice, it upset me that Boro Mama and everyone else had taken me away from him. That they had subjected me to Boro Mama as a foster parent, as if Abbu had been insufficient or incapable.

I said goodbye and put the handset down, almost missing the switch hook. I saw on the table a small yellow notepad with hurried cursive letters that spelled "No one is home."

I sat back down on the bed and this time allowed myself to sprawl across the whole of it. Suddenly, my body began to give into the stillness of rest. Rapid heartbeats calmed like softening drums. My appetite still left somewhere on a side street, far away. I closed my weary eyes, my brain still twitching like a lightbulb about to go out. I let it do its thing, until I couldn't feel it anymore.

I woke up in the middle of the night to the aroma of melted cheese on some type of fish. I lifted my weighty legs and dropped them onto the carpet. I sat upright, fighting gravity every step of the way.

The white walls with cracked paint whirled as I walked over to the bathroom and splashed a handful of water over my face. I ran back to the table and fiddled with the Styrofoam box, which contained a tuna fish sandwich. I hadn't eaten for days. I filled every inch of my mouth with tuna and bread.

After a level of satiation, I began to notice the darkness of the room, how it crept over me, half sinister, half comforting. The sky through my window was pitch-black, too, I thought, until I saw a few glimmers of light.

When I returned to my bed, it occurred to me again that I had no plan for what I'd do next. Certainly, I couldn't even think beyond the night, to the day after or the day after that. I had missed half a semester of school, and I would be heading

into my second year of university where I needed certain pre-
requisites. What would I do if I couldn't go to school? How
would I pay my tuition if I would already be in debt from this
semester's missed classes? For some reason, all this still mattered so much.

My thoughts spun and I felt a cold chill. I wanted to talk to
Abbu again, so I called him.

"I am so glad you called me back," Abbu told me. "I am so
worried about you. Tell me what you need. I'll do anything you
need. Just come home to me, please," Abbu pleaded. "I cannot live
without you."

"And I without you, Abbu," I responded.

Abbu didn't live in the house in North York. He lived in my ear-
drum, offering me advice and reminding me that he would always
give me his support. Ammu was in me, too, but I felt her more in my
blood, her vicious stamina. I was the daughter of both these forces.

"Your relatives want to see you. The officials asked the family
for your belongings. Sweety Khala's husband will drop off your
suitcase. Will you see him for a few minutes?"

"No," I told Abbu. "I don't want to see anyone."

"Well, what about your Boro Chachi? They just want to know
you are okay."

"Abbu, I was manipulated. If I speak to anyone, they will try
to sway me one way or the other. It was all a big manipulation."

"They told me that you agreed to see Shoaib multiple times
and that you said you liked him."

My voice now raspy, I shook my head in disbelief and then my
whole body started shaking, I shot back, "You don't understand, it
was a trick, how they did it."

I told him I needed to rest, and he replied with "Please come
home. I promise I will not let anyone harass you again. I will see
to this."

After that call, I cried for him and then myself, because Abbu actually thought he had power over the situation, and I wasn't so sure he did. A thought passed me then that I might never really know what he truly felt about everything. The pang in my chest told me not to ask.

I called Bhav again, who was also relieved to hear my voice. I told him that I had spoken to Abbu and what he had said.

"It's your choice," he said. "Whatever makes you feel safe, and whatever you are ready for."

"I think tonight I will sleep and tomorrow morning I will decide what I want to do."

With that I crawled back under the covers. It was hard for me to draw out thoughts and feelings that belonged to me. The voices, now faint — Bhav's, Abbu's, Ammu's, Boro Mama's, Sweety Khala's, Shoaib's, and the world's — had been louder than Dhaka streets mere hours ago. Then there was Shoaib, who crossed my mind for the first time that evening. What was he now thinking?

My thoughts on a reel, round and round they went. Edges of the off-white wallpaper were peeling off the surfaces they had been stuck to. The lightbulb above my head flickered like a bad itch. As it burned out, so did I.

From: ███████████████████████
████████████████████████

Sent: October 31, 2005, 4:54 AM

To: ██████████████████████
███████████████

Subject: RE: Please

As I'm sure you've heard, we found her and spoke with her. She is with us at the High Commission and we are giving her some time at a hotel to think about what she wants to do. She will get in touch with you.

█████

From: ████████████████████
████████████████████████

Sent: October 5, 2005, 5:31 PM

To: ████████████████████
████████████████

Subject: Funds for Sumaiya

Hello ████████,

As per our telecon today, I'm very pleased that Sukmaiya is now safe and preparing to return to Canada. She will need money for her tickets home, and maybe a new passport. It's very good to know you are here to help.

Attached is the form for you to complete and sign, which authorises us to debit your credit card. Once we debit your card, the money will be available to our High Commission in Dhaka. They will arrange tickets and anything else necessary so Sumaiya can fly home to Canada.

I am hoping to have the full costs available tomorrow, and will let you know as soon as I do. However, I looked at flights on Travelocity.ca, and while there are several on Thurs 03 Nov from $1221.00, most are $1500 and up. Usually flights are cheaper when purchased locally, so hopefully the price will stay under $1500, but of course it does depend on the day of the week and the airline and routes etc.

Please note that there is a consular service fee of $75.00 to be added to the amount needed for Sumaiya's expenses.

Thank you for your kind assistance.

██████████

I stayed in the hotel for almost two weeks before deciding to fly back to Canada, to return to my parents' home. I made this choice after much thought, because I had faith that everyone could seek resolve and heal together. It was important to me not to abandon anyone, including myself.

It was my first time alone on a plane. I was wearing a green-and-black *salwar kameez* with gold print and open-toed sandals, even though I knew there might be snow in Toronto. My hair was in a bun. Next to me sat an Asian man, maybe in his late thirties or early forties. He reeked of cigarettes, salt, and pepper when he leaned in closer. I shifted my eyes to the window. With uneasiness, I pulled the blinds down.

"You're going to miss out on the beautiful view," he said. I could see the glint in his eye, of interest and curiosity.

I was worn out like his faded black shirt. I hoped he would leave, go away. He didn't. I just smiled and nodded, then swiftly looked away.

"Why are you alone?" he asked me. "Do you not have a husband or a father?"

I almost choked on my own saliva. "I'm just alone."

He smiled, as if to suggest, *I can be your father or your husband, or maybe something else.*

I cringed, thinking he might do something worse, maybe even wink. I wondered if there was something about me that asked for the companionship of a husband or a father. Or perhaps it was him, and what he expected or wanted. What he thought I wanted or needed. It was interesting to me because, for the first time, I found a small space in my consciousness, a loophole, perhaps, through which I could slip through. Where I could get away from however it was that he expected me to perform.

The man continued talking. He told me that he had a business in Singapore and travelled often for it. He was a single man looking to settle down, although I wasn't entirely sure I believed that. He had a ring or two on his fingers, but I politely didn't point that out. He told me that I was beautiful and that I was always welcome to contact him if ever in Singapore. He gave me his business card and I took it as a memento, of my first solo ride on a plane, and under such circumstances. He had no idea what I had just been through. I smiled an unfeigned smile and nestled into my seat. Draped a blanket over myself. I was safe for now.

Quatervois

I bumped into Ammu and my siblings at the baggage claim of Toronto Pearson International Airport when the plane landed. I speculated whether they had been on the same flight as me. We didn't say anything to each other, other than Ammu asking how I would get home and suggesting that we could all ride together.

In the taxi, I noticed the streets were just how I had left them. Things seemed to move as they always did — the buses, the crowds, the leaves of trees lining streets.

When we got to our somewhat suburban neighbourhood in North York, I noticed the green leaves of the vines that climbed the house's red bricks had fallen off, the roses on Ammu's lawn were no more, and the snow on the car window had not been cleared.

I knocked. Abbu opened the door with frail hands. He appeared smaller than usual. He probably hadn't eaten or slept for days. His hair was now almost past his chin. The lower half of his face was dotted with grey stubble.

Inside, the house looked like a storm's collateral damage. There were long-distance calling cards scattered all over the floor. The plants were all dead. Photograph frames on the walls and the *almari* collected dust. There was a tower of dishes tilting in the sink, and the beds were unmade.

I entered my old room, a seemingly average teenager's room: clothing over the bed, movie posters on the wall, novels stacked on my night table. I closed the door behind me. When I sat on the bed, it creaked. I titled forward slightly then flung myself backward onto the mattress, which bounced me a little. It was such a relief to be back in my own room.

This bed would be where I would find myself for the next few days, under the duvet with the curtains drawn. It had been so long since I'd been able to navigate space freely that too much of it made me uncomfortable. I heard the floor creak when people moved. I watched the white walls watch me. I breathed. I spoke with no one and no one spoke with me. The betrayal had drained me, and the estrangement left the rooms of the house barren. Still, the house was a busy house. There was noise, despite all that went unspoken.

I remained like this, doing nothing while the world spun around me like a carousel. Underneath my skin I could feel my dying cells. Necrosis. The cell membranes swelling then bursting, one by one. A white noise began to spread. I heard the pulsing of blood vessels at my wrist, even more acutely.

During one of these days, it came to me that in this nothingness I was continually being reduced to, I was also being reborn.

I had thought of Bhav every single day for the last five months, and now that I was back I would finally see him again. I wondered how it would feel to once again have his hands cupping my face. Would the warmth be ferocious and overtaking or would it feel different? How crucial was it, this thing we called touch, that had the power to not only prolong our life but mould our bodies so we anticipate and expect certain possibilities?

I wanted to hear his voice. I didn't have a phone. I didn't want to ask for the password to the home computer so I could send an email. So, I waited by my window every night, hoping Bhav would appear. He would have been notified by the High Commission officials that I had arrived. This time, I would not just talk to him from my window but actually come down to meet him, without caring if anyone saw us. He didn't come.

So, in a few days, I trudged downtown to the University of Toronto, where I was still a student — I hoped. Downtown looked how it always had, steel and concrete. Corporate automata dressed in black and white. Wide-eyed or underslept students, the business-men in their suits, mothers with yoga mats, skateboarders, drag queens, the forgotten homeless. All the people I knew and didn't know had gone about their lives.

At the Registrar's Office I'd have to inquire what my status was. I knew the deadline for a tuition refund had passed. Thousands of dollars that I would have to eventually pay back. I also knew that I probably wouldn't be able to enrol in the current semester or next, that I would probably have to wait a whole year before I could continue my studies. All this I thought with a nagging frustration, as the delay in returning to Canada wasn't my doing and because my education was important to me. I'd always tried hard and done well in school. Still, I had to make do with the situation.

On my way to the Registrar's Office, I stopped at Robarts Library, shuffling through the rotating doors and passing the students flipping pages of their books and scanning their computer screens robotically.

At the computer desk, I opened Internet Explorer and then my email inbox. I took a deep breath. Although I had been awaiting, with great anticipation, for the moment to see Bhav again, I was now at a loss for words. What could I say to him? It was the mere act of writing an email — I had done the same thing almost a year ago here in this library, and the difference between that time and this time seemed so little. Well, maybe I was moving slower these days, second-guessing my thoughts more, having to do double takes at people because a fundamental trust had been broken.

I typed my email to Bhav. I asked him to meet me at the Humber Valley Pond, which was close to where I lived. My hands were clammy against the keyboard, and as I typed I realized that when I thought of Bhav now, I didn't necessarily think of him like my hero or saviour. I was now more concerned with becoming a heroine to myself. The strong instinct to protect, to *live*. A distinct cleaving from what was on the other side of my skin — was it my awareness changing or the reality I was in? A newfound independence, perhaps, or a type of self-preservation.

After, at the Registrar's Office, it was confirmed that I would miss almost a year of university without getting any money back. I clutched my paperwork and left. Outside, I looked back at the entrance. How many futures did this institution and these university employees shape without ever truly knowing the person's circumstances? More than ever, I felt like a number. As I watched the students pass by, looking ahead as if they were following a very straight line, one by one, walking behind one another on the street, I wanted to touch the space between them. My surroundings seemed two-dimensional, like flat paper. Then there was a light tug of determination. I would find a way to complete my education no matter what.

∞

When I saw Bhav sitting on the park bench from afar, I ran through the snow toward him. When I reached the bench, he stood up and we hugged. He then picked me up and twirled me around. "I am so happy to see you again!"

As we twirled around, his warm breath on my face, I did feel as if I had found a part of myself that had been stored away for a while. The discovery of an old dusty box with keepsakes under the bed, or in your dresser. Somehow, however, there was a sadness. That part was either gone or had changed, and so the joy I felt at the discovery was rather fleeting.

I thought that perhaps the trees surrounding us would bow down. I thought the spiral arm of winter's milky way would wrap around our bodies to keep us warm. That the smoke from the chimneys would dance in the sky in the shape of figure skaters. Our arms would intertwine like branches of a wreath. The joy of a magical winter evening and the joy of two lovers reunited.

Such didn't happen. Yes, the season had changed, and the nights were now pale. Bhav still tasted like roasted coffee, the type that would give me solace when waking up every morning. Indeed, and without doubt, this was a comfort very specific and individual. For me alone. Yet, the rush toward him hit more like the rocks along the shoreline than the ocean's water itself — there was a certain durability but still some erosion. Surges slowed. He and I had endured together such a tragic event. In this test, we had made it back to each other. Yet, what did *back to each other* mean? I didn't even know who I was anymore.

I saw in his beard a couple of shiny strands, which I pulled out. "It has been five months and you've already gone grey."

He laughed and I thought, *This man is so beautiful. I remember why I was so crazy about him.* I wanted to tell him then everything I had seen and felt. Would it make sense to him? Would it scare him away?

"We haven't lost the battle," Bhav declared.

To which I nodded. "Do you think we will make it? Where do we go from here?" I asked.

"What we've always done. Hold on," Bhav said.

"For how long?" I asked him.

"However long it is," Bhav assured me. "We won't lose this battle."

The cold breeze that slid toward us and rested on our cheeks was a stark awakening — I no longer saw it this way, this *us against the world*, although in Dhaka I might have felt that.

"Will you tell anyone?" Bhav asked, peering into my eyes. "About what happened to you?"

I shook my head. "Maybe to a couple of my friends, but no one else."

"Well, you know I'll always be here for you," he said.

When I left, Bhav's words were like drumbeats at the base of my ears. I was glad to be back. However, in the solace, there was still a lingering dissension.

During one of these early days after my return, I went with Bhav to his friend's home. His friend had recently married his girlfriend, and Bhav wanted the same for himself. I knew this by what Bhav had said during the short stroll we took in the park near this friend's home, and the beautiful ceramic ornament he had given me of two white doves joined by the beaks.

"Birds symbolize peace, but also transformation," he said. "I want us to grow together. We can put this on the shelf of our future home that we will build together."

Our future home, he'd said.

Bhav held my hand, my fingers intertwined with his, and I shuddered like the surrounding aspens that shook their leaves. My skin suddenly stiff like bark.

"I have to finish school, and about us —" I said, almost stuttering.

"Yes, of course," he replied.

I didn't elaborate then on some thoughts I had been having about going on to do a master's degree after completing my undergraduate. I was considering becoming a therapist.

Bhav's eyes dropped then to the grass, but all I could feel in my chest were all the tumbling buildings ever bombed in the name of faith or love. As we stood there, Bhav's fingers framing a side of my face, I almost tipped over.

"You don't look too well." He wrapped his wool jacket around me and took me back inside his friend's home, where the social gathering was still going on. My eyelids opened and closed, closed and opened. I heard Bhav in the next room after, with the other people. I couldn't make out the speech; there were whispers and then laughter. Who was there and what were they saying? Suddenly the tan walls of the living room pushed in and against my lungs. "Stop!" I yelled, and he came in running.

"Nothing is right," I said.

"You're safe," Bhav said. "I'm here, I'm here. We will make it."

I thought, *I'm not the same. I'm not the same.*

On our drive back, I did not say much, just looked out the passenger window at the bleak roads. Then the strangest thing happened. I saw a floating ball of light in my periphery. It beckoned me to follow it across the road and I wanted to. If I did, I would gain access to a certain truth. I felt so close to it yet so far, as if it just slid through my fingers before I could clutch it.

"I thought," I heard Bhav say, "that you would have fun. Be happy. You just always seem down."

His voice interrupted my concentration on the ball of light. It went away.

"I don't know what it is. I just feel sad," I replied. I didn't go on to explain any more than that.

Bhav and I knew we still owed some money to the High Commission of Canada, but we hadn't received any instruction. So, Bhav wrote them a letter:

From: ██████████████████████████████ ████████████

Sent: December 7, 2005, 11:04 PM
To: ████████████████████████
Subject: Important

██████████████████████ this is ██████████████████,
I recently opened a case for Sumaiya Matin she was in Bangladesh and in need of the embassy's services to get her to a safe place. She stayed at a hotel and we owe you guys around 2600.00. I spoke with ████████ a few weeks ago and she said she was going to mail me a bill indicating the remaining funds we owe and how to pay it. It's been at least 2 weeks now and I haven't received anything. And today Sumaiya has told me that her house received a phone call of someone saying we owe them the remaining funds … we are both worried that interest is being added on and we can't make payments because I haven't received any bill.

I will also forward you the letter I sent ████████ on November 23.

My address again is ████████████████████████

██ █████████████████

My cell number is ████████████

Sumaiya's Cell number is ████████████

Can you please look into this for me and please email me back as soon as possible?

From: ████████████████████
Sent: December 8, 2005, 2:34 PM
To: ████████████████
Subject: RE: Important

Dear ████████,

Thank you for your e-mail. I am aware of Sumaiya's situation and the outstanding bills. I will speak to our accounts section right away and advise they contact you directly. I will also ensure that phone calls and bills are not directed to Sumaiya or her home, but to you at the mailing address provided below.

Sincerely,

████████████████

We waited tensely. Neither of us had the money. I strived to keep much of this away from Ammu and Abbu for fear of further stressing them about the situation. The distance I espoused may have felt like a coldness, but that was what we needed to establish a boundary; me around my faith in particular and how it was interwoven with my individuality.

Then and beyond, I began a deep quest, learning about all religions and the ways that people could extricate themselves from the world, which, to me, seemed temporary and added to the sneaking discomfort that wouldn't quite go away. I also began hopping houses, living in different places, staying in the homes of friends. Eventually I contacted the university administration to discuss my situation and intention to get into graduate school. I was able to live in residence for about six months, and to pay for living expenses I worked multiple jobs: teaching, research, and legal administration.

It was during this time, as I tried to put my life together, bring about a certain stability in the present while focusing on my future aspirations, that I watched as I took care of myself as if my survival depended on it. It sometimes took me longer to discern more clearly what I had seen or heard. To feel safe, protected. There had been an injury, and I was coping.

The High Commission of Canada got back to Bhav and I. Apparently there had been some sort of a mistake in our payments.

ATTN: ▮▮▮▮▮▮▮▮▮▮

Below is the receipt Sumaiya received on January 20th 2006. I think I may have miss lead you when I told you Toronto passport office … I checked the website just now and she actually went to the North York office located at Suite 380, 3rd Floor

Joseph Shepard Building, 4900 Yonge Street. I'm really sorry, I said Toronto, I'm just so familiar with it I assumed it was the only one in Toronto. I think that's why you didn't see a record of payment.

Sumaiya is going to make another 1000.00 payment this Friday February 3rd at the same location. They told her to tell the guard that she has to make a "repatriation payment" and the guard will direct her. I hope that everything is ok now; once again I'm really sorry for saying Toronto.

From: ███████████████████████
██████████

Sent: January 20, 2006, 23:09
To: █████████████████
Subject: Our First Payment

Hey ███████ it's ███████████████ again, today on January 20, 2006 Sumaiya went to the passport office in Toronto and made our first payment toward our bill. We made a payment of 1000.00 dollars and they told her that they don't know when you guys will get the money but we made the payment today. Sumaiya received a receipt and I will feel more comfortable faxing you a copy is this fax number correct ████████████████
██████████

They also said that they wouldn't be able to tell her the remaining funds next time we make a payment they told her that we'd have to ask you to find out the remaining funds. We plan to make 500$ payments every 2 weeks, my concern is that as of tomorrow interest will be charged and we are worried that we won't know what exactly we'll have to pay because the interest will be added on. What's the best way for us to make payments and know our remaining?

Thank you for everything,
█████████

We were informed that the debt we owed was around $2785. It was our utmost priority then to pay it all off. Gathering the money and making the arrangements to pay was an inconvenience to say the least, but we were grateful that we had had the help of the High Commission of Canada, that I had made it out of Bangladesh safely. That was really all that truly mattered. During these challenging times, I often found Bhav distraught, despite his having it together for the most part.

One night, he called me in the middle of the night. It was from somewhere where there were a lot of people outside. It sounded as if he was maybe on his knees, fighting the urge to throw up certain parts of himself.

"Today I had a fight with my brother. I broke his chin, because I couldn't break anything else."

I was under the duvet and using the new cellphone I had purchased. It was noisy. The wall clock ticking, the slight buzzing of the electric table alarm, the wind hitting the window.

"And you, well, I want to see you planning for our future, as if you want to be my wife. But you're still crying about the past. Just move on from Bangladesh. Fuck!"

As Bhav yelled into the phone I could only see a snapshot of that moment: me, under my duvet, and Bhav, in some park, a drunken mess. I couldn't connect this snapshot to events of a few months ago, or even a few years. If I tried, I would certainly get a headache. I longed to just feel like a *whole person*, to follow my string of experiences to a place that made sense or was somewhat grounded. But there was no string. I was floating, hearing the pronounced wall clock ticks and the slight buzzing of the electric table alarm.

"Okay," I said.

"I went in front of a mosque today. I yelled, 'Fuck all religion!' I hate these *jihadis* and bombers killing people and fucking up the world."

Perhaps I should have felt something more in response to these words Bhav spoke, but somehow I'd understood this would happen, and to an extent I could comprehend why he said what he did. I, too, hated the bombers who killed in the name of religion, but it was the thought of Bhav tying this to what had happened to me that blanketed the rest of my mind in a cold chill. As if the reason *jihadis* killed people was the same reason my wedding had occurred, as if violence were somehow implicit to Islam, which it was not. I needed him to see faith separately, the way I did. I hoped he'd understand my *Muslimness*, and not just tolerate it. Whatever it meant to me, that was.

I imagined Bhav wiping his mouth with his sleeve. On the other end of the phone, I heard the clanks of bottles. His drinking was becoming increasingly intolerable. I had never been comfortable with it; it was always something distant from my world but somehow deeply associated with his. I could see he was in pain, like I was, but I asked myself what I was supposed to do — acquiesce, ignore, or more clearly name that what was happening was not okay? It was clear: we both needed help.

As I listened to his heavy breathing on the other end of the line, I heard the echoes of Sweety Khala's voice in my ears. "Punjabi men like to drink. What if he becomes an alcoholic?" I shook my head at the stereotype, and now, I shook my head to get rid of her *I told you so* voice. Voices merged onto a single plane and I heard them all at the same time.

My dreams at night had become much more frequent, and somewhat terrifying. In one of them, I was walking through a yard. There was an orchestra of crickets surrounding me. Against the night's light, everything looked like charcoal etchings, even the fireflies passing by. I came to the middle of a field, about eight feet long and three feet wide, bordered by albino redwoods.

I fell onto my knees, then started digging into the ground with my nails, which felt like claws, with a hostility I'd never experienced before, tasting the flying dirt that landed in my mouth. When the hole in the ground was large enough, I toppled over and into it. I shut my heavy eyelids.

"What's your name?" I heard but I could not answer. I believe I was about to climb out.

I thought the answer was easy, yet I couldn't quite recall. A thousand pins in my brain hitting nerves, a sharp then dull sting, then the lightness of heavy fog.

"I don't know," I said.

The albino tree branches caved in and swayed. I felt hair strands across my face.

This is how I awoke, my forehead warm and my hair tangled. I tiptoed out of the room, squinting the whole way, searching for specks of light, arms outstretched to befriend objects, walls, people, really anything in the way. I woke up in the living room, where I found Rayleigh hues splattered across the grey canvas of the sky: reds, blues, yellows, and oranges. The sun commanding everything as it rose.

One day Bhav was driving, and I was in the passenger seat. He gripped the steering wheel tight with his left hand, his right laying loosely on his thigh. The road we were on was made of bumps and holes. My whole body juddered as I looked out the passenger seat window: streetcars with red-and-white markings, swarms of people in lines and crowds holding coffee cups and clutches, buildings old and new, reddish-brown or pewter hues, other cars, some bikes. A whirlwind around us.

We were having the same conversation we'd had many times before. *You're just not the same anymore.*

I could tell Bhav was distressed. He had lost his job and was going back to school to start a completely new career. His mother's mental health was also getting worse. However, these were all things he could express only through a short temper, which reminded me not just of Boro Mama, but the anger in me that I had disowned.

"So," I asked again, "can we please try to talk?"

Bhav's nonresponse filled the car.

"Please tell me," I pleaded.

He clutched the gear tightly. The flames in my core rose up to my throat and I remembered again what it was like to not be heard. In that moment, perhaps I didn't care whether or not the car crashed at all.

"Listen to me!" I shouted.

He lifted his hand from the gear and pushed my head. My face hit against the window. It didn't have to hurt physically to hurt. On the other side was still an inappropriate normality: streetcars with red-and-white markings, swarms of people in lines and crowds holding coffee cups and clutches, buildings old and new, reddish-brown or pewter hues, other cars, some bikes. A whirlwind around us. Car horns honking, tire wheels screeching, people shouting. On my forehead, a tender patch. The passing thought: *Who are you?*

"Take me home," I demanded.

When the car stopped, I kept looking at his profile, a cut-out from the background of a dark evening. He turned from ahead to my face with a drilling stare. I quickly shifted my line of sight to my lap. I squinted as I looked up.

Then I saw the two sides of his face split apart and come together again like a double exposure photograph. I blinked with the suddenness of a camera shutter. How strange it was, to see him this way, divided, and in between there was a kernel of truth. Had I been seeing him accurately all this time?

It is said that one form of sorcery is trying to break two lovers apart; making a person think their lover has become someone else. Suddenly, they don't know who the person is anymore. Their face changes, as does their nature. The person can no longer feel love, just a sudden estrangement and a little bit of fear. Had Shoaib or Boro Mama or some other person in Dhaka who had felt betrayed put a curse on mine and Bhav's future? Were there ill-intentioned jinns interfering? The thought crossed my mind, but I pulled it back. It wasn't that, it was something else, and I felt I should find out. How was it that a person so close could suddenly become a stranger, and just like that?

I moved my right hand to the car door and floundered with the knob; it was stuck. My other hand sat composed, delicate on my lap, within the creases of my scrunched yellow skirt. The rest of my body inert. The air in my lungs travelled up and then down again, stuck midway. I needed to get away from him. Who was he to me anymore? He was the same as all of them, my family, the people at my school, the government, everyone. I pushed the door. It flew open and I jumped out of my seat. I ran for two blocks without looking back. Quicker and quicker, my boots clickety clacketing, matching the panting of my breath.

The leaves on the big trees appearing vacant, as if the green had been sucked out and all that was left was a vague greyness, the lights of the houses dimming, the world slowing. The night wanted to sleep. I could no longer see. I didn't know where I was at all, on the side of some nowhere street.

I eventually stopped running and found myself on the bench of a nearby park. I lay on it, sinking into a fetal position, my spine curved forward half-moon, knees up, two arms together against my chest. I tucked myself into the blanket of darkness.

I was back here with him, the man I had longed for for months, and who had helped me back to safety. But he seemed like someone else. The realization that filled me with a desperate, yearning sadness and a very specific kind of grief. I no longer wanted him.

In the weeks that followed, I saw Boro Mama again, not in my nightmares but as a memory that insisted on inserting itself into every thought I had throughout the day, as if my mind instinctively understood his authority and committed itself to carrying out his bidding. When his image conjured itself, I, too, scrunched my eyebrows like his, clenched my teeth just the same. I tried at times to walk like him, too, wide strides. As if all space, any space, was mine to take. I pulled my shoulders back, raised my chin, raised my two arms above my head, to grab the anger, which followed me like a cloud everywhere I went. I grabbed it because I could, because in his hands anger was exalted, in his hands it was dignified. Whereas in mine it was out of place. But I was now him.

As I took my steps like his, I mimicked his words, "These are the rules." I laid down the rules with my hands out on the wooden table, then pounded it, as if not to care that anyone heard. Then I'd thrash the same table against the wall with a deafening scream. The chair's spine would crackle into smithereens. *Ha,* I thought, *and without any consequence.* Like him, I also lit a cigarette, held it between my fingers, angled it to the ground, let the smoke fill the space. Then I brought the cigarette to my lips.

How did Bhav feel about it? Perhaps confused. He was more careless with his words, negligent even, but yet couldn't seem to fathom why I was so immersed in myself, my every thought and emotion no longer focused on catering to him. He missed the girl who saw him as the beginning and the end of all matters of the heart. How great it must've been for him to see himself through my youthful eyes. And then I started wearing the shortest halter dresses I could find, open back, barely reaching mid-thigh, stilettos that added three or four inches to my height, and painting my lips blood red. When music came through the speakers, I pointedly swayed my waist recklessly to the bass. I was suddenly overcome with a ferocious desire to test the limits of my very own mortality, to live uninhibited. This was how I was supposed to free myself, apparently, as a woman. Yet, despite the thrust of activity, of taking every opportunity, of trying to think differently, I still felt *uncured*. So, on a trip to Italy, at the Piazza del Campo, I sat with the blue- and green-eyed people who were all bare-backed and pouring wine. On the red brick pavement, I looked up at the vast sky and Tuscan landscape and thought, *Where within me is home?*

Later, in a bar in Italy, I sat at the wooden table with a glass of water in my hands. The girls I met on the trip were also students, curious, carefree, and smart. They left the place late, walked the dark alleyways, found their way to the hotels of their new lovers with little help. I remained there, soon after dancing, Italian music blasting and overtaking my body like the darkness of the night outside of the sienna pub walls. Did Bhav know the British boy I danced with wasn't the one I wanted? I pulled away, he pulled me back again, and I stormed out, bewildered by what I had done.

After I flew back to Canada and agreed to meet Bhav at our usual bridge at the Getaway, he asked, "How could you betray me?"

"Like your words did," I searched his eyes to find the part I still knew, but instead found my own reflection. I looked different.

We both turned our faces to the cascades before us. I could see the traces of tears on his face, and he saw mine, too. He put his hand in his pocket and pulled out two pennies.

"Here." He handed one to me. "Let's make wishes together. Because, you know, we'll make it."

I reached my arm out to grab the penny, but instead pulled his hand and brought him closer to me. I dug my face into his chest with force, mussing my hair. He returned the embrace.

"Would you consider therapy?" I asked Bhav.

"Okay, I don't know who your friends are these days," he replied.

"What do you mean?"

"You sound whiter by the day. Therapy? I don't need to pay a stranger to tell me how to live my life."

I thought, *I'll do anything to make things right again.*

It was important for me to become more of an agent in my own life.

I made my way to therapy, all the way from St. George and Bloor, passing all the cafés, alternative health stores, independent video and record shops, and vintage clothing swaps. When I passed Koreatown, whiffs of *japchae, bulgogi,* and *hoeddeok* overtook me like a spell; I, immersed in my solitude and its irresistible taste.

The name of the therapist I was going to see was Amna, and she was of South Asian descent and Muslim. It was possible she had Indian or Pakistani heritage. I never asked. She specialized in brief treatment modalities, including grief recovery, which she paired often with psychodynamic, open-ended psychotherapy. She was not new to the field, nor was she a veteran.

When I reached her office, I took a seat in the waiting room. I sat on a wooden chair with uncomfortable padding and stared at the corkboard ahead of me. I read the text on the pinned business cards and on the flyers, all advertising programs and services to unlock a better life. Beside me, there was a soggy mat with a pair of boots. I imagined it belonged to Amna's other client, the one whose murmurs I could hear from down the hall, on the other side of the closed office door. I looked at my watch and tapped my fingers on my thigh.

When I got inside, Amna welcomed me in. I said my pleasantries, as did she. We did our introductions. After which I poured out everything and concluded with, "The thing that stands between him and I is his *manhood*, you know, his silence or maybe his pride. But I can tell he is suffering. How can I help him and help him help me if he won't even let me and just blames me for everything?"

Amna, in her therapist chair, nodded away.

It became a ritual, two times a week, taking this walk along the road, finding myself plotted on Amna's grey couch, telling her everything. About Dhaka, and about Bhav and I. I had found her name on the internet, and as a brown Muslim woman, I thought she would understand. Low-pitched in tone, and gentle in her movements, there was a tranquility about her that allowed me to believe everything was manageable.

Whenever I stood on the prayer mat — the one I had was made of velvet, black and gold, rather symmetrical, and with the *mihrab* sitting neatly at the top, pointed toward Mecca — my toes would sink into the warp and weft, and all else would fade. And in *sujud*, when I brought my forehead to the ground, a sense of calm would wash over me like a lavender shower, loosening my muscles, relaxing my breath. I would think then how grateful I was to be alive, to be safe again. There must have been a purpose — and not just for me but for everyone else.

However, as the months passed I sometimes could not help but ask, *How could You let this happen?* On the prayer mat, when I stood, my eyes closed, I almost fell over. In *sujud*, with my forehead on the ground, I could only hear the grinding of my teeth.

I wondered if Allah truly did love me, for some tribulations seemed far too long or great. However, I didn't want to be severed from what I innately knew, despite the spiritual abuse I had both witnessed and experienced. I remembered Iblis, who closed the chambers to his wildfire heart. For me not to end up the same way, and feel Allah's love as unrequited, I had to try harder to remember all the ways I had been blessed, privileged. I was alive, I was breathing.

"And I'm sorry," I told the sky, "for the times I may have forgotten you, or didn't trust you. For the ways I may have wronged, despite having the best of intentions."

It was hard to say these words; they gnawed my teeth as I released them, and the soot that had begun cloaking my heart crawled into my throat. However, something deep inside told me that I should try my best to surrender to what was happening. As I stood on the velvety fibres, the white rayon curtains with royal-blue floral print fluttered, and the scent of tulips and lilies crept through the room. I breathed it in with the morning sun. The floor's mahogany wood blushed a deeper tone. The room was smitten by the sun's morning flirt.

I told Amna, "If I express my anger, it comes back to my own shortcoming. And if he is angry, he says it's because I made him this way. Why can't I be angry at him? Why can't I be angry, period?"

I rubbed my eyes. The office was like a nineteenth-century apartment: semi-dark lighting, an ivory carpet patterned in Bakshayesh Herati, replicas of Victorian artifacts, cherry-oak shelves with dozens of books, and a feathery fern enclosed in a Wardian case. Amna herself had matching black-rimmed glasses and a dark-brown bob. The ambience of sophistication in the lap of comfort.

"We were so attuned once, as if he could often read my mind. Now there's estrangement," I told her.

"The ruptures we feel in our relationships, when abrupt or strange, leave us struggling to make ourselves whole again. They take a big toll," she replied. "Do you think you are seeing who he is *now*?"

I looked down at my feet. Underneath, I thought I saw tectonic plates shifting and the flames of the Darvaza crater, rising up to me.

"Well, do you feel safe with him? Do you want to be with him?" Amna raised one eyebrow, her thin lips like pungent red chili.

"I don't know," I replied. "It's hard for me now, to feel safe. And who he is now — it's disappointing. After everything we have been through, after the way I had longed for him."

I fixed my gaze on the white wall behind Amna and did not move or say anything for a minute. I was stock-still, like the woman I had met in Bangladesh.

Then, I blinked, and Amna leaned in, pulling me back into her face as she said, "Tell me what he means to you, as a lover, and nothing else."

One night I called Bhav. Told him I needed him as my whole body rattled, my head in my hands.

"It's this feeling I get, as if I'll be left in a dark room with no way out. And I can't see anything."

"Again, this Muslim thing," he shouted.

It hit me then that perhaps I had relied on him too much, to the extent that my *yaqin* had diminished.

∞

"Your sadness and tears seem to mourn the loss of something very important to you. They express the yearning for what's gone to come back." Amna handed me a tissue.

I wiped my eyes.

"I believe you sought your father in him, when your father withdrew his love. Then your mother in some ways. You were left with a very strange choice. You could have your mother, or your father, or him, but not all. Perhaps, as you're seeing yourself more for yourself, you're also seeing more of who Bhav is."

One day Bhav called me and said he really wanted to talk. I remember the mist on the car window; I dragged the tip of my finger across it. And then I saw on the other side of the smudged window, dancing glittery graupel.

This meeting wasn't too long after the day I tripped and fell on the downtown Toronto pavement. I had called Bhav to tell him I had just gotten into graduate school. He yelled so loud all the passersby could hear.

"We are supposed to get married and just move on, like everybody else." He sounded like Boro Mama, stern and disappointed that I wasn't moving in the direction and at the speed he saw fit. "If I'm not in your future, then you can fuck yourself."

I wanted to tell him then that I felt vulnerable in my womanhood, that I needed to experience its strength before I could relate to him again. Something about it had been deeply endangered, almost taken away, like a poached pearl. I wanted to protect myself because I wasn't sure a man really could.

I opened my lips to tell him, but it was right about then that I fell on the pavement, the phone still in my hand.

Bhav laughed, then said nothing. I thought, *I mustn't ever show him any weakness at all.* That's how it began, the heart closing, and my commitment to not let him become the reason for the full extent of my happiness.

But then, on that foggy night, he said, "It's just that I tried my best to fix you, but I couldn't."

I finally saw it: Bhav's mouth forming the same shapes, his fingers fidgeting, and his distant eyes as if he was looking at someone else. I thought, *You're talking about your mother, aren't you? Everything you said.*

Bhav was fighting the urge to rescue me, and then, right then, I was certain that I didn't want to rescue him, either. We both needed help that we couldn't give to each other. Even if we were both already whole, fully realized adult human beings, we needed to find it for ourselves independently. My journey was mine alone, however much I loved Bhav. And I did love him.

There was a story Abbu told me often. Folklore, if you could call it that. It was the story of two young lovers, a village girl and a village boy. The young girl told the boy to prove his love, and he responded that he would do anything. The girl decided to test him, so she asked him to rip out his mother's heart and bring it to her on a platter. The boy contemplated her request for a couple of days, for he was conflicted. His mother would only live for a few more years, but he could have a whole future with the girl.

One day his mother found him at the gates of their straw hut looking distraught and distant. She asked him, "What's wrong, my son?"

The son looked up at his mother's concerned face.

She continued, "You know I love you more than anything in this entire world. Whatever it is you need I will give it to you. Tell me how you are doing, because you seem distressed these days."

The young boy didn't respond at first. He looked at his scrawny feet, now muddied. "I am fine," he muttered.

That night, in the midst of villagers' snores and howling animals nearby, he tiptoed out of his bed and across the yard to his mother's hut, where she lay in sound slumber. He towered over her. She was an angel wrapped in her white cotton sari. She didn't have a husband. The boy didn't have a father. Mother and son had raised the animals and crops on their farm together. Her cheekbones carried a sort of defiance — defiance of a world that denied her joy merely because she was a widow. She was like the character Bali from the renowned book *Choker Bali* written by Tagore. Bali was a widow who had taught herself to read English, despite her lower position in society. Similarly, this boy's mother nurtured joy despite her fate, like she did the farm, with her son by her side.

The young boy imagined his mother dreaming of corn fields underneath a blazing sun — a life of abundance. Then, slowly, he drew out the butcher knife sitting between his belt and bare back. He wished that she remained in her peaceful state permanently and then uttered, "I'm sorry, Mother."

With that, the butcher knife came raging down into his mother's chest. The sacrifice would be like the sacrifice of Prophet Abraham, except that he would do it for the love of a woman, who he then saw as God.

The next day, he found his lover by a willow tree, carving her name in the bark. She turned to look at him when he entered with a silver platter covered with a red cloth.

"What's that?" she asked.

The boy removed the cloth to show his mother's now dark violet-red heart sitting at the centre of the silver platter.

The young girl gasped in terror. "What did you do?"

"I did this for you," he explained.

"I don't want you. I was only joking." She strutted away.

"Wait, you said that you would —"

He ran after her, and she yelled, "Murderer, murderer!"

He lost her, but then later found her at his doorstep with other villagers. They all dragged him out, including her, and then shoved his head through looped rope. The boy was hanged.

The boy had lacked empathy for his mother. He focused instead on how the girl had betrayed him. As if all of his actions were predetermined by women and he had no free will.

How I left Bhav was gradual and sudden. I felt we had already left each other by the time I finally forced myself to do it, by moving to another city, as everything reminded me of him. It was the only way to make peace with this decision I had made, based on the realization of what I already knew: my faith was integral to me, and so was my self-respect. These things I could never compromise, no matter how alone I felt. It would only hurt him and I to hold on. Like I walked away in Dhaka, I'd walk away again, however excruciating, to live by the values, the principles that made up who I was. It was a vow I made to myself.

In the new city, away from every familiar face, it was still a tug of war getting myself on the prayer mat some days. One of the mornings, just a few minutes after *fajr* prayer time started and the room was still a pitch-black, I woke to the sudden feeling that someone was standing over me. My heavy arms and legs were being pulled off the bed and onto the ground. It wasn't a sinister presence, no, just a gentle observance and perhaps reminder. I thought then, *I should get up.* So, after *wudu*, I found myself on the prayer mat. I said, "Dear Allah, he is gone, as are so many other things that I thought perhaps would stay the same. Dear Allah, if there is one thing I wish, it's to have you in my heart always and to never leave, to strengthen my ability to intuit the signs of what I need to do." I rested my head on the *mihrab*, deducing that our desires in life are never stronger than what Allah wills.

Duniya Ke Kone /
Corners of the World
(दुनिया के कोने)

One day I visited the Chokhi Dhani Village in the pink city of Jaipur, India. I was volunteering at a local non-governmental organization that supported Delhi street children. On this particular day I was wearing a black-and-red *ghaghra choli* with *shisha* work, mica mirrors handstitched in cotton, which trapped with their specular reflection the evil eye of onlookers. On my arms were matching red bangles.

I had bought the ensemble a few days prior in a market in the city for a hefty price. The shop was owned by a local man who appeared to be in his late forties with rusty bronze hair and one bronze tooth. When I walked in he stood in the middle of the room, his two arms wide open, as if he'd just met his long-lost sister.

He walked me over to a stool facing multiple large wooden shelves standing side by side, with an assortment of garments folded and packaged in plastic. From the ceiling with the hasty fan hung a long rope, which spanned across the room. On the rope were sample garments for show: a caramel *kameez zardozi*, embroidered with gold thread and sequins, a fuchsia tie-dye sari, a long red cotton and silk *kurta* with patchwork techniques, and the black-and-red *shisha ghaghra choli*.

When I reached to touch the *ghaghra choli* the man said, "That's a special one, to ward off the evil eye."

I looked at the dress, intrigued.

"You're not from here, are you?" he asked.

I told him I had come from Canada, to which he chuckled and said, "Then you definitely must not believe in what I just said. But the irony of it is, Westerners don't know anything themselves."

I smiled, then turned my attention to the royal-blue cotton crepe fabric spread across the bed-like cushioned structure on which the man stood.

"You could be right. It could be true," I told him.

"Have you been, madam, to the home of Mariam-uz-Zamani? The wife of great Emperor Akbar. It is not too far from here."

"Yes, I will be going there soon," I told him.

"Their love, it was a grand story, the coming together of two cultures and two faiths, and it only benefited the Indian economy." The man pulled from his shelves three or four plastic packages holding the sequined saris. He unpacked the saris and laid them on the bed. I placed my fingers over the *Maharani* sari, the peacock spreading its golden sequins plumage.

"Sometimes it just doesn't work out that way," I muttered. "Anyway, I am sure it was also a political alliance that motivated the acceptance of that relationship."

I was surprised at how jaded I sounded.

"The trouble with Westerners, they have such little faith."

"Well, you're open-minded. I didn't quite expect that. What can I say? I guess I've just learned that it's hard to build anything pure when the basis is bloodshed."

"Are you talking about what the white people started?" he asked me.

"Oh, yes, but you know everyone plays a part. We're all part of this mess now."

I bought the *shisha ghaghara choli* from the insightful shop owner, who understood colonialism and imperialism without ever probably knowing any academic institution. I thanked him for his service and was on my way to the village of Chokhi Dhani.

Chokhi Dhani was rather touristy. Yet, I couldn't help but revel in the Rajasthani folk dances. The women were also wearing *shisha* and had *ornas* draped over their faces. They swung their hips from side to side, performing *Kalbeliya* and *Nagin* dances. I revelled also in the brick masonry that enveloped me, made partly of traditional cow dung, and the murals that hung on the walls made of relief, stained in geru, ochre, and white clay. In the dining room, called *chaupad jeeman ghar*, I sat on a straw mat, saw palm leaves plastered on the walls. The roof was made of bamboo net. I rolled the *dhaal* soaked rice with my fingers on the palm leaf plate, the aromatic spice blend — cardamom, turmeric, cumin, and whiffs of ginger — soaking the roof of my nose and my mouth.

After the meal, I remember passing by the blue pottery *Koftgari* art and puppet making, until I saw a lone man sitting by a stall with *barmeri* cloth for sale. He gestured me toward him, and at first I avoided him, but then I was compelled to hear what he had to say.

"I have to tell you something very important," he said. His moustache was black, the ends twirled upward. He was wearing a plain *dhoti kurta* and a multi-coloured *pagri*. With a rather pensive face, he investigated the curiosity in my eyes. Who was this person and what would he say?

"The sorcerer's knots, you are bound by them," he continued. "Someone close to you is holding you back from change, from movement. From love, from marriage."

The words from his mouth tasted familiar in mine, and as his glower grew I stood there frozen. I remembered then the Shayṭān Bride, how she stayed stuck and could not *move on*.

It is true that I sometimes felt like I remained in the same moments, feelings, and thoughts, despite years having gone by. Every decision I took felt as heavy as the one I had made in Dhaka. I wondered, *Where is she now, the Shayṭān Bride?*

"What do I have to do? To untie the knots? To move?" I asked the stranger.

He took a moment to fix his *paghri*.

"Tell me when and where you were born," he instructed as he ripped a white piece of paper from his tatty notebook and pulled out a ballpoint pen. "It will, however, cost you a few rupees."

I scrunched the sides of my skirt. It wasn't acceptable in Islam to have your fortune read by third parties. However, I was curious, so I agreed and handed a few rupees to him.

He accepted them with one hand while he scribbled with the other. He mumbled indecipherable words under his breath. After a few minutes, maybe five, he took the paper and folded it as if doing origami. Each fold left my breath heavier and back sweatier. I wanted to know the secret to truly moving in flow, like *barakah* when it touched a person.

He finally handed it to me and said sternly, "Do not open this."

My eyes opened wide and I asked, "Why not? How will I know the answer?"

"Keep this for seven days, and without opening it. Then, on the seventh day, find a body of water, water that moves like a stream, a river, or the sea. Not water that's held down in a perfect container by gravity. When you find the moving water, put the paper in it while reciting a prayer. Let the water take the paper away."

I listened to him intently, nodded, then went away.

Over the next seven days, I thought of this paper that I carried in my purse. Conflicted, because I knew that no third party could necessarily know the truth of my soul, especially not a human, and that this would be considered *shirk*. I thought whether or not I should let the paper go, maybe fly away like the papers that flew around in the corners of Delhi slums.

I decided to bury it. One day as I walked over to and past an old lady who sat on the steps of Jama *Masjid*. I buried the paper in a small hole in the ground, then gave the woman, the witness to the act, a few rupees.

I settled my restless heart into her wrinkles when I asked her for her prayers; a respite for me at the time. I could have taken the paper with the prayers, found a way back to the Shaytān Bride, and given it to her, but I didn't. I thought perhaps what would be more important was the story I'd try to tell.

I didn't know that only a few years later, India would pass a law that would discriminate against Muslims by granting citizenship to all religious minorities except them. I didn't know that the United States of America, founded on values of freedom and opportunity, would do a similar thing, banning travel from Muslim majority countries to the U.S. Later I would wonder how my experience in

India would have perhaps been different, knowing anti-Muslim immigration sentiments were rising even there. I would wonder if it was 1947 again. And I'd wonder again if we had come any way at all, in all these years. Still, I'd remember my conversation with the local store owner in Jaipur, and the mysterious fortune teller man. I'd remember the unique ways the architecture, customs, and languages had blended difference. The stories of Nana, Nani, Ammu, and her elder siblings swimming in the rivers to Malda, simply having fun.

Revolving Doors

It was a strange homecoming when I saw Bhav again, familiar yet as if I was meeting him for the first time. It was 2013, and I had just returned to Toronto after completing my master's of social work in Windsor. The idea to reconnect came to me when I passed by the Getaway during a drive.

The last Bhav had crossed my mind was during the tumultuous period where my stored anger would erupt like lava — sporadic, scorching — flashbacks that would hit like meteorites, damaging whatever sense of normalcy I had. For years I remained angry at the strange situation I had been in: that in order for him to feel seen, I had to validate the pain he was expressing through abuse and, in doing so, minimize myself and normalize what was not right. This was not the face of love. I could no longer carry others' feelings — I had to focus on mine. Perhaps I was expected to be selfless as a woman, but I hoped Bhav and everyone else around me could understand that my selfishness, my own self love, would be how we'd all survive through this. Loving myself would preserve the humanity we had left. So, this grief that I experienced like natural disasters was tied to difficult decisions that involved a disentangling of myself from all those I loved more than life itself. The boundaries I drew were important for containing the *ghadab* (intense anger) there was, the type that destroyed the highest of characters and damaged the best of relationships — which is what the Shayṭān probably wanted.

So, all this accompanied me while I gulped Red Bull into the late hours of the night as I was writing term papers and when I ran group therapy at a women's shelter.

Just to say hello. I can see how he is doing, I thought. But why? I didn't know.

We met at Tim Hortons. I waited at the window seat. I noticed it was raining outside. The ambience of the place was the usual, laid-back and casual. Stereotypically Canadian. Top-100 musical hits through the speakers, customers dressed in everything from sneakers to stiletto boots. People rolling up rims to win, biting into grilled cheese sandwiches, and sipping iced caps while they pressed on their laptop keys with haste. I perused the room until Bhav strolled in.

He looked as he always had, except with a few more lines on his face and pounds around his belly. He sat across from me. It was uncomfortably formal, considering all that we'd shared.

He was quiet but vigilant, as he usually was, and I was curious, as I usually was. He fidgeted a little bit with his hands, which indicated that his thoughts were chronicling. I remembered that the last time I saw him, I feared him. But now he appeared to me quite unthreatening.

"It is good to see you again," Bhav said. He was calm now, and settled.

I had already ordered my tea.

"You, too," I replied. He nodded and said he'd get himself a cup.

I wasn't sure what the purpose of our meeting was or what I thought I could get out of it. Our souls had been contracted for almost eight years. What could I want or need? Why was I there, really?

When he was back, he still had his black leather gloves on, the kind that showed the tips of his fingers. He pressed those fingers into the paper cup in his hand as he angled it closer to his mouth. I could taste the warmth of the coffee in my own mouth as he drank it.

"How are you?" he asked. "You seem well."

Yes, I was. So, I told him about completing my master's degree, something he'd originally contested because he wanted me to settle down with him. I told him also about the new person I was seeing, and that I was still writing.

"Well, I expected no less." He looked around the room, then put his cup down. "But I have to say I am a little disappointed. You're doing it again. The person you're seeing. It sounds like trouble."

I smiled at him smiling at me. "Things just seem to happen for me this way." I followed up with, "And you?"

Suddenly his lips contracted and a blankness fell over his eyes. "Marriage is no longer for me." And I thought that it was a shame because Bhav had one of the most loving souls I had ever met.

"Why would you say that?" I asked.

"Because you give, and you build, but then your castle falls down. People can change any time and decide to leave all of it. Life is far too short for pain."

I thought then that this was true; the molecules of the cells in our bodies were constantly changing. Like these cells, we died and were rebirthed throughout our life span. There would always be mourning, but also celebrations. Recalling this, I remembered *Al-Wahhab*, the continual giving of blessings without expectation or return. This remembering grounded me in the sense of *it will be okay*.

"There isn't a restraint to love because it's everywhere, it's plentiful," I told him. We sat quiet for a moment while Drake's new song "Started from the Bottom" played through the speakers.

"I'm sorry," I said.

"Why are you sorry?" he asked.

I saw my reflection in his eyes, which appeared the same as the reflection in the cup in my hands, the one I saw past the rim: I was relaxed. He didn't apologize for all he had said that had marked my soul, shaken my psychological, physical, spiritual safety. But that was all right. I believed he may have forgotten everything he said, but it didn't matter. When I had arrived at Tim Hortons on that day, I had already forgiven him.

A few years ago, after a quarrel or disagreement, we'd sometimes be sitting in similar coffee shops. My body would be slouched, my eyes searching his face heedfully.

It was as if I was joined to him the way a woman would be joined to the rib of a man. As if my arms were twisted and my legs were intertwined, forming a shape similar to that of a snake, my entire body cramped in between his ribs, the bridge of my nose against the hard sternum. Perhaps it had been snug, and perhaps because of my position I had no choice but to see the world through his gaze. I couldn't exactly feel my own body, the one I was then in.

Over the years with Bhav, my limbs grew and stretched. His chest cracked open and I walked out. He often used to say, "You made me this way," after his outburts, and so it seemed he felt entitled to blame me for this separation, as if his rib was where I was always supposed to be.

In the Tim Hortons, I closed my eyes, sitting with this for a moment, drifting in and out of a fantasy where I saw the backdrop of Salvador Dali's *Metamorphosis of Narcissus*. On the dirt ground of this painted place, beside the mountain, the lake, and the sprouting flower emerging from the cracked egg, I saw the bodies of men sprawled out with their ribs cracking open, out of which climbed bare-bodied, long-haired women. In bands, they dragged the bodies of men to the lake, left them there, then walked away.

"You seem back to where you started. Calm. Alive. Happy. I'm proud of you," he said.

I thought, *I have my resolve, knowing I did everything I could.* I wanted to tell him that he, too, didn't have to lose hope. As much as the story of creation, as told in popular culture, blamed women for the original fall of humans, I knew innately that that was not how it was written. According to my faith, the two souls in any pair were equally accountable.

We spoke for a couple of hours. He held my hands in his at some point, leaning in closer then away. I felt nothing other than a tremendous amount of appreciation that he had once walked into my life. In seeing his fallibility unfold, I more clearly noticed my own, our deeply flawed selves — an enactment of pain from our childhood, our present, our human limitations, our misguided beliefs that we knew certain things when we really didn't — that we just did not want to face.

I wanted to share with him a gift of some sort. I wondered if there was something I could do to make him change his mind, so that he believed he could love again. *Forgive yourself,* I had wanted to say. *But not in self-aggrandizement or self-disdain. Just for being limited.* Because I was, too.

That day I left the Tim Hortons remembering that when we first met, I had deduced that we were meant to heal each other.

And although between the fine hairs of a second I felt an unsurmountable urge to once again do the same, I remembered that it was not my place.

The warm coffee in my hands had got cold, yet I took the cup with me when I left. It was a strange homecoming, that familiar smell of his cologne, the exact width of his chest, the beard stubble that now climbed past down his chin. His outer shell, the perfect shelter; under his sheath of bravado, against the storms. But now, in my body, I had found both. My very own.

It's 2020 and the entire world is in the middle of a pandemic. Covid-19 has taken the lives of many people. I'm in a condominium at the intersection of McCowan and Highway 401, looking out into the deserted streets.

My editor, Julie Mannell, has informed me that the missing piece to my manuscript is the story of Bhav and myself. She tells me she needs to know who Bhav is, and I think this may be as challenging as undoing world wars, because I had tried very much to bury him in order to survive.

I'm tapping my ballpoint pen on the hardcover of my journal. I'm sipping my fourth coffee. I'm taking a break to fiddle with the keys of my new harmonium, brought in from India. I'm listening to the late Tagore's *Majhe Majhe* and eating a box of Ferrero Rocher to soothe my melancholia.

Why aren't the memories coming to me like when a word lost in your memory returns to the tip of your tongue? No, the memories are lost somewhere, and hence so is the awareness of certain parts of me that have grown into something else.

I flip the pages of my journal open, a fresh, crisp page, and I try to capture what I can remember. How did our story start, Bhav and I? How did we meet? Who was he to me?

My brain is foggy. I rip up the page. I get up and blast Punjabi music to maybe be reminded of him. I sway my hips, I twirl, I raise my hands to the sky and then down as if it's *garba* night. Nothing comes.

I will find, maybe, an old photo of him or an old email, I decide. But I don't have any photographs of us together. They are all stored in my old Hotmail account titled *Shahrukh's baby something*. Yes, what a ridiculous name, and how unoriginal. *After a Bollywood star, of all things*. I shake my head. The hardcopy photographs are with Bhav in the many albums with narratives I had created. He had asked me to pick them up from him, I remember, when he was distraught and wanted nothing but their burial, but I had ignored the plea. What had he done with them?

I open up Internet Explorer on my laptop and type hotmail.com in the address bar, but I am redirected to Microsoft Outlook. I try Google and type in "How to retrieve a Hotmail account" in the search bar. It tells me to enter my username and password.

Okay, this is useless, I think. How can this even be considered an option if I don't have any of this information? Furthermore, why is it that most South Asian women through the generations have experience with some form of love letters that eventually become inaccessible? Letters lost during the war, letters hidden by family members, letters diverted from their destination by purposeful plotting of enemies. And now Snapchat messages that can be deleted within a span of six seconds. Did such fate only serve to confirm that sentiments are meant to be passing illusions or dreams never lived out?

I put the laptop away. The deadline to submit my manuscript is in few days. I am pacing back and forth.

Traces of touch arrive and leave my skin. I forget him again.

I think, *I must bring the dead back to life*.

I'm looking at my cellphone. A missed call from Ammu, and a text message, too. *How are you feeling?* she is asking.

I stare at the keypad and think, *What is his number again?* I lie to myself that I don't know. I have it memorized, and why wouldn't I? All the calls I made to him before and after I came back from Dhaka, and from Dhaka, too. Calls about our dreams or our agony or just simple greetings. There were many. It was possible, however, that the number had changed. I dial it, anyway.

The phone rings twice, and then I hear him.

"Hello?" His voice sounds the same.

I hang up. This is just too strange. I am not even sure what I will say.

I drop the phone by my pillow and just lie on the bed. I stare at the ceiling. A sense of déjà vu washes over me.

My cellphone is ringing. I'm looking at the screen. It's Bhav.

"Hello?" I answer.

"Sumaiya?" he is asking.

"Yes."

"You called?"

"Yes, that was me. Just, you know, wanted to see how you were doing."

"Okay." He sounds a little flabbergasted. "You remember my phone number."

"Yes, I do."

"Are you okay?"

"Yes, I just called, you know, to say hi," I tell him.

"I am well, and you?"

"Fine. Is this a bad time?" I think I hear a woman's voice.

"No, I can speak. Are you okay?"

"Yes," I repeat. It feels impossible to continue the conversation without sharing the purpose of my call. In fact, I feel almost sly. "Well, I'll just tell you. I'm a writing a book about what happened to me in Dhaka. A memoir that captures that time of my life. As you know, that time of my life includes you."

"Oh," Bhav is silent. "Well, I am not surprised. You always loved to write, and that story is very important to share."

"Yes," I sigh with relief. "There are gaps in my memory about us, before Dhaka happened. Would you be willing to help me restore those memories? A walk down memory lane?"

Bhav laughs. "My memory is not that great, either, but we were something."

"Yes," I say. "Will you help me? I will understand if it's too strange for you, to do such a thing."

"No," Bhav says. "I will help, but let me first ask my girlfriend. If you're with someone, you should perhaps ask them, too."

"Oh," I say. The last time we met, he was single, and I had encouraged him to find love again. I'm not hurt but I do feel a little strange, as if I just stepped onto a whole new plane and I'm trying to orient myself to a new scale of gravity.

"I did always like that about you," I tell him. "Your loyalty, and your consideration."

"But," he continues, "I am not sure where that is going."

I don't know what to do with this information, so I say nothing, other than, "Okay, please do get back to me."

"I will," Bhav replies. "But we can also talk for a bit now if you like."

"Yes."

"I do have emails that I had sent to the High Commission of Canada that includes the text messages we sent to each other when you were there. I also sent them a list of key dates, which outlines what had happened."

"That would be really helpful," I say. "Because it's really hard for me to remember certain details, like timelines or order of events. In fact, it hurts my head if I try."

"I understand," Bhav says.

There is a discernment in his voice, and a fondness I remember from pre–2005 Dhaka days.

"I want to tell you something before I share anything else," he declares.

"Okay," I say. I am speculating about what he could possibly say after all these years. It has been almost ten since the last time I saw him.

"I would like to apologize to you. I'm sorry," Bhav says.

Ten seconds slip by within which we are both silent.

"When you came back from Dhaka, you were going through quite a lot. Post-traumatic stress, I did look it up. I know you needed me to be there for you, but I wasn't. I was going through a very challenging time in my own life," Bhav says.

There were many nights I had given company, many nights of suffering, wishing for the utterance of these exact words, and now he is saying them to me. I don't know what to do with them right now.

"You didn't deserve it, how I treated you at the end."

"Well," I say after taking it all in, "that means a lot to me. More than you can imagine. Thank you," I tell him. How stoic I sound, and that I should. We had moved on, but does anyone forget the first pangs of their heart ripping apart? Prolonged pain echoing into eons, eroding the sense of time itself.

It was strange indeed, having thirsted for an apology that I once thought could allow my soul to be unchained, but I never received it and therefore had to remove the shackles myself by giving my life a new meaning. An arduous act for those of us who are stubborn in our sentimentality and romanticization of that which we are fond. And those of us who have been through so much — we cannot take one more loss. However, I am aware that many of us seldom do receive apologies such as these. So, as Bhav spoke the words, I felt nothing but a showering of *Alhumdulillah, he has seen me.*

It is a gift which at this point in my life I don't necessarily need, but which brings me hope in human beings. The current time in human history is dark, but also one of resilience. His words remind me that people are capable of self-awareness, of reflection, and of new beginnings. That one can battle their own pride for love; if not love, then simple decency and respect. Kindness. *I see you, a human being, the person I once loved.*

Bhav tells me then a few more things about what he remembers, and I jot them down while listening. As we do this, a thought crosses my mind: *What would my younger self have thought of this?* The one who held onto the promise ring in the storage closet in Dhaka, wailing, recalling every detail of her lover's face that she had memorized? Bhav, who always had his disposable camera ready to create memories so they would never be limited to time and space? Oh, young love, dreams, and promises. Here we were, trying to pull together all of the pieces of a puzzle that now seemed ancient. Did we ever think we'd be doing this?

"What about all our emails, our letters? I know we had maybe ten thousand or more," I ask him. I want to find relics of who I was at the time.

"I deleted them all out of anger," Bhav says, then sighs.

"What?" I ask. "Were you that upset?"

"Weren't you? What was I to do? Remember how I had a box?" Bhav says. "The one with all those albums you had created? The dove I gave to you? And so many other things?"

"Yes?" I ask.

"I drove to where you lived that night, but you wouldn't come out and take it from me, the box. I don't know why. Do you remember? I called you maybe twenty times."

"I didn't want to because I wasn't ready to —" I start then stop.

"I cut you out of every single photo I had."

"That's a lot of photos. Almost eight, nine years' worth of photos," I tell him.

"I know," he says. "I cut you out of every single one."

"Why?"

The floor creaks. I see from the corner of my eye that night is falling.

"Because I loved you more than anything in the world, and it broke my heart to lose you. You left me at the end. I didn't think you would. You were so loyal. You would die for me, that's how much you loved me."

"I thought we left each other," I say.

"I pushed you away, but I didn't think you'd leave." His voice is mellow. "In all of these years, whenever I hurt you, you didn't say anything. You just asked me to listen, and you were so patient. I didn't know how to handle everything. I didn't want you to go."

"After what happened to me," I tell him, "I wasn't going to take anyone's abuse or disrespect, especially from the person I loved."

"I know." Bhav's voice is soft and pensive. "It's the last thing you needed. I should have been there for you. And I know I was stubborn, putting my need to be right, my ego, before what you needed, what you were suggesting. You were always smarter than me."

"Despite you being the old man." I am laughing. We are both laughing.

"You always knew how to put what you felt into words. I struggled with that."

"It's something," I tell him, "to fight fate so hard while fighting to keep your faith, and just ending up in a place where all you have is a grieving heart in your hands." I touch my face and I think I feel the dried tears from that time gone by. But then I realize, *In these losses, I have gained so much.*

"I buried —" Bhav tells me.

"Me?"

"No, the box, with all our things." He is changing the subject of our conversation, diverting it just a little bit. "I buried it at the Getaway."

"You should have burned them," I tell him, but then I remember he couldn't have, and neither could I. I decide not to entertain the idea of tracking these mementoes down.

So, we continue like this. Bhav tells me what he remembers, and I continue noting it all down. I had buried so much of these recollections in order to make room for the visions of how I wanted to live. I write the memories into chapters and send him paragraphs. He shares any information he thinks I may have missed. We laugh at the poor grammar and ridiculous slang words we used in our text messages and emails. We bring up old jokes that still seem new. He tells me he carried his promise ring around for a decade after our separation, imagining we could be reunited one day, although he wasn't actively seeking such an ending.

"Wouldn't it be something?" he tells me. "If we were to end up together, after your book comes out?" To which I laugh.

I ask him instead how his new love religiously and culturally identifies. He tells me she is a Muslim, and that he is once again trying to make sense of how to navigate an interreligious relationship.

"Why would you do this to yourself?" I tease him.

"Well, I guess the heart just does what it wants," he says. "Takes you in circles and you just end up in the same goddamn place."

"That's the definition of insanity," I say. We laugh, and then I become serious. "It's a beautiful thing, when we can appreciate the good in all faiths. There are so many miracles, when we just believe."

"I am blessed and honoured to have had these calls with you," he says, and I concur.

It is indeed rare that previous lovers can still see each other as gifts, but some unions do survive somehow — they just take on different forms.

I say goodbye.

I open my email soon after and I see Bhav has sent me all the text messages and emails he sent to the High Commission of Canada. He even had old poems I had written during troubled times. I read them. My head spins. I get up to drink a glass of water, thinking with each step forward that in these poems, I had inked my desperation to be seen.

When I come back, I continue scrolling through all the emails he has sent me. I open up one titled *Dates*, which I desperately need to give an accurate sense of how the events unfolded in Bangladesh. Here is how that email reads:

> On Wednesday July 27th 2005 Sumaiya boarded a plane to for your trip to Bangladesh.
>
> On September 17th 2005 Sumaiya texted me saying her uncle beat her ███████████████ and her head was bleeding. I left Franks work that day raced home, changed her email password and opened the case for Sumaiya with the counselors officers in Ottawa, who then passed it on to the Bangladeshi embassy.
>
> On October 3rd 2005 family took her to meet the guy.
>
> From a lot of pressure and abuse, from her uncle and no hope of her ███ ever letting her come back without getting married. She had to accept the proposal and the wedding date was initially set for November 9th 2005.

The wedding date was bumped up to October 31st 2005. I finished school on October 21st, which gave me a week to figure out a plan to get her back. On Friday October 28th 2005, Sumaiya told me gave me the address to which I can tell the embassy to go get her. Unfortunately, the embassy said they needed to hear from Sumaiya but her cell phone wasn't calling outside nor could she text ████.

From October 28 2005, I told everyone I know to pray for Sumaiya and for the Canadian government to get her out. On Saturday night Sumaiya gave me the last hope to call the embassy and ask them to come get her. It clicked in my head to get ████'s cell phone number and forward all the text messages from Sumaiya to her. On Sunday 9 pm (which is 8 am in Bangladesh) I called the embassy and spoke with ████, told her Sumaiya's only got till 12:00 in the afternoon before they will move her to another address. ████ got her team together and got to the house at 11:30. Sumaiya called me early morning before she took her shower, to say her final good bye, that's when I told her that they were coming and I told her to stall and not leave the house. Sumaiya sounded dead, it felt as though everything we've built together, our characters and our behaviors, they were able to literally destroy it.

So, at about 12:30 am Toronto time, which is now October 31st Sumaiya's wedding day, ████ called me and gave the phone to Sumaiya. That was the

second time I spoke to her. She didn't know what to
do, I told her she had to leave, that the government
people won't come back. She called ███, and
then later made the decision to leave, for her own
safety. Before that she called the guy to explain.

As I read the email, certain fragments of memories return to me.
My shoulders loosen, my jaw loosens. These accounts are painful to
see, written the way they are, objectively. They account for a reality
that I did not want to believe for the five months I was in Dhaka.
There must be some sort of misunderstanding, I had always thought. My
anger is not here, it has been morphed into the life I have built for myself. I am looking around the condominium I now live in. The musical instruments, the shelves of books, my work laptop on the table,
a fridge full of food, framed photographs, and a *jai-namaz* next to me.
I have lived and that was how I forgave everyone, including myself.

I open up another email. This is the one Bhav sent to one of the
contacts at the High Commission that gave my consent, for them
to get me from Boro Mama's house.

Hi ███ this is ██████████, I've opened
up a case for my friend Sumaiya Matin (DOB)
██████████ ... she is currently in Bangladesh.
I spoke with her on Wednesday September 28,
2005. She wants to get back to Canada but she
doesn't want you guys the Canadian government
to get her. Because she worried that if that happens, first she'll never see her brother and sister
again because the father that is here will just move
there and live there. Second she just doesn't want
to take that route because her parents will hurt. I
know that's what she said and in a perfect world

it will happen like that ... but I think she's just avoiding the truth. I tried to tell her that there is no other way to get back without someone getting hurt. I really don't think she's thinking logically over there ... I know she loves her parents and she doesn't want to hurt them with you pulling her out but I also think she's getting manipulated over there ... with all the negative comments and abuse and not eating or sleeping. Her plan is for me to go over there ... her to sneak out and we come back. She is absolutely smart, but that's the stupidest thing she ever told me ... and I'm worried that she losing her self over there.

Anyway, below are the conversation I had with her ... I'll copy them just as I see them.

At 4:08 PM
Tue Sep 27

Don't talk to any of my cuzins serious backtstabing pressure if I say no [no to a marriage] they will leave me here go bac home sel house n cum here

At 4:26 PM
Tue, Sep 27

Babee we need to think how do I get bac without embasy cuz my fan

At 4:39 PM
Tue, Sep 27

(1/2) How do I get bac without that can u come after some run away how can u wait everyl cryin how do I get them not to cum [how do I get them not to move to Bangladesh]

At 4:40 PM
Tue, Sep 27

(2/2) here pls no embasy dad will die

At 4:54 PM
Tue, Sep 27

Wut if my peeps go bac we wait a while then u cum n I run away nutin to publicly show

At 5:03 PM
Tue, Sep 27

(1/2) Babee I love u so much I'm saying no so much pressure saying I'm heartless everyl cryin u come here I sneak out but after bro and sis go

At 5:05 PM
Tue, Sep 27

(2/2) home tell ███████████. [███████████ was her childhood teacher and a special friend to her and the family. She had asked me to find her and tell her how her family is trying to move back to Bangladesh but I couldn't find her]

At 5:45 PM
Tue, Sep, 27

(1/2) Babe it will be too hard on my peeps if we tell embasy I just have to get bac if I get stuck here can u

At 5:47 PM
Tue, Sep 27

(2/2) Cum here after a while babe its so hard 4 me

At 5:59 PM
Tue, Sep 27

(1/2) No sleep no food I'm dead babee if u cum
here we cud run away I cant leave publicly babe it
is hel here I wish I was home the prob [problem]

At 5:59 PM
Tue, Sep 27

(2/2) is everyl luvs me too much so no one can let
go how r u doin without me

At 6:03 PM
Tue, Sep 27

(1/2) Wut wil u do if I never cum bac to u babe
we need to think of sumtin don't talk to my cuzins
that u

At 6:04 PM
Tue, Sep 27

(2/2) did b4 they insulted me n my mom

At 6:20 PM
Tue, Sep 27

(1/2) The Dif is that that wil hurt more knowing I called cops [High Commission of Canada,
they will think she called you] babe these ppe

care about me but they jus hav a dif idea of wut is good 4

At 6:20 PM
Tue, Sep 27

(2/2) me babe its really hard 4 me here the situation got twisted ppl think I'm nuts

At 6:25 PM
Tue, Sep 27

(1/2) pls find ████████ don't get dad involved with govt we hav to avoid that I'm scared.

At 6:26 PM
Tue, Sep 27

(2/2) Don't text to other no ever [that number that I had given you guys earlier was a cell phone of one of her cousins was one that she said was safe but no she says those cousins can't be trusted and she said never text there. This cell phone number is a girl cousin of hers but I don't know how safe is its now … I don't text it unless I receive one from her first]

At 6:38 PM
Tue, Sep 27

(1/2) To be honest I don't kno exactly it is 5 in the morning me wil send after babee how can u wait 4 me this culture is so strong

At 6:39 PM
Tue, Sep 27

(2/2) That ppl have to care wut others say my bro
n sis wana go home but I luv u they cant accept so
they wil do anything to keep me

At 6:52 PM
Tue, Sep 27

I live at many adres change house one is at lalmatia I dun kno now wil give next time I promise [I
guess that's one of the cities she staying in]

At 7:15 PM
Tue, Sep 27

(1/2) Babee if they move here I wil not stay that's
wen u come I wil sneak out run away with u if I
can jus make it to Canada once babee

At 7:16 PM
Tue, Sep 27

(2/2) ppl r getting fed up wit me so many fites I
hate this I cry al day

At 7:19 PM
Tue, Sep 27

████ al I kno if I say no they r leaving me here
6 months later they comin here babee think of
sumtin pls I love u

At 7:23 PM
Tue, Sep 27

(1/2) ▬▬ I have to go I hear sumone don't text anyone or talk to to cuzin I love u so much babee pls don't ever stop luvin me we will

At 7:23 PM
Tue, Sep 27

(2/2) find a way.

There were a lot more texts I had originally from that Saturday that I first called you guys, but I had to erase it to receive these latest ones. Well as you can see she doesn't want to go the route I want to but if at all possible can we please keep her case open. I told her I won't tell her address unless she wanted me to tell you guys to get her out. So next time she text I'll have the address, hopefully. Well I guess I'll just continue to email you with whatever she sends me and when she wants to get out and can't just walk out the door I'll email you her address and a text message from her saying she wants to come home. But please if at all possible can you please keep her case open because I know there is no way for her to come back peacefully and in one piece with out you guys.

......

Hey, this is ▬▬▬▬▬ a few weeks ago I opened up a case for my friend Sumaiya Matin DOB ▬▬▬▬▬. I have had contact with her in recent days, she's still unsure as to what she

wants to do, but she has given me 2 addresses. I
told her today to call you guys, she said she will
tomorrow, but I don't know if she will … cause
that way you hear it from her I know its best for
her to get the embassy but I can tell you right now
that will be out of the question there is no way
they will let her out of their sites.

I pull down my laptop screen. I can't read anymore. As a writer, the poor grammar and misspelling of words is a slow death.
There is a part of me that remembers watching all of this as it
unfolded. She asks, *What could I have done differently so that this didn't
happen?* Sometimes it feels as if I now have a defect of some kind,
that I cannot live life at the expected pace, or relate to others in the
ways they want. She also says, however, that I should be easier on
myself. That the life event had moulded me a certain way — the
considerations I make, how quickly or slowly my heart beats, how
I am in relationships, the trajectory of my life — but it does not
have to define me.

I skim the emails again. I read between and on the lines: the
pressure I faced in Dhaka to make a decision when I didn't have a
real choice, yet was made to feel as if I had one, therefore render-
ing the wedding an event I chose and encouraged. My behaviour
then was considered inconsistent, and the anger I expressed, my self-
assertion, my loyalty, and my longing for who I loved were all considered a sign of jinni possession (although I couldn't rule this out
— who was I to say?). My persistent will, even in my small acts of
resistance, was not something anyone expected. Irrespective of how
ill-informed or troubled I seemed at nineteen, or how terrible I was at
garnering trust with my kin, everyone who had participated in one
way or another sidestepped their accountability, or just believed they
were somehow saving me, acting in my best interest. I am grateful,

however, for the family I have. Over the years our efforts have become greater in understanding each other, and this has brought us closer together. The strength of our bond is continually tested, and we continually seem to find a way back to each other. *Matin* means *strong*, and that, I believe, is what we are as a family.

Alhumdulillah. I close my eyes. I fall asleep.

I text Bhav the next day, *I know it has been over ten years, but I am still hurt.*

Bhav writes back, *I understand. If we were going to end up in the same predicament, we should have just ended up together but we didn't.*

No, we didn't. I have moved on. Allah knows what is best.

Still, I ache, looking out onto the 401, the cars passing by. Remembering the deep devotion that I once felt, I think that I'm still not an expert on love, nor can I really define it, but what I do sense deeply within my core is that it is not bound by these tests, nor by space or time or a physical, gendered body. Love shows its face in places and during ages one can never predict. When Allah writes people into our lives, even for a short time, there is a bigger reason.

When on the phone with Bhav again, he says, "I think you should kill Bhav."

"What?" I am confused.

"Bhav, in your book. Kill me. He needs to die."

I remind him my book is non-fiction. I don't love him that way, but it still hurts. And then, while resisting the urge to fall on my knees, I ask myself, *Is it possible that all those who have touched us coexist in our hearts, simply because their essence is really a manifestation of the attributes of God?* It's what the person gave us, their gift, something that we needed to see and experience at a particular point in time, and becomes a part of us. When we own that part we can let go, but would that mean we love less? We can still appreciate their gifts from afar with a certain tenderness. The people I loved, the people for whom I am deeply grateful.

Still, I ask him, "Do you want me to kill you from my consciousness?"

He is quiet. He says nothing.

"Thank you," I tell him. "You were what I needed then to be who I am now."

He reminds me that I've always been a strong, loving, intelligent woman, and that no life event should convince me otherwise.

We say goodbye. I hang up.

I close my eyes. On my back of my eyelids, I see the ending of this story, not as the South Asian women of our previous generations saying, *I am glad you didn't end up with him. This is what happens when you disobey your traditions, and do not follow your religion.* Nor do I see the end as women of the generations after saying, *Hail love over everything else,* because that could also be an illusion. I see the ending as the simultaneously ugly but beautiful truth that life is a revolving door, and the opportunity to keep this door open is the greatest gift that has been bestowed.

Jajabor / Nomad
(যাযাবর)

It had been about fourteen years since the phone call to the High Commission of Canada from the corner of Boro Mama's bedroom, using the rotary phone, now archaic, placing my finger in the holes of the dial and rotating it, breathing so heavily, saying "Hello?" as if it were a wish.

I was back for my younger cousin Maryam's wedding, a grand ball, close to the country's Victory Day, a celebration of the win allied forces had over West Pakistani forces during the Liberation War in Bangladesh. The people in the streets were hanging red and green lights on the buildings, wrapping them around the streetlamps. Just a few blocks down, the Bangladesh armed forces were practising for their military parade. I could see already that some smaller flags had been hoisted, green backdrop like the land, the red dot in the middle the marker of blood. Nine months of massacre; I considered all the lives lost.

"Victory! Victory!" I heard some of the workers say. A couple of them I saw had paint spread across their faces in the shape of flags, and writing that said "Victory Day 2019."

I was looking at all this from the balcony where I was standing. It was evening. Down below, at the hemlines of the street, I spotted shattered glass on the roads and heaps of plastic on the road edges. The storefronts were defaced with slander and vandalism, as a form of propaganda or free expression. An election was on its way. This land, although free, continued to be in a state of survival, recovering from the negative impacts of oppression, the lateral violence it had been subjected to and was now subjecting onto others: the Rohingyas, the people of the Chittagong Hill Tracts. Another complicated hometown, and I looked at it like a voyeur, with curiosity, yet unable to participate in it fully.

What relationship did I now have with this place? Did it scare me, being back here? Yes, to an extent. I had avoided it for fourteen years out of a fear of being trapped again. Now, here I was, being reacquainted, a sadness falling over me like the black velvet evening sky above my head. The realization that in my avoidance, I missed so many years of truly knowing the place, helping it rebuild in some way. Each time I visited, another family member or relative had left the country, or someone had died, or I had less information about what every day was like for the citizens.

∞

It was the evening of Maryam's wedding. I was wearing a maroon velvet *lengha* embroidered in gold. On my ears hung pearls placed on a golden frame the shape of paisley, dangling. I walked into the grand hall, where from the high ceilings hung what seemed to be gilt chandeliers. The main stage where Maryam and her husband sat was a cut-out of a Mughal palace — arched doorways, windows, and balconies swathed in roses. I stood in the middle of the hall, surrounded by over a hundred tables, my eyes trailing along the gold-tinted runway in front of the stage.

Her wedding, she said, hadn't been arranged, although she found her now husband's biodata in a pile of twenty other ones handed to her. As she looked at it, she realized he was actually a distant family friend. *Meant to be — fate.* When she met him for their first date in New York City, their veins jolted like the ever-lasting electricity running the Times Square billboard lights. The city that never sleeps. That night she put checkmarks next to the criterion that she expected of him, that she expected of herself, that was once expected of her; these three things now one thing. *Meant to be — fate.*

And now they were situated in what appeared visually as a fairy tale of sorts. Should I have been envious, especially after having been carelessly forced into an unwanted wedding myself? *Hasad*, like the type Iblis had for Adam? I couldn't. By now, I had realized I loved myself too much to put myself through such self-sabotage, not trusting in the greater order of events. Standing there, I was overcome, actually, by exhilaration. I was happy for Maryam but also myself, that I had learned so much since the last time I'd been in Bangladesh, and this would serve me, I was sure. I felt stronger than I had ever felt.

I reflected on marriages in Canada. Such occasions were not nec-essarily this big, and almost half of the people I knew who were around my age were still unwed. I thought about the late-night bars where people searched for solace, and those who also reviewed the criteria of potential mates like Maryam, headhunters looking at resumes, just in the form of *swipe right or left*. I wondered then about the complexities of love and the process of finding marriage, and the multitude of ways that it had been framed. The multitude of ways people found each other and somehow decided to be together, for a time.

There are so many factors that shape the process of finding marriage or companionship for those who are looking: the neighbourhood one lives in, citizenship status, employment, socioeconomic status, heath, and other resources. There's also the way societal structures work and how communities are organized — for example, consumerism and capitalism impacting the way we think about and interact in the personal, domestic sphere.

And then I thought about arranged marriages — the Duggars and their *19 Kids and Counting*. Chaperoned courtship. The arranged marriages of Hasidic Jews starting in the late teens. And the many Hindu societies where unions are often determined by caste or the stars.

I wondered then about the complexities of all of this. How much was love an environmental set-up as it was a mysterious inner calling that answered to no one but itself?

The multitude of ways people found each other and somehow decided to be together, for a time. How much of it was predestined, and how much of it was free will?

The twinkle lights flashed and I closed my eyes. I climbed up onto the stage, went down the shiny runaway, the golden hemline of my *lengha* skirt gently brushing against the floor. The twinkle lights sparkled and there was a lightness at the soles of my feet. I could almost run like the character Paro from the film *Devdas* then, my arm extended, shouting "No, stop, come back!" He once had too much ego to make her his, so he drowned himself in his despair, drinking, eventual death.

I thought about Iblis. There's no such thing as tragedy in Islam, but I couldn't help but wonder if Iblis was really a tragic romantic hero after all, like some Sufis said — forsaken by the one he loved so much because he wouldn't bow down to someone else — before the door of Paradise was closed on him. I thought about the betrayal, then, of women becoming demonized and of God not yet correcting the wrongs done toward them in His name or in that of something else. It was possible to free ourselves from all of this, I believed, but not by subjection to those pretending to be God and the ideas they perpetuated, and not through Shayṭān's vengeance, either, but by Iblis's independence and ability to truly trust ourselves. And divine decree.

I twirled my *lengha* skirt under the chandeliers. Pins pressed against my flesh; my exposed midriff momentarily caressed by a passing breeze. The moment within which I twirled felt like a century.

I took a red car to Boro Mama's new home. I had avoided this moment for many years, but now it had come. This new flat he lived in was a few miles farther away than the old one. As I sat there, in the leather back seat of a red car, I barely noticed the half-naked boys and girls that passed by. I concentrated instead on how Boro Mama's face would now look, seeing me suddenly walk through his doors, once again under his roof. I closed my eyes tightly, conjuring up the image I remembered most vividly: Boro Mama towering over me as if he were ten storeys high, fury between the eyebrows and lining his jaw, teeth clenched, dark-brown pupils sinking deep into an abyss of a face. He looked down at me, I looked up at him, and between us the friction of two clashing wills.

The red car came to a halt before the teal-painted iron gate. Sweety Khala's driver, in his grey dress pants, half-sleeved white cotton collared shirt, and fine black dress shoes, walked out and over to the gate guard. He explained who I was, pointing at me as I stood by the car door, once again shrinking, the building towering over me like Boro Mama would. Sweety Khala's driver slicked his hair back as he nodded, listening intently to the white-bearded senior in his matching beige shirt and slacks who was sitting sluggishly on a salmon-pink plastic chair.

Sweety Khala's driver gestured me to get back into the car, which I did with relief, suddenly regretting the decision to see Boro Mama again. I had been in Dhaka for almost a week now and I was planning to stay for only one more. I was at first reluctant to meet him, but later thought, *Who knows when I will see him next?*

I got in the car and the driver followed behind. He pressed the pedal with his right foot. I saw him in the rear-view mirror, checking on me, me fidgeting with my white *orna* draped over my chest. I was wearing a blue-and-white *salwar kameez*.

The teal gates opened, and the red car pulled in. We parked in one of the parking spots, and I stepped out of the car again, the driver gesturing me forward now. I followed him to the elevator, my heartbeats increasing in pace as if I was back in Toronto on the treadmill of my condominium gym. The elevator stopped. Its doors opened, a little too slowly for my liking, yet giving me a few minutes to gather my thoughts, which I so desperately needed. Somehow, I had not prepared for this moment at all in the last fourteen years. What would I say to him now? What would he say to me? Would he express disappointment? Or perhaps apologize? In what ways had I ruined his life, as he had claimed I would fourteen years ago?

Sweety Khala's driver was a quiet man, or so it seemed. When we got to the right floor, he gestured me forward as if to say, "You can do this," but what he actually said was "I will be downstairs. When you are done, please let the gate guard know, and I'll prepare the car for your departure." I watched him hurry down the stairs. I wondered how bored these personal drivers were as they waited for their employers and how they used the time they had.

The sound of the driver's footsteps faded. I made my way to Boro Mama's rosewood door.

I closed my eyes, clenched my fist, and knocked. Mami opened the door, wide-eyed as usual, as if the past seven hundred and twenty weeks had not even gently touched her with age. She beamed still, like a halo, sunny citrus mid-tone yellow, as if she truly belonged somewhere up in the sky. She was in her usual floral maxi, a cup of *doodh cha* in her left hand with the twinkling red nail paint, ordering about the four maids, who were meticulously sweeping corners with straw brooms. I'd only really heard Mami's voice when she complained to these maids about the spots they left untouched, or the rotis they accidentally burned, or the bedsheets they left wrinkled. Occasionally she yelled at her three sons, but mostly related to their performance at school or their *adab*. I wondered about Mami, her selective expressions of frustration and her silence; if it was really buried rage that showed its face in seemingly mundane activities. For I couldn't see her expressing any dissatisfaction in Boro Mama's presence. Most of the time I saw her dressed up and attending fancy events, eating well, preparing food for charities, and going for weekly spa visits, among other activities. Her life seemed balanced. She seemed, in general, happier and healthier than many women I had met in North America. Mami's sons were now abroad — England and Australia — and I wondered what it was like now for her to have them gone.

Mami screamed when she saw me, the *doodh cha* spilling on the floor and soiling her floral maxi. I was astounded by her reaction but before I could ask her why, I saw in the hall mirror from the periphery of my left eye a glimpse of my own reflection: the Shaytān Bride. I was dressed in a maroon *katan* sari, golden embroidery and narrow fringe, the blouse slightly past my shoulder. Vivacious lips, gold bangles, and golden *nath*, long black hair pulled over my left shoulder, and deep kohl — the kind made from burning oil-covered monosha leaf in a mud lamp.

I reached out to Mami, her mouth agape, she turned her back to me and darted away. I stood there looking back at the reflection of myself, dressed as a bride as if it was fourteen years ago and I was getting ready to be married.

With my last blink, I was back again, in front of the door, my fist one centimetre away from the rosewood. This time when Mami opened the door, after I knocked once or maybe twice, she simpered as usual. She appeared as I had imagined before, but this time less threatened.

"You were able to make it. That's good. How are you?" she asked me, gesturing me in. The new flat looked slightly smaller than their previous home. I supposed it made sense, with her sons now gone. There was a small kitchen, where I saw a little girl, maybe twelve or thirteen. A maid. She chopped onions with one hand, and wiped her eyes with the other, using the trail end of her orchid *orna*. I speculated about what had happened to Bilkis.

Passing the maid in the kitchen, I followed Mami to the wooden dining-room table, on which laid an assortment of dishes: rice, *dhaal*, fish, egg, chicken, shrimp curries, *bhortas*, sautéed and roasted vegetables. As I sat down, she pulled out a white plate from the pile of plates, placing it in front of me. She covered it with food, and I repeated, "No, no, I can't eat much." And yet I did, the intense aromatic spices now beginning to warm up my blood.

"Your Boro Mama is just finishing up some work. He will be out in a couple of minutes. You enjoy your meal."

She sat there watching me eat, as if to observe my every flinch, to her food or the whole awkward experience, I couldn't tell. Did she remember anything, or had she forgotten? She seemed somewhat genuinely relieved that I had come, as if it were a dishonour to not have a meal by her hands after having come all this way. She did not say much, until she'd left the room for perhaps a minute or two and then came back to say, as she poked her head from the doorway, "When you're done, feel free to make your way to the living room. Your Boro Mama will be waiting for you there."

As I stood up, the curry on my lip now tasted saltier. I wiped it off with a tissue and went to wash my hands. Soon after I was on my way to the living room, my heart thumping with each step. As I walked into the room I saw Boro Mama sitting there on the light-mauve sofa, his right ankle piled on his left knee. His arms were outreached on the sofa, he leaned back in the self-assuredness that I knew him to have. As I stepped forward, I could see more clearly that age had begun to settle on his skin like invisible dust. His face had withered slightly, and his stature, as well. He looked, in fact, quite small.

"*As-salam alaykum,*" I greeted him. I would be polite.

"*Wa alaikum salam.* Have a seat." He gestured to the seat across from him. I walked over to it and sat down.

"How are you doing? How is all?" He asked me, and I wondered how I could articulate for him all that had happened in the last fourteen years in a way that he would understand.

"I am well. How are you?" is all I said, because I couldn't gather myself to say, "Your actions really impacted by life, you know?" And, "I did think about everything we talked about, even years later," or, "I just needed guidance and support, but not to be pushed away, demonized the way I was," or, "It's true, I was stubborn, but I'm that way about the things I believe in, about protecting the people I love. I suppose the passion runs in our blood," or, "I have forgiven you, even though I haven't forgiven the action you took, despite you believing it was for my own good. Will you forgive me, too, if I've hurt you?" and, "I'm afraid, though, that I can only be myself. I'm afraid, I can no longer apologize for this."

"So, you came here for Maryam's wedding. Wasn't it a beautiful wedding indeed? You see, you have to marry right," he said.

I nodded. My conversation with Boro Mama didn't last beyond simple formalities, despite all that was simmering in my heart.

I accepted this because I knew that there was so much about the world that drove people to do terrible things for the best of reasons, and the best of things for the most terrible reasons. I knew that I was not responsible for all of it, other than my own actions. I still believed in holding people accountable, the ones who inflict harm on others. In this situation with Boro Mama, I had decided to leave it up to God.

When it was time to take my leave, however, he stood up and looked me directly in the eyes. His own were of pure surety — the way they had been when he saw me off at the airport, when I was emigrating to Canada. He said, "You are an intelligent woman. I trust you and the decisions you'll choose to make. I hope to hear lots of good things. Please, come visit me again. Now, you take care."

I left the place, and there was something so pure about the liberty I suddenly felt as I made my way back to Sweety Khala's red car, her driver turning the wheel, stepping on the gas pedal, the teal-painted iron gate opening, us driving out into eventful streets.

Boro Mama passed away on November 2, 2020. When I found out, the pink petals of the carnations on my espresso-brown bookshelf were dried and falling off. The stems were wilting, just at the glass vase rim. By the vase was the poetry book I had been reading, *Radical Love: Teachings from the Islamic Mystical Tradition.* A poem each morning.

That afternoon Ammu had texted, "Boro Mama died," after calling a few times when I had been preoccupied writing.

When I first read it, it's as if gravity itself wanted to punish me. As if all my blood had gone to my feet, and the floorboards of the building had collapsed.

"How?" I texted Ammu back.

"A heart attack."

To which I thought, *The part of people he wished to quiet seems to have sought its vengeance.*

I shook my head. *Astagfurallah, I shouldn't think such ways.* Keeping *bughd* (hatred) out of my heart, for him and others, was important. The only thing to do was to wish others well, even if I was in pain.

"*Inna lillahi wa inna ilayhi raji'oon,*" I said. *I loved my dear uncle; he was once my friend. May his soul be at peace.*

And there I was, standing over my carnations, placing my palms over the hardened petal fibres.

I ripped the petals off their stems and threw them everywhere, because sometimes when I'm alone I express a dramatic flair. I had wanted to have a heart-to-heart conversation with Boro Mama someday, when we both could be open. I wanted to talk to Nani, too. And now this could never happen.

Forty days later, December 12, 2020, I was in my kitchen preparing my *cha*. I was having it black. I stirred my tea with a silver spoon, which clanked against the cup. I dropped three brown sugar cubes in, bubbles forming and swivelling like clouds of a hurricane. I thought I heard someone pass by. Somehow, I smelled petrichor. A thousand fragrant flowers that unravelled their petals at the same time. Roses, lemons, cedar, and something more tonic seeping into the soil is what I whiffed. The same fluid found in the veins of Greek gods. Survival.

Who is there?

It is said in Islamic faith that when the soul is separated from the body after death, it visits its family on the seventh day and on the fortieth day. I sit on my wooden chair, disappearing behind the fumes of frankincense.

The ghostly spectre of Boro Mama's physical absence in my life and maybe soul presence on this fortieth night reminded me that our histories could still haunt us. But when the frankincense smoke enveloping me like a container slowly started to dissipate, I remembered that change was always possible.

I sipped the tea; the sugar storm clouds were now in my mouth.

I gulped them down. "May you rest in peace. *Inna lillahi wa inna ilayhi raji'oon,*" I said again.

During the two weeks I had remaining on my 2016 trip to Bangladesh, I visited the Shah Jalal Dargah, home of the Hazrat Shah Jalal, a Sufi saint of Bangladesh. Although it isn't clear, many scholars think Hazrat Shah Jalal was born in Turkey and raised by his maternal uncle in Mecca, Saudi Arabia. He knew the Quran by heart and spent years learning Islam and meditating. Ammu, my two paternal Chachis, a few cousins, and I drove for over a day to visit this *dargah* in Sylhet and pray. Sylhet, from the Arabic term *Serhad*, meaning central town, is a city in northeast Bangladesh, sitting on the bank of River Surma.

Our journey started in Dhaka. We took the Dhaka-Mymensingh Highway, including Airport Road, to Uttara, a suburban area of Bangladesh bursting with educational institutions, shopping complexes, and a string of homes running through relatively quiet roads. I sat in Choto Chacha's white BMW, which he drove himself to take us to his home. Choto Chacha was Abbu's younger brother. We were going to pick up his wife, Choto Chachi, as well as his daughter. Before Uttara, Choto Chacha lived in New York. He had moved back to Dhaka because to him it felt more like home. I recall looking through his car window to see heaps of garbage lining the edges of the road, almost like a fort around the city. The feeling of being startled when I saw the pollution — so stark, so unheeded — never got old.

My hands shook a bit, and I felt a heavy weight, like the anchor of a boat sinking deep into the water below. This thought kept resurfacing on this trip: *What have I really done to help the country of my birth?* I thought at the time about the climate change issues in the context of Canada and their neglect — both countries, in their own ways, running toward the future without nurturing the conditions that would take them there.

When we arrived in Uttara, though, I discovered how quiet and capacious it was. I likened it to Mississauga or maybe Vaughan, or perhaps another small town or city in Ontario.

Choto Chacha's flat was spacious. Beside his balcony was a sturdy tree with almost-ripe mangos, which I ogled from afar. Choto Chachi, who was bubbly with beady eyes, followed my line of sight to the tree and then disappeared into another room. When she came back, she had a net attached to a long stick, which she gleefully used, rather patiently, to reach and yank a couple of the mangoes from their source. When she caught one or two, her son and daughter, and Ammu and I, yelled in elation, "Success!" She cut the mangoes up into a few slices and we suckled them as we sat on the balcony. It was a wonderful welcome indeed.

The next evening we set out in a big black van from Uttara to the Shah Jalal in Sylhet. We headed farther and farther northwest. Since we were travelling at night, we saw not much other than the pitch-black night holding us, rocking us gently as the sounds of Hindi melodies reverberated through the van speakers. We sang loudly together, then separately under our breath, the tunes and words adding to our personal inner stories. I slept only for a couple of hours, revelling mostly in this sensation of being somewhere new and seeing something different, being together.

Soon the sun rose, cascading red, orange, and gold hues washing over our van. I looked around at the unbound pastures: small, tall trees of a thousand kinds, and peeking floras embellishing select branches and bushes. I saw also women making their way across the hilly terrain like floating dots, and two men on a tractor steadily driving along the dirt paths.

"We are in Srimangal now," the driver told us, and it was perhaps the first time I had heard him speak. A few of us first opened our eyes to his shrill voice, and then looked around to see the tea plantation.

"These tea gardens are remnants from the days of the British Raj. They were started by the British. Do you see those white timber bungalows over there? The managers live there," the driver continued to share.

Soon we touched the tea leaves with our own hands, when we wandered out of the van and onto the dirt-ridden path. We followed this path deeper into the interior of the gardens, until I was immersed in a botanical heaven. Suddenly I remembered what it was like, sitting in the storage closet in my Boro Mama's home fourteen years ago, just desiring to be shielded by the mountains of suitcases and buried in dust.

Now, I stood between the leaves, breathing in Bangladesh, my feet grounded in soil that seemed safe once more.

Ammu appeared next to me and pulled her arm around my mine.

"How are you?" she asked. "Isn't this beautiful?"

Later, when we hopped back into our van, we headed to a nearby café for some Sylheti tea. It was a cute little place, with a roof made of straw. Out front was a little stall with savoury and sweet snacks, and inside, just a metre past the entrance, a man with a full head of hair and glossy skin. His head bobbed up and down as he took notes on stained lined paper on the shop's latest sales. Behind him were stacks of colourful packages which read "Famous Sylheti Seven Layered Tea." Ammu, my two paternal Chachis, my cousins, and I found ourselves a mid-sized table from which we could see the open parking lot that had in it a couple of scooters, our van, and a motorcycle. We sat there agreeing on the surrealism of the tea gardens.

"This must be why Sylhet is known as the spiritual capital of Bangladesh," Boro Chachi said. Her slender fingers were covered in jade, and she had shiny cherry-red nails. She smiled often with her eyes, bashfully yet invitingly, and when you looked at her it was as if you were on the Mediterranean Sea, whiffs of sulphur and jasmine combined, a briny sweetness.

We all sat there, sipping the warm black *cha* that had just been served.

Ammu watched me watch my two Chachis, as they shared stories of their childhood and experiences of similar places they had visited. Ammu pulled up a chair beside me and said, "I'd like to sit beside my own daughter from now on."

What made Ammu long for the daughter she had almost lost? Over the recent years I had seen this longing grow. It matched my very own longing for a mother I had almost lost. The more I had dug and dug and dug to find the voices of women within myself, the more I started to see behind Ammu's tough love. Suddenly, my heart just warmed toward her, like years ago when I was a child. After all the coldness, some distance, and my continual discovery of womanhood and how uniquely it was experienced by every woman, I was more able to come closer to Ammu.

I thought about that feeling, of women sitting together like this, having *cha* while sharing stories. I longed to be surrounded by these women and other women like them in Canada, congregated, banded, undivided by the race of who had the most material goods or status or opportunity or love, or even safety, in a shifting world captured through screens and ordered by stock markets. Undivided by the colour of their skin, how they practised organized religion or dressed, whom they loved. Talking about how to harness their own power, help other women harness theirs, creating a new world order.

And when we finally got to the gates of the Shah Jalal Mazar Sharif, coloured a capri blue and white, I walked toward it slowly, bringing my light-gold *orna* over my head. As I entered through the arched door, I saw a wide-open space and what seemed to be marble floors. Quickly I removed my sandals from my feet and held them in my hands. First and foremost, we decided we would pray. So I walked alongside Ammu, my two Chachis in front of us. We looked for the sisters' entrance. We found it soon; it was an adequate space and the women in it — heads draped in hijabs, *ornas*, and *abayas* — stood in rows, some with hands on their hearts, others flipping through pages of the Quran or making *duas*. Congregation of women together, meditating.

I sat next to Ammu and I felt her rock me gently from side to side. I joined her. That day we both had the same prayers in her our hearts: *May I find peace, and may I find the love for me who is meant to be, safety and protection, and Allah, your guidance forever.*

We were near a window with iron bars. On the other side was an empty corridor with seafoam-green walls and what appeared to be cedar floors. The footsteps of the many visitors before who came to decant their souls, soft treading at the base of my ears. Had they found their resolve?

Hazrat Shah Jalal himself held the soil he was given by his uncle in cupped hands, and travelled all over South Asia looking for a similar soil to settle and plant his love for Islam. He had ended up in Sylhet. I pondered then the extent to which human beings go to share their truths.

The treading footsteps called out to me, too, as if to say *We have been with you.* Suddenly, I felt overwhelming gratitude for the opportunity to have loved at all as well as to have lost. What followed was a thought, a reminder, that parked itself at the forefront of my mind: nothing was ever truly mine to begin with.

"Return us back to a place of peace," Ammu said.

"Ameen," I said.

When Ammu and I left the mosque we retrieved our shoes from down the stairs at its entrance. We looked across and ahead together to see the *jalali kobutors*, the pigeons descended from the pigeons gifted to Hazrat Shah Jalal by the Sufi Nizamuddin Auliya, whose *dargah* I had once visited in Delhi. These *jalali* pigeons were in a flock, fluttering their wings in unison, flying up into the air at the same time. Ammu and I had to started to become increasingly in union, not because I was her daughter and she my mother, but because we had started to recognize each other's souls.

"My daughter," she said, "that time we were here last, we didn't know any better. We were just scared."

I held her hand. Ammu and I would now share with each other everything in our hearts, so that the doors could never close, not even be left ajar.

"I want to see her," I said. "I want to see the Shaytān Bride."

"Who?" asked Sweety Khala. She had one of her legs folded on the wooden base of her sharp *boti*, the other was outstretched. She was gutting a hilsa, running the *boti* blade through its middle, the metallic lustre of its scales appearing like diamonds in her hands.

I walked over to the counter and saw a burnt-umber notebook flipped open to a page with a hilsa recipe:

1 *ilish* (hilsa) fish cut into steaks
½ cup mustard oil
½ cup of mustard seeds (ground into paste)
6 whole green chilies
1 teaspoon red chili pepper
1 teaspoon turmeric powder
4 tablespoons ginger paste
1 large onion diced
salt to taste

"I won't be needing that," said Sweety Khala. "But tell me, what were you saying about a woman and a jinni?"

I looked around the room to also see two large red buckets with sizzling warm water. I walked past them to the little balcony, as wide as two human adult bodies. The balcony had a large faucet protruding from a wall in an open space for dishwashing. I looked over the railing to see, a few miles down, the colourful hoods of tents, jam-packed over muddy ground.

"The woman who wouldn't marry. The one who sat in an unhinged marble state. Remember, she stared at the walls all day. She was numb, pale, and unmoved, often silent."

Sweety Khala kept her eyes on her fish.

"The woman who people said had fallen in love with a jinni. Or had been a victim of sorcery."

Sweety Khala was now washing her hands in the sink, the hilsa steaks a half to three-fourths of an inch thick. "Her. Yes, she went away."

"To where?" And now I was on Sweety Khala's tail.

"Somewhere in North America. She got married and left."

A thick cloud of malaise suspended in the air, but also joy. I looked at Sweety Khala, who now poured fresh coriander and the juice of lemons from her morning Mohammdpur market run into the thick brown broth in the steel wok. She stirred the concoction with her wooden ladle while I conjured the strength to speak. How was the Shayṭān Bride so close but I did not know? I had wanted so much to have a cup of *cha* with her. Other than her lover and her marriage, I was curious to know what else made her who she was. There was much else that was just as important, that the people had forgotten to mention. What gifts did she bring into the world? What did she think was her life purpose, really? I wanted to share with her the new books I was reading or films I had watched, the adventures I'd been having, in new cities and close to home, the projects I had started, and the new people I had met. There was a lot to explore. Yet I was also relieved that she was gone. She had found a way, it seemed, to carry on.

"Who did she marry and how?"

"I'm not sure, but I don't think she was happy about it. Here, why don't you taste-test with curry that I made, and then tell me how it is."

"Tell me the details. I want to know," I said.

"Once a girl is married, no one really cares. Now, you go and get ready, we have guests coming over today."

I left the kitchen, leaving Sweety Khala to prepare her feast, deciding that she already had enough on her plate.

Later that day I asked again, this time to Ammu, who said, "You're a grown Canadian woman. Why are you even asking about this? Jinns and such, *chi*. You have more important things to worry about than this nonsense."

I raised my eyebrows, recalling that just a few months earlier, when I was looking through one of Ammu's wedding albums, I came across a photograph of her on her wedding day in a red *Banarasi* sari. When she saw me admiring it and came closer to take a look herself, she shrieked, pointing to the small woman sitting next to her. The woman, also never married, was said to have a jinni in her.

On the plane back to Canada, I looked out the window and saw the buildings, mostly white and beige, stacked next to each other, human-made reservoirs of green waters and a twilight sheen signalling the sun's departure. In all of these years, I could perhaps have come across the Shaytān Bride at some point without having known it.

If I had seen her, I would have whispered to her, "Read my lips: you have the rights you most desire."

I wanted to tell her that I believed in her, what she knew, and that she could choose herself.

Then I saw the reflection of my face on the window of the airplane: black hair, curious eyes, Darvaza flames as strong as the longing for love and life.

Conversations with Trees
(Part Two)

It was a summer afternoon in 2016 and Zahara, my cousin, was driving me from the Thunder Bay International Airport to Pori and Ahsan Khalu's white house. I would be meeting some family members there for a short reunion and we'd be spending a few weeks out in Ahsan Khalu's cottage, fishing, cooking, and conversing together.

I hadn't seen Zahara in years. She was now a junior architect, following in the footsteps of her father, still quiet and observing with her large eyes and cautiously donated smile, frugal about the information or sentiments she shared. I wondered how her friend Annabelle was. It had been so long since my brief time there, who I had been then, the era before English when my days passed slowly, snowily, and I mostly spoke with trees.

As Zahara drove, I gazed out the car window. The roads weren't as wide as I remembered, except the buildings that bordered them were just the same: small, single storeyed. The grandiosity of the Thunder Bay captured through my childhood eyes shrivelled down two-fold. The bungalows passing like stories of lifetimes that bobbed beyond reach.

We'd pass the Kaministiquia River, where dead bodies of Indigenous children had been found. One of the largest inquests in history was happening. And not too far away, Kakabeka Falls, underneath which were ancient fossils. Just further down, closer to the harbour, one could also see the mesas that form the shape of a giant laying on his back. The Sleeping Giant, it was called. I had heard the name came from the Ojibwe Oral Tradition that had to do with giving away secrets to colonizers.

The house was not too far from the grand Mount McKay. As we got closer, I could see the mountain from a distance. Thunder Mountain, *Animikii-wajiw* in the Ojibwe language, the mountain where sacred ceremonies take place.

As my eyes feasted on the Canadian landscape, a sense of wonderment was reinvoked in me. I remembered the mountains of my childhood. The ease with which I seemed to fold into nature, my awareness of my oneness with the earth and the amplification of that oneness as I navigated my world. I remembered also sitting alone and watching all the people.

When Zahara and I finally arrived at the white-brick house, bordered by garnet roses, amethyst lilacs, and emerald bushes, I hesitated before going in. Wasn't it here that I last truly felt cohesive? When was it that the geography started imposing itself on me? Calling me into its predatory winters? It hadn't killed me, but it could be said there was a fracture. Things that once seemed solid could break into parts. How many pieces do I contain? Am I like others? Am I a good person? Are my decisions flawed? Would it be better to change or stay the same? I had read somewhere that freedom was a series of decisions. What would I decide each day?

For a moment, I also thought about all the ways I had been privileged, which allowed me to survive the quietus that I had; in this lifetime, and for now. I reached my hand toward the door but heard someone calling.

Sweety Khala? Ammu? Nani? It could be the Shayṭān Bride, one of them, all of them, none of them.

Had someone truly cried out to me? All around the land was empty and frozen and quiet. Who here would know me as one to call out to? Yet it seemed so clearly directed toward me. That cry had carried a startling urgency that compelled me to stop and turn. My heart thudding. A brief glimpse of my hands, shaped like the hands of my family.

I spun around to see a V of Canada geese twist and turn around the pine trees like a mutating double helix. My eye lingered at the front, the point of the V: beyond the uniform of drab goose feathers there was a strikingly familiar startling shade of green. I cannot be sure of myself, as we all have ways of seeing what we need to see. Memory imposes itself on every landscape. I am the snow. I am the trees. I am the Canadian birds in a V, at the tip of which I swear I saw a parakeet.

Acknowledgements

There are several wonderful souls who have contributed to the shaping of this book and at various stages of its development.

First and foremost, thank you to my friend/professor/mentor/editor, Julie Mannell at Dundurn Press. Julie, thank you for believing in me, my writing, and the potential of this story. You are intelligent, funny, and incredibly talented. You've done more than just edit this story — you've helped me piece together floating memories into something I could share with the world.

The entire team at Dundurn Press has been so supportive of *The Shayṭān Bride*. Special thanks to Jenny McWha, the project editor who worked patiently and diligently to address my last-minute requests as we raced against the clock to get this book ready for publication. Words cannot describe how appreciative I am of your work. Thank you also to Kristina Jagger, Laura Boyle, Heather Wood, Scott Fraser, and all the other folks at Dundurn Press who I didn't work with directly but who were behind the scenes making this book happen — thank you so much. Julie and I have always thought of this debut book as an artifact. You've all been so responsive and handled this book so carefully. I am deeply honoured that *The Shaytān Bride* is one of Dundurn's first Rare Machines titles — I cannot think of anything more fitting.

I want to acknowledge also my Ammu and Abbu: I wouldn't have been able to see this book through if I wasn't the daughter of strong forces like you. Thank you also to my biggest supporter and sounding board, Vishaal.

Before my manuscript was submitted to Dundurn Press, I was part of several writing groups where I workshopped content from this book. My wonderful classmates from the Autobiography and Memoir class I took in 2019 at George Brown College provided their critical feedback and touched this story with their spirit even before it was fully conceived. Their encouragement and honest feedback strengthened my belief that there are people out there waiting to read a book like *The Shaytān Bride*, and that the time to get the book done was the present. I will never forget these souls and the beautiful, thoughtful, funny, and deeply moving life stories they shared with me.

It was in this class that I met activist/writer/academic Mandi Gray, who always supported my work by sending me relevant articles and connecting me to other activists, academics, and writers. When I joined Mandi's creative writing group, I had the opportunity to receive feedback from talented writers like Nilum Panesar, Alex Wilson, Leigha Comer, Megan Kinch, Andrea Brockie, and Kelly Skower. During our biweekly calls, these savvy and thoughtful scribblers always left me with questions to ponder or pointed out my blind spots, which challenged me to grow and improve my craft. Thank you. Marlene Malik, whom I met at another writing group, was also kind enough to review a few chapters. Of course, there was also Michele Byrne, my colleague, friend, and cheerleader, who gifted me with her discernment and compassion whenever I shared a few pages with her. It means so much to me to be around such wise women.

Before writing this narrative as a non-fiction book, I tried to write it as a fiction. Although my mentor, Shyam Selvadurai, at the Humber School for Writers did not work directly with me on *The Shaytān Bride*, his insights and encouragement on my fiction book were helpful to my creative process and influenced my final decision to share this narrative as non-fiction, and for that I am grateful. ·

Thank you also to my friend Tahbit Chowdhury, who was always available when I wanted to bounce around ideas and get feedback. Tahbit, your humour and insight made the editing process fun.

When it comes to marketing myself and my work I am not the greatest, so Tasnim Jerin, Karam Masri, and Lainey Cameron's Writers Support Group — thank you for sharing marketing/promo leads and ideas. I'm deeply appreciative of your contributions. Silmy Abdullah and MCIS Language Solutions, thank you for your help with the translations.

I believe there are many more characters in my life who have somehow touched this book (even before it was written) for I do believe every book has a destiny of its own, even separate from the author.

Of course, there is Allah, who opened the pathways for this to happen.

And thank you to my readers who spent their time and attention reading this book. I am deeply grateful and honoured that you chose it, and that it chose you.

About the Author

SUMAIYA MATIN is a writer, part-time social worker/psychotherapist, and strategic advisor for the Ontario government who has worked on a wide range of public policy files, including anti-racism. She was born in Dhaka, Bangladesh, and emigrated to Canada at the age of six. Sumaiya has worked on various projects internationally and locally that support marginalized populations. She is particularly passionate about spirituality/faith, intersections between gender and religion, cross-cultural communications, and mental health. Sumaiya loves exploring new and unique places, as well as the terrains of her mind on rainy days through good books and mind-boggling thriller films. She loves music and is currently picking up where she left off with her childhood harmonium lessons. You can find her in the kitchen trying out new recipes or on long hikes in the middle of nowhere. Sumaiya lives in Toronto.